The Seventh Babe

The
Seventh
Babe

 A NOVEL BY

Jerome Charyn

ISBN: 978-1-955398-10-7 (pbk)
ISBN: 978-1-955398-11-4 (ebk)

For information about permissions, bulk purchases, or additional
distribution, write to
Summer Game Books
P. O. Box 818
South Orange, NJ 07079

or contact the publisher at *www.summergamebooks.com*

I would like to thank Bill Crowley and the Boston Red Sox for letting me visit the tunnels and playing field of Fenway Park in August, 1978. Roaming through those tunnels helped me write this book.

Publisher's Note

The Seventh Babe is a remarkable novel. The prose is crisp and the characters are memorable. Skinny 17-year-old Babe Ragland makes the 1923 Red Sox as a walk-on. "Rags" is quickly immersed in the ugly reality of early 20th century baseball. But as the narrative goes on, that reality begins to take increasingly magical turns.

But while Babe Ragland's journey takes many magical turns, the descriptions, settings, and dialog of the book accurately depict the life and language of the rough-and-tumble world of major league baseball in the 1920s and the surrounding American culture.

Part of this reality is the pervasive racism in society and baseball at the time, both the segregation on and off the field, which plays a central role in *The Seventh Babe*, and the language used by the ball-players, some of which is now considered highly offensive, and rightfully so.

The use of these offensive words presents a dilemma—to remain true to the original version, or to change the objectionable words. While both choices represent important principles, we have opted to change the offensive racial terms, including words that begin with "n" and "c," which have been changed to "Black" or "Blacks."

Readers of the story will see that the most admirable characters in the book are the African American ballplayers, whose skills not only surpass those of their white counterparts, but whose play is infused by a great love and devotion to the game. Despite frequently using makeshift fields lit by headlights, they are dazzling performers whose seasons have no beginning, middle, or end. They just play.

And this is perhaps the most important theme of the book—the grip that baseball can have on us, the power the game has to make us put aside everything else for another chance to step onto a ball field.

Ragland of the Red Sox:

BOOK ONE

1

THEY were the laughing boys of the American League. Footloose imbeciles, they couldn't hit, they couldn't field, they couldn't run. These were the Red Sox of 1923. They'd bartered half their club to those rich kids, the Yankees of New York, who fattened themselves on Babe Ruth and other Boston throwaways.

The Sox had been a dynasty six years ago, with Harry Hooper, the Babe, and Sad Sam Jones. Then their owner, Hollis McKee, decided to break them up. He allowed that beer baron, Jacob Ruppert, to steal his best men away. The Sox became a talent farm for Ruppert's Yanks.

Managers quit on Hollis, or else they were fired. This year the Sox had Briggs Josephson, who'd played third for the Brownies before his ankles chipped, and hobbled him for life. Briggs never argued when Hollis wanted to sell a man. He fielded a team and detached himself from the fact that he had ragamuffins instead of ballplayers. What was the use of bringing a boy along? Hollis would give the boy to the Yanks if he showed the least bit of promise.

The boss saves a penny wherever he can.

Hollis avoided the expense of a Florida training camp. He brought his team to Sackville Forest, a godforsaken hole on the other side of Hot Springs, Arkansas. It was still freezing in March. The Sox had to play on grass and rubble that were bitten with hoarfrost.

One day, when the frost disappeared from the ground, Briggs ran a pathetic tryout camp. Hollis pushed this on him. "You have to be kind to local talent. Give some of the rubes from down here a chance to play. People like that. It gives them a feeling of power, seeing their own boys scrappling with my Red Sox."

So Briggs went through the bother of watching a bunch of Arkansas rubes bat, field, and pitch. He didn't expect it to be anything more than a clown show. Briggs couldn't take his vengeance on the Yanks. But he could copy from them. He hired a hunchback named Scarborough as mascot and bat boy to the club. Scarborough was pretty old for a bat boy. It was hard to guess his age, with the seams under his eyes and that hump. But he had to be over forty. Briggs didn't care. He had a hunchback on his team, like the Yankees did.

The players despised this Scarborough. The Yankees could afford to travel with a freak. *Their* hunchback had brought them two pennants in a row. But Scarborough would only bring the Sox to perdition.

He was a helpful brute. He carried a load of bats on his shoulder and a bag of old, squashy balls for the Arkansas boys on tryout day. He encouraged them, giving them pointers on how to hit. It was comical, watching Scarborough swing a bat. He had a cross-handed grip; the hump would move down his back at the end of the swing, with his wrists knotted against themselves. "Babe Ruth," the Sox would scream. "Babe Ruth." But Briggs was pleased with him. It helped pass the time, having Scarborough around.

The rubes had no more finesse than the hunchback. Still, Briggs got all their names on a slip of paper. He wanted proof for Hollis that he'd kept his word and drilled every rube that came to him. The last boy at Briggs' tryout camp was a beanpole in a ripped flannel shirt. He was tall as Briggs, five-foot-ten or eleven, but he couldn't have weighed more than a hundred and thirty pounds. You could see how sharp his elbows were under that shirt.

"How old are you, son?"

"Seventeen," the boy said.

"Are you from these parts?"

"No sir. I come from Baltimore. I heard about this tryout the Sox were having, and . . ."

Briggs had to laugh. "You mean, the news got to Baltimore?" He nodded to his own men. "Heck, we must be getting famous."

They crowded up to the boy, Germany Stone, the team's first baseman, Hooks Poland, and Chicken Stallings. "What's your name?"

The beanpole looked at them. "Babe," he said. "Babe Ragland."

Briggs scratched his head; he couldn't get out from under the grizzly shadow of Babe Ruth. The Babe's disappearance from Boston had ruined the Sox. That big monkey was the rage of the whole frigging world. He'd turned the National League into a cemetery. It had no Babe Ruth. And the American League existed as a playpen for the big monk. It was Babe this, and Babe that, and now Briggs had Babe Ragland in the middle of Arkansas.

"Hey," Chicken Stallings said, "how many Babes they got in the big leagues?" He used his knuckles to count on. "There's the monkey himself. There's Babe Adams of Pittsburgh. Babe Winters, Babe Pinelli, Babe LeJeune . . . Briggsy, whatever happened to Babe Chicote?"

"The Giants picked him up."

"Well," the Chicken said, after counting twice and pointing to the beanpole. "This one's the seventh Babe. But I can't figure on it. He's all elbows, and them other Babes are big, round men."

Germany poked Ragland with a thumb. "Kid, don't you have a regular name? Is it George Herman Ragland Ruth?" Briggs told Germany to leave the kid alone. "What's your position, son? Where do you like to play?"

"I'm a third baseman, Mr. Briggs."

He took a crusty leather mitt out of his shirt pocket. It was a fifty-cent glove. It had no cushioning in it. The glove couldn't have stopped a dying ground ball. Ragland put it over his right fist. The players looked back and forth between Ragland and his glove. They were waiting for Briggs to grab him up and hurl him out of Sackville Forest. There was no such thing as a lefty third baseman.

There had never been. You couldn't perfect the double play throw-ing with your left hand; you'd lose a step every time you went into the hole between third and short, because you'd have to make a backhanded stab at the ball with that glove on your wrong hand. Christ, they didn't have to lecture Briggs about it. He was on the Brownies fifteen years, the best corner man in the league. But he didn't even holler at the kid.

Ragland went to third, and Briggs himself hit grounders to him. The beanpole gobbled them up, and Briggs said, "Okay, I'll carry you."

His men couldn't believe it. "Briggsy, should we cover first and second for you? Don't you want to see if he can make the throw?"

"I saw enough," Briggs said.

"Briggsy, let him grab a bat. He could have a hernia, or a wood-en leg."

"What do I need his bat for. Chicken, when I have you, Germa-ny, and Hooks?"

The three of them walked away in disgust, but there was noth-ing strange about Briggs' choice. He promised Hollis that he'd keep one rube from the tryout camp. It would make the locals happy.

The team avoided Briggs' seventh Babe. A left-handed third baseman meant rotten luck, like a catcher with a missing pinkie. No one wanted him. So he had to room with the hunchback. The Sox wouldn't let him near the batter's cage while they were being drilled. Ragland took his batting practice alone, with Scarborough as his mate. The hunchback was a crazy hurler. He couldn't throw the ball overhand. That hump would get in the way. He had to use a sidearm delivery. The Sox would die laughing when they saw the brute throw. He would wrench his body, twist halfway around the world, to get that ball across the plate. Ragland would choke up on the bat, peer out at Scarborough and paw the ground like the great Ty Cobb, and smack the ball over Scarborough's head. The hunch-back had to jump off the pitching hill and retrieve the ball.

They were a comedy team, Ragland and the hunchback. Briggs could always use a pair of clowns. That's how he justified holding on to a third baseman who wore his glove on the wrong hand. "It's early," Briggs assured himself. He was waiting for a good prospect to arrive. His scouts tramped east and west, looking for desirable boys. "Give me a young ballplayer who's alive, and I'll drop Ragland in a minute." But the prospects never showed. Better teams were grabbing them up. He shaved a knuckleballer from his lists who'd been recommended to him by his most reliable man in the Southwest. The knuckleballer was gray around the temples, although he swore to Briggs he hadn't turned twenty yet. His scouts were bringing grandfathers into camp.

Briggs got out of Arkansas with his club and went down to New Orleans. Hollis had arranged for the Red Sox to travel around the country in an exhibition series with the Boston Braves. The Braves were as feckless as the Sox. Both teams occupied the cellar in 1922. They were natural rivals: the eighth-place wonders of the American and the National League.

Briggs would have preferred to link up with his old club, the St. Louis Browns. But the Brownies trained in Florida. They wouldn't have trekked to New Orleans for a series with the lowly Red Sox. The Boston teams were stuck with each other like a brotherhood of crippled cats.

The bleachers were empty when they played. The Pelicans, a minor-league club, owned New Orleans. The Pelicans outdrew them every game. If you didn't have George Herman Ruth, you couldn't even gather the mice into a ball park. Briggs tried to cancel the tour. Hollis wouldn't have it. "The Pelicans are shitbirds," he said. "We'll draw, you'll see. New Orleans was always a dumb baseball town."

How the hell would you know, Mr. Hollis McKee?

The fans had loved Briggs when he came to New Orleans in 1920 with the Browns. They didn't need Babe Ruth. The Pelicans wouldn't have dared to schedule a game while the Browns were in New Orleans. But Briggs only nodded to his boss. "It's a dunghole, you're right. We'll do better in Mobile."

They surrendered New Orleans to the Pelicans and got on the Alabama Express. There wasn't any more tolerance for Boston baseball across the Louisiana line: they were flops in Mobile too. The Braves would drift in and out of ice-cream parlors searching for applejack and fickle wives. The Sox kept to their hotel. They grew mean in Alabama. The boredom of an idiotic rivalry had turned them in upon themselves. They were without the usual factions that other clubs displayed. Veterans didn't have to band together and thwart rookies that might take over their jobs. Rookies were hard to find.

But cliques did develop on the Red Sox. The team was split in two. College men and country boys. The country boys made up the weaker side. They were led by Germany Stone. Stone had Chicken Stallings, Hooks Poland, Nemo Leibold, and Frank Howe in his camp—utility infielders and journeymen pitchers, most of them. They didn't amount to very much.

College men dominated the club. Hollis McKee was a Dartmouth man, and he preferred to surround himself with college players. He might get rid of a baboon like Babe Ruth, but he would never give a college man away. Seaman Schupp was from Notre Dame. Briggs' fireballer, Sheriff Smith, had gone to Gettysburg College. Tilly Young held a Phi Beta Kappa key from the University of Alabama. Ross Barnett and Snake Attreau were sons of Princeton and Cornell. Alvin Critz had two years at Florida State. Blondy Cutshaw, Steve Dubec, and Garland James were Dartmouth men, like the boss.

The college men looked to Garland James. Garland played center field for the Sox. He stole thirty bases in '22, and hit seventeen triples. He was the last piece of artillery the Red Sox had. The Indians would have traded Smokey Joe Wood for him. The Browns offered Baby Doll Jacobson and cash. The Tigers would have let Hollis pick any two men on their roster for Garland James. Hollis refused them all.

Maybe it was the idea of being untouchable that turned Garland into such a brat. Five years ago, on the Washington Senators, he'd been a modest young man who learned how to blast triples and play the center field wall. Then Hollis brought him to the Red Sox, and now he was the bully of the club. He made life miserable for Briggs' country boys. He laughed at them in the dressing room, reminding everyone how illiterate Chicken Stallings was. "That chump can't read his own contract. Lord, he wouldn't wear shoes if Briggsy didn't make him." The Chicken would have to fight. He'd get a bloody nose, and Garland would walk away without a scratch on him. That's how it was with those Dartmouth men Hollis loved to buy. They'd rather punch you in the face than swing a bat.

Garland wasn't going to chase after whores in Mobile, Alabama, or drink bootlegged mountain whiskey. He would read Plato before a game, tell Germany and Hooks Poland how dumb they were, and then destroy the Boston Braves with doubles rifled off the left field wall. It gave him little pleasure. There wasn't a pretty girl around. Hollis would have done better to bring the circus into Mobile.

The teams crept up to Birmingham. They didn't sell enough tickets to pay for their hotel rooms. "Things will liven in Baltimore," Hollis told the Braves. "That's no dead rabbit town."

Both teams were glum when they arrived at Union Station. Garland wouldn't allow a porter near his bags. He made the hunchback bend over and grab them up. "Go on, Scarb'ruh. Bat boys gotta earn their keep. I'll give you a silver dollar, you ugly son of a bitch."

The Sox were staying at the Kernan Hotel, and Scarborough had to carry those bags up to Garland's room on the eleventh floor. He went downstairs with the silver dollar clutched inside his fist. He wanted to treat his roommate to a chocolate sundae at the Kernan's soda shop, but Babe Ragland wouldn't slurp ice cream that had come from Garland James' pocket. "Carrying his bags is one thing, but why did you take money from him? He thinks he's such hot pants. I could hit just as many triples as that college baby if Mr. Briggs would let me try."

And Ragland went up to his room. Scarborough followed the surly boy upstairs after his fifth chocolate sundae. He was drunk on the juice of those maraschino cherries he had swallowed. His hump swayed in the halls of the Kernan Hotel. Ragland had to put him to bed. Scarborough had an idiotic luster in his eyes. "Rags, aint your people from Baltimore?"

"Stop mumbling, you, and go to sleep. You took a silver dollar and stuffed yourself with ice cream."

"I thought Baltimore was your home," Scarborough said. He was growing alert. The wine from the pickled cherries had begun to wear off. "I aint deaf. I heard you tell Briggsy you come from Baltimore. So why are you staying in a hotel when this is your own town?"

"Because I don't have people here. I went to the bad boys' school . . . like Babe Ruth."

Scarborough tossed his covers off the bed. The whole world knew about the Babe's origins. He was a foundling who'd gone to St. Mary's Reform School, where he studied how to be a tailor and throw fast balls and the curve.

"Rags, you mean you aint got a mother and a father? . . . you're one of them bastards the school took in?"

The hunchback got dressed before Ragland could determine what was in his crazy head. "Come on. Rags, we're going to St. Mary's."

"What for?"

"I want to see where you and the Babe went to school." Ragland had to accompany him, or the hunchback would have beaten down the hotel walls. They climbed on the Wilkens Avenue trolley, a seventeen-year-old boy in a baseball cap and a forty-five-year-old brute with deep lines in his face. Passengers twisted their bodies away from Scarborough and the kid, who had the back of the trolley to themselves. In his excitement Scarborough dipped over the side of the car. You could see his hump ride in the air.

"How far is it?" he asked. "How far?"

Ragland told him. "The school's at the end of the line." The trolley didn't waver its course. It bumped down Wilkens Avenue mile after mile. Passengers began to drop off from both sides of the trolley. They arrived at the bottom of some vacant hill in a deserted trolley car. They jumped off, then the conductor and his mate turned the trolley around on its axis; the wires crackled once, the trolley pole dipped and then stood upright, and the car made its return run into Baltimore.

Scarborough was confused. Rags had brought him to a wasteyard at the edge of town. "Look up there, you dope!"

Scarborough turned his head. He saw a brick monster with a church at one side and a tower in the middle, all at the top of the hill. But he wasn't going to be tricked. "If it's a reform school, how come it doesn't have a fence?"

"They don't need fences, Mr. Scarborough. Where else does a bastard have to go?"

The hunchback seemed satisfied with that piece of news. "Well, Rags, take me up the hill. Show me them Catholic brothers what taught you how to play third with your left hand. They must do miracles at St. Mary's school."

Ragland refused to go. "I aint getting inside there again."

The hunchback stamped on the ground. "You took me this far. Can't I watch where the bastards eat and sleep?"

"No. The brothers don't take to visitors. It riles up the kids."

"You're no visitor. Rags. You're an alumnoos. You made the Red Sox, goddamn. The brothers can show you off. Who knows? They could be raising a team of lefty shortstops right this minute."

"You shut up."

They had to wait for another trolley to come and turn itself around, so they could ride up Wilkens Avenue to their hotel.

The Sox and the Braves began a five-game series at Black River Park. Spooks could have been on that field. There wasn't a stir when Garland hit the ball into the bleachers for his second home run of the day. Studying the flight of that ball must have reeducated the owner of the Red Sox, because Hollis McKee called off the series with the Braves.

"Thank God," Briggs said. "I'd like the men to stare at a human face once in a while."

They got out of the Kernan Hotel, cursing Black River Park and the ungrateful fans of Baltimore. The Braves were going to Pittsburgh to try their luck at Forbes Field, but the Sox went straight to Boston on the Seaboard Special. The team invaded the club car and finished twelve rye breads and every slice of roast beef on board the train. Briggs' men lumbered out of Back Bay Station with their bellies hanging low. A trolleybus brought them to the Sox's headquarters at the Brunswick Hotel on Brookline Avenue, opposite Fenway Park.

Ragland could see the flags on the stadium roof from his window. Fenway was a wall of red bricks on the Lansdowne Street side. The hunchback wanted to nap, but Ragland was the curious one right now. "This aint Mobile, Mr. Scarborough. It's Boston, home of the Sox. Why does every rabbit on the team live at this hotel? Don't they have sisters, girlfriends, wives? . . . what about you?"

Ragland heard a voice from under the quilt. "There's no such thing as a married man on the Red Sox. Oh, Hooks Poland was married once. His wife left him after three weeks. We're vagabonders. It's trains and hotels, trains and hotels."

"Could be. But I'm going to find a rooming house somewhere in Boston. I aint living across the street from Fenway Park."

"Go 'head. Landladies don't cotton much to ballplayers. They'll charge you double the rate and call you a bum. It's rookie fever you got. Rent your little old room with some widow on Marlborough Street. She'll fix you up with curtains. She'll make you pots of tea. You'll have to stand in line with twenty boarders to take a leak. You'll come back to us. The Brunswick's home-sweet-home for the Red Sox. It's always been that way."

Rags was getting furious with the hunchback. "*Always* been? How the hell would you know? The skipper only brung you to the Sox last year."

The furrows began to darken on Scarborough's head. He could have been eighty, looking at him. The sun poured into the room, but his face was in some deep hollow that had nothing to do with Boston weather and Boston time. Ragland felt ashamed.

"I know lots about the team," Scarborough said. "Skipper told me."

Ragland tried to make amends. "What did you do, Mr. Scarborough, before the skipper picked you up?"

"I lumberjacked."

He's lying, like always, Ragland thought. How could he swing an ax with that hump sitting on his shoulder? Briggs must have swiped him out of the Boston freak show.

Ragland decided to live with the Sox. A team of bachelors was good enough for him. Briggs began to drill in earnest for Opening Day, and Ragland had to scamper around Fenway with the full squad. Briggs cut three pitchers and a utility man who couldn't turn over the double play. But he didn't break up his comedy act: that brute and the beanpole called Rags kept playing pepper ball in the shadow of older, established men. The Dartmouth faction wouldn't condescend to notice a rube at third base, and the country boys, Germany, Chicken, and Hooks, didn't needle him very much.

Ragland could have been a groundkeeper for all they cared. No one bothered to breathe the word "rookie" at him, or nail his shoes to the clubhouse wall. Why razz a boy who didn't have a monkey's chance of getting into a game?

Garland read Plato in Greek and patrolled center field. He had no time to think up pranks against the hunchback. It was April, and Garland had to take care of his batting eye. The Indians were coming to town.

Opening Day was a disaster for the Sox. Cleveland's young righthander, big George Uhle, shut Boston out. The Sox bought one hit, a scratch single that splintered Hooks Poland's bat. A famine at the plate wouldn't have angered manager Briggs. When big George Uhle had his "smoke," he could put anybody's bat to sleep. But the Sox had murdered themselves. Their infield behaved like four ruptured chumps. Alvin Critz made three errors at short. Germany Stone couldn't trap a ball in his first-baseman's mitt. Seaman Schupp and Snake Attreau collided on the grass.

Five thousand fans snickered and booed. It was the smallest Opening Day crowd in Red Sox history. Hollis McKee had spooked the turnstiles on Lansdowne Street. He made his Red Sox into the dogs of the American League.

But five thousand fans seemed like a mob to Babe Ragland, who sat in the dugout by himself, because the hunchback left him there. Scarborough wasn't simply the mascot who had to hang off the dugout roof and point his tongue at opposing teams until they couldn't stomach the sight of him. He was the bat boy as well, and he was forever shuffling on and off the field to bring this man or that man his favorite piece of wood. Garland James had ten different bats, and Scarborough had to remember which was which. He couldn't entertain the rookie, he couldn't sit still. He was sweating in April, on Opening Day.

Rags would have liked to help his roommate carry bats and rosin bags, and shinguards for the catcher, Tilly Young. But not even the obscurest man in the major leagues could fool with a bat boy once the warm-ups were over with. Baseball had its laws: players didn't tamper with the necessary flow of a nine-inning game. The bat boy had his special place. You didn't want to get him out of his groove. He could kill whatever string of luck you had.

Briggs had none. The Indians didn't have to worry about a brute and his rosin bags. They took four from the Sox. They were a contender this year. And they'd never catch the Yankees if they couldn't run over the boys from Fenway Park. Briggs went to his secret book on the Washington Senators. The Senators were weaklings. But they had a stable infield, and that was enough. Boston could only manage one win out of five.

The Sox were deep in the cellar after nine frigging games. Briggs had to do something when the Tigers arrived. He took Snake Attreau off third base. The Boston faithful, those three thousand fans that had come to the park, couldn't remember a game without Attreau. The Snake meant glory to them. He'd been on the championship clubs of '15, '16, and '18. He was the last of the Sox to know what a World Series was.

The Boston announcer, Weingarten, stood at home plate with his beautiful megaphone and didn't mention Attreau. Hollis had lured this chubby little man away from the Athletics. Bull Weingarten was the surest megaphone man in the league. His voice could carry to the roof in center field. He would yell the Boston lineup once and only once. He knew how to capitalize on the absence of a name. "Batting eighth for the Red Sox and playing third," Bull said, with that megaphone high in the air, "we have the seventh Babe. Not Babe Pinelli. Not Babe Winters. Not Babe LeJeune. Not Babe Adams. Not Babe Chicote. And not Babe Ruth. But our Babe, Babe Ragland of the Red Sox."

The fans yelled back, "Snake, Snake, Snake," but they couldn't get to Bull. He finished up and withdrew to his tiny chair on the foul side of first base.

That echo wouldn't cease. "Snake, Snake, Snake." It shook the dugout walls. Briggs sat on the bench with his legs crossed. "Heck," he said. The fans weren't going to make his lineup card for him. They could yell their heads off. Either Hollis found a decent crop of ballplayers and held on to them, or Briggs would be obliged to play that young freak, Ragland, at third. The Sox had a chump's infield. So why shouldn't Briggs use a third baseman who did everything the opposite way?

But Briggs' juggling of his men couldn't ease Ragland's pain on that wretched infield grass. The beanpole hadn't expected to play. The skipper never revealed what was on his lineup card. Rags had to learn from the croaker. Bull Weingarten, that "the seventh Babe" was bumping Attreau off third. So he picked up his glove that was patched with Band-Aids and he ran out onto the field with Briggs' other men. The shortstop, Alvin Critz, set a wide corridor for himself and left Rags with a stingy bit of land around third base. Ragland hugged that coffin of dirt. It was the one protection he had. The fans were screaming for Snake Attreau, and unless he dug in with his spiked shoes, their voices would have sucked him off the grass.

The Tigers were coming to bat. Boston's fireballer, Sheriff Smith, went into his windup. The ball disappeared inside the crook of his arm. The pitch was released, and the Tiger shortstop. Topper Rigney, swung at a ball that danced in around his knees. Rags was shivering in the jersey under his short-sleeved blouse. "God," he mumbled, "please, please, let him bang it to some other guy."

He heard a hollow pock that told him the ball wasn't going very far. Rigney hit a high popper into foul territory. Alvin Critz leered at Rags. "Chase it, you dope. That's yours." And Rags started to run. He didn't have his eye on the ball. But he could *feel* a crazy shadow on him. He ran headlong into the Tiger dugout on the third-base side of the field. He stuck his glove hand out. The ball plopped into it like a lazy egg. Rags tripped on the dugout stairs; he fell and his body twisted around, but that glove stayed over his head. The third-base ump scrutinized him and signaled that Topper was out.

Rags had scraped his leg on the concrete floor. The blood pounded like a savage in his skull, and for a moment Rags couldn't decide where he was. He could have fallen into a spider den. The Tigers didn't offer to pick him up. Ty Cobb and his ferocious men would have loved to spill Ragland's brains under the dugout bench. Whoever heard of such a catch? Only a baseball monkey would dive in among the Tigers for a foul ball.

Rags shook the dizziness from his head and pulled himself out onto the field again. He didn't hear the chant of "Snake" anymore. The Boston faithful, scattered in a park that could seat thirty thousand souls, had gone wild. "Rags," they screamed. "Rags, Rags, Rags." It was their fickleness that disturbed the manager in the home-team dugout. Briggs understood: one catch, and they forgot Snake Attreau.

Rags didn't see another ball in the next two innings. He came up to bat at the bottom of the third. Scarborough had given him a piece of wood to carry to the plate. That blond stick wiggled on Rags' shoulder. It seemed like a puny weapon to use against Detroit's big righthander, Herm Pillette. The enemy catcher, Larry Woodall, was singing to Pillette. "Dumb kid here, dumb kid here." It was a language some catchers employed to calm their battery mates and pester the hitters. Woodall's song got to Rags. His shoulder felt stuck. Pillette scorned him from the mound. How could Rags face up to a big guy standing on a hill?

That first pitch floated up near the letters on his blouse. Rags thought it would never arrive. His ankles crossed as he swiped at the dead air around home plate. The ball was in the catcher's glove. Herm had given him a slider to eat.

"No bat," Larry Woodall sang, while Pillette went to his fast ball. Rags heard a strange wind. He blinked once, and the umpire yelled "Strike two!"

Ragland would have liked to vomit into one of his red and white socks. He couldn't swing at a pitch he never saw. He waited until Herm was in his stretch. As the ball left Herm's fingers, Rags closed his eyes. That wind had a cleaner sound. He lunged with his blond stick. He could feel a sweet vibration in his wrists. Hell with Ty Cobb! Rags got a piece of the ball. It looped over the first baseman's head. Bodies were moving in the outfield when Rags opened his eyes. The seventh Babe had bought himself a hit. He dropped his bat and strutted to first base.

Briggs grew forlorn in the dugout. He was mumbling a prayer. Briggs believed that every baseball city had gods of its own. And he begged the gods of Boston that this crazy-handed kid at third wasn't *too* good, or Hollis McKee would send him away to the Yanks. Hollis only cared about his Dartmouth men, and Rags was no college beauty. He was a country boy from Baltimore, like Babe Ruth.

"Gods of Fenway," Briggs muttered to himself. "Let me have this boy."

2

The Fenway gods were kind to manager Briggs. They shielded Ragland from Hollis McKee. The gods saw to it that Hollis wasn't around when Rags made his miracle catch in the Tiger dugout. The owner's box behind third base was empty for the series with Detroit. Hollis had gone to New York with a case of Broadway fever. He was looking for backers to help him mount a musical comedy. It was to be called *Eveline,* and the idea of it swelled in Hollis, clutched at him, as it always did. *Eveline* was about baseball wives who banded together and consoled themselves while their husbands were on the road. Hollis couldn't have been dreaming of his own club. The Sox were without one legitimate baseball wife.

The unmarried bandits split four games with Detroit. Ragland's hitting leveled off; he had two more singles in his maiden series, and went three for twelve. It was his fielding that surprised. He didn't lose a step at third, crazy-handed as he was. He was more agile than Snake Attreau had ever been at turning over the double play. But Briggs still had his chump's infield. Critz, Schupp, and Stone fell behind that maddening rhythm that flew out of the boy's hands. So what? The Boston faithful had told their friends about this Ragland boy. There were over ten thousand in the park for the last game of the series.

Rags swiped the left side of the infield from Alvin Critz. Alvin had to retreat into a small pocket in back of second base. He was lucky to have this end piece of his old corridor. It was pathetic to watch him now. Before Alvin could make that first push into motion, Rags was in the air.

Briggs' men, his coaches, his hunchback, and the tiny band of journalists that still went on the road with the Sox, met at Back Bay Station and waited for the Liberty Bell to arrive. The Sox had three cars. It wasn't a night train, and they didn't have to scramble for upper or lower berths. The Liberty Bell seemed to exist for the comfort of Garland James. Garl was adored by the journalists. They compared him to Tris Speaker, who had played center field for the Sox at the beginning of their glory days. "Yeah, I like Tris," Garland said. "But have you noticed, boys?... the old Gray Eagle has lost a step. He can't swoop down on those fly balls like he once did."

"It's true," the journalists had to admit; at this moment, in 1923, Garland James of the Red Sox played the shallowest center field in the American League.

"What about the new kid, Garl? The busher who's replaced Attreau at third. Where the hell did he come from? He wasn't on the roster of any minor-league club."

"You mean Rags? The skipper picked him up in Arkansas. He was planting weeds somewhere. You don't have to worry about the Snake. He'll get his old job back."

The journalists were skeptical of anything to do with Attreau.

"We hear Hollis McKee has it in mind to dump the Snake. Hollis is working on it. He hasn't found a taker yet."

"Boys, somebody's been feeding you a dumb line. This Ragland is like those other beauties. They come up swinging a big bat, they feast on grounders all April long, and then they disappear. He won't last into May, I'll telling you." The Liberty Bell made a special stop at Mott Haven, in the Bronx, where two small buses took the Red Sox to their hotel, the Concourse Plaza. The Plaza overlooked the new wonder of baseball, Yankee Stadium. The Yanks had been tenants at the Polo Grounds until John McGraw of the Giants kicked them out. So the Yankees moved across the Harlem River and established themselves in the Bronx. That sly Colonel, Jacob Ruppert, built a concrete stadium that dwarfed the Polo Grounds. The Sox had never played in the Colonel's white horseshoe. They were used to the wind blowing off the river and into the Polo Grounds. The stands would shake during a hard blow. Water would seep up through the clubhouse floor, and the Sox had to come out onto the playing field in wet shoes.

The Colonel's horseshoe was warm and dry. The wind couldn't bite through concrete. The Yanks scorned the Harlem River. The only thing that river got to see was the curve of a thick, thick wall. The grass wasn't yellow, like Fenway grass. The pipes didn't gurgle and sweat. The numbers on the scoreboard in center field had a whiteness you could find in no other ball park. The Sox marched into the dugout in those gray knickers a team had to wear on the road, and they couldn't believe the wide girdle of Yankee Stadium. You had to twist your eyes to locate the uppermost deck of the grandstands.

Rags caught the hunchback muttering to himself. "What's in your head, Scarborough?"

"I'm counting straw hats."

"How many did you catch?"

"Half a million so far."

The Yanks had their murderer's row of Ruth, Bob Meusel, and Wally Pip. Then there were the "cousins" they inherited from the Sox: Jumping Joe Dugan, Wally Schang, Everett Scott, the Bambino himself, and four starting pitchers, Herb Pennock, Sad Sam Jones, Waite Hoyt, and Bullet Joe Bush. The Sox were left with Dartmouth boys and the dregs of both leagues.

Briggs searched for Hollis in Colonel Ruppert's box. Hollis wasn't in the park. He was still busy with his *Eveline*. "Good," Briggs spoke into the wall of the dugout. "Maybe he won't scalp us on this trip. We might get away from the Bronx without losing a man."

He could sense a furor in the crowd. Yankee partisans didn't give a damn about the third baseman Briggs had unraveled. He was just another kid to them, no matter what hand he picked for wearing his glove. But they were irate over the hunchback. They jeered at Scarborough the first time he emerged from the dugout. The Yanks had their own brute. His name was Henry, Henry Watteau. The crowd loved his savageries, his willingness to fight lemonade boys, raucous fans, and enemy players. Henry would wag his buttocks at any umpire who made a rotten call against his team. He was vicious with children and all kinds of girls. He had no respect for the women who had come to watch Babe Ruth with their parasols and their white gloves. They didn't belong in Yankee Stadium. Henry would shout into the box seats. "Hey, you slits up there, leave the Bambino alone. Don't you make eyes at him. The Bam can't concentrate with too many slits in the house."

Nothing enraged him more than the sight of another brute. Scarborough was an affront to his dignity. Boston had mocked the hump on his back by bringing that creature to town. He didn't intend to stand for it. Twice he tried to enter the Boston dugout and wrestle with Scarborough, and twice he had to be restrained.

"It's me or him," he warned Miller Huggins, the Yankee skipper, who was even more of a shrimp than Henry Watteau. Huggins would have waved Henry off the field and banished him to the clubhouse for the *whole* Boston series, but he couldn't go against the fans. They were having a perfect day adoring Henry and reviling the Boston brute. They hurled pop bottles at him the moment he wandered from the dugout. And Henry kept aiming practice balls at his head. The brute was terrified. With each step he took, he could have been broken for life.

The stadium had gone berserk. You couldn't get through an inning without another rumpus featuring Scarborough and Henry

Watteau. The umpire had to act. He tossed both brutes out of the game. The fans hissed and then grew quiet as the hunchbacks were forgotten.

The Bambino slapped a long triple at the bottom of the sixth that fell into the alley off right center field. The fans marveled at the flurry of Ruth's ankles as he rounded second base. Rags watched, like everybody else. He could hear the churning music of that enormous body. The nostrils were widening in front of Rags. The Bambino yelled at him between snorts of his nose. "Look out, you're in my cocksucking way."

Rags didn't mean to challenge the Babe. He was watching the big man run, that's all. Those nostrils widened in deep anger. The Bambino knocked Rags down with a flick of his shoulder and continued on to third. The fans were delighted to see Ragland lying in the dirt with pebbles in his mouth.

The Babe was jovial once he got to third. He stood on that base with his belly rumbling under the stripes of his Yankee blouse. "Sorry, I decked you, kid. But this aint a traffic circle. It's fucking third base." Then he danced on the bag and took off his hat to the crowd.

Rags turned eighteen on the road. He passed his birthday with the hunchback in a Philadelphia hotel. Scarborough had smuggled a pint of rum into the room. "Wish I was eighteen," he said, with those marks on his face looking like battle sores.

"How old are you, Scarborough? Fifty? Forty-five?"

"I'm twenty-three."

Rags started to laugh, but a sadness gnawed at him. How could a grizzled brute, with seams and pits all over him, have the nerve to claim he was twenty-three? Did he pull himself out of his mother's womb with a hump on his shoulder, a lot of sores, and a head of thin gray hair? Rags had never seen the hunchback without his clothes. Scarborough would undress in the bathroom, and come to bed wearing an ancient brown robe. He wouldn't display his hump to anybody.

"You don't look twenty-three."

"Well I am. All lumberjacks age pretty fast. Hell, a bat boy's like being on vacation."

"How long were you a lumberjack?"

"Ten years."

Scarborough had trapped himself with a stupid lie. "Ten years? That's nice. Did you go from the cradle to dropping trees?"

A rage was building under Scarborough's lip. His jaw began to shiver in Ragland's face. "Don't give me any cradles. You can't lumberjack before you get to be eleven."

It was silly trying to untwist the words of a brute. Rags drank his rum in silence, while Scarborough searched for his disgusting brown robe.

The rum didn't hurt. Rags got two hits the next day at Shibe Park. He was like a scorpion in the field, robbing Philadelphia of doubles and triples with that crazy throwing hand and his flimsy glove.

The Sox returned to Boston in seventh place. There were articles about Rags in the *Herald,* the *Globe,* and the *Evening Transcript.* The *Globe* called him "a foundling who had made good." For the *Herald* he was "that mysterious boy without a minor-league record." The *Evening Transcript* proclaimed in thick black type that Rags had jumped from an orphanage to the Red Sox. All three papers likened him to Babe Ruth. Heroes out of Baltimore, they said, and St. Mary's "college." George Herman Ruth and Boston's seventh Babe.

The stories disgusted Rags, who had hidden himself from the journalists and granted no interviews. He caught Scarborough near the bat rack in the Boston dugout. "Who told them bigmouths I went to the bad boys' school?"

"Briggs."

"And who told Briggs?"

"Me," Scarborough said. "He's the skipper. He has a right to know."

That rage against the journalists and their stories spilled out of Rags. He grabbed the hunchback by his ear. "What I say to you is private, understand? It's got nothing to do with Mr. Briggs or any bigmouths from the *Globe*."

The other men heard Scarborough howl, and they slapped their knees and delivered horselaughs at the spectacle of a dumb brute with a fist clamped to the side of his head. That horrible sniggering of the team killed the anger in Rags. He saw the veins stand in purple knots on Scarborough's temple, and he let go of the ear. He should have questioned Scarborough in the hotel room, and not around the bat rack, where college babies and country boys could laugh at them.

"Didn't mean it, Scarborough," Rags said. "I shouldn't have touched your ear."

The hunchback drew his crippled shoulder away from Rags, and pulled two "black beauties" out of the rack for Garland James. Rags felt a shiver when the Sox took the field. He wasn't in the mood to crouch like a monkey, with his arms dangling, and his legs splayed, so he could gobble up any grounder that spun in the grass. He was as much a bully as Garland was. "Orphan," he muttered, "orphan Rags," hoping to work his mind back into the game.

Mr. Briggs' old team was at the park, those tough guys from St. Louis. The Brownies owned the bases. They could run you to death, charging at an infielder with their spikes above your throat. It gave them pleasure to rip a man's cheek. The Brownies, with Dutch Schleibner, Homer Ezzell, Baby Doll Jacobson, and Hank Severeid, loved a good brawl. They twittered at Ragland from the steps of their dugout.

"Love a hunchback," they said, making noises with their mouths inside their fists. "How's your roomie, little orphan boy? Do you grease him right? Hey, Rags, does a hunchback taste like snow?"

Their evil clucking only got Rags to play. He went into that crouch of his and denied a bunt single to Baby Doll, galloping and throwing to first in one great blur of motion that was too pure an act for anyone on the Browns to comprehend. Baby Doll had dropped a perfect bunt, and the ball arrived at first base before he did. There was a silence in the dugout.

St. Louis couldn't get a ball through the hole. Rags was always there. So the Brownies looked to Garland James in short center field. *The college boy thinks he's the old Gray Eagle.* The bench climbed on Garl. "Hey, Tris Speaker, how you doing, Tris?" Dutch Schleibner drilled a double over Garland's head. Garland tripped and tore the seat of his pants while running for the ball.

The Browns had made him appear ridiculous. Garland didn't blame them. It was Rags who had shut him off from his natural boundaries in the field, Rags who was forcing him out of his shallow spot. No center fielder running with his mouth to the wall could compete with a crazy-armed kid.

Rags wasn't thinking of Garland or the Browns. He noticed two women in Hollis McKee's box. They were like witches with hair on fire. That's what the sun behind third did to redheaded girls. Rags could see the quiver of their eyebrows as they talked to Hollis. They didn't bother with parasols and straw hats. They let the sun fall on their eyes and their lips. They had beautiful, sharp noses and little ears, the girls with Hollis McKee. Rags went over to his bat boy after the Brownies were retired in the fifth. Scarborough was still gloomy with him. Rags kept his distance from Scarborough's ear. "Who are the girlies with Hollis?" he asked.

"Them's the Cottonmouths," Scarborough said. "They live on Beacon Hill."

"They twins, or something?"

"No, no. They're a mother and daughter team."

Rags couldn't believe it. "They look like they're both your age, Scarborough . . . twenty-three."

The hunchback made a fat lip. "Iva's fifteen. And her mama's thirty-five, I expect. Marylou."

"Which one's the mama?"

"She's in the middle."

"Her? She aint mama Cottonmouth. The other one's older, you ask me."

"You're blind," the hunchback said, starting to move away.

Rags pulled him back with a shout. "How come you know about their histories?"

"Everybody knows. They're Hollis' pets, them Cottonmouths. He brings them to Fenway all the time."

And Scarborough finally got away, carrying out a rosin bag for Germany Stone.

Rags would look and look for the Cottonmouths, mixing up mother and daughter in his head. Marylou had the smile of a girl; Iva pouted like the matrons of Beacon Hill. Red hair on a woman could inflame Rags and weaken him for baseball. Hollis' pets, the hunchback crooned. Rags had to take his eyes off the Cottonmouths.

There was dissension on the club. Garland had tolerated Rags while he was a curio, but now he was a rookie that refused to disappear. Garl had been wrong about the kid. Snake Attreau didn't get his old job back. The Snake and Nemo Leibold were sent to Washington for a pittance, a small bundle of cash. The skipper was giving them away. He picked up Ira Flagstead, a journeyman outfielder from Detroit, but he held with Babe Ragland at third. All the catches Garl made, coming out from behind the flagpole in center field, grabbing balls off the tongue of his shoe, were meaningless with the kid around. The Royal Rooters, those raving boys in red coats, who abandoned the Sox after Hollis sold Babe Ruth and butchered the club, were coming back. The Royal Rooters could get little solace at Braves Field. The Boston Nationals had lost a hundred games in 1922. So the Rooters took up their old seats at Fenway, near the Boston dugout, to watch that strange kid Hollis had brought out of the hinterland. They were touched by the story of a foundling Babe.

"Bastard" became their call word. The Rooters had nothing for Garland James. He could stand in the outfield forever, in wind, sun, or rain, and they wouldn't have noticed him. They had an affliction for Dartmouth men. None of the Rooters had been to college. It was sissified. They were from South Boston, where all the "John Harvards" were afraid to go at night.

Garland felt undermined. Why should he let a busher from nowhere usurp his position on the club? He began to pester Briggs. "It's trading time, skip, that's what I hear. Me for Baby Doll. You'd better talk to the Browns."

"Don't be silly, Garl. Hollis wouldn't think of losing you in a trade."

"Well, do something about the busher then. Take him off third."

"I can't, Garl. I don't have an infield without him."

"It's too bad, skip, because all the commotion that busher makes, all his jumping around, is gonna ruin my batting eye someday. And we'll really be in trouble."

Garland had other resources than Mr. Briggs. If the busher wouldn't stop his monkey dance, Garl had ways of quieting him. He broke into Rags' locker and tore the kid's uniforms with a razor blade. He filed down Rags' spikes to little stubs that belonged in an old man's mouth. He put wounds in the kid's three bats, shaving

their barrels until the polish was gone and you had naked wood,
with splinters on every side.

The kid tolerated these shreds and ruins. Rookies weren't supposed to bitch. They had to cow before veterans if they wanted to
stay alive. That was the law of the major leagues. But Garl's wrath
went outside the expected boundaries of baseball gear. He slapped
and kicked Scarborough for rooming with Rags, and then he stole
Scarborough's shirts, hats and pants from the hotel and burned
them in a trash barrel at Fenway Park.

A day after this bonfire, he discovered that his two favorite bats
were missing. A groundkeeper located them for Garl. His "black
beauties" were now charred sticks. Somebody put them in the same
barrel Garl had used to burn Scarborough's pants. He moaned at
the image of his two dead bats. No one had ever seen a Dartmouth
man cry. "Who did it?"

"Me."

Rags was pointing to himself. "I don't think black wood be-
comes you, Mr. James. It gives you a bloated look when you swing
at the ball. Blond wood, sir. I'll make you a present of blond wood."

Garland leapt on the boy and tried to tear off his mouth. His
own allies had to pull him away. It was ten minutes to game time,
and the Sox had to be out on the field. The fans would have despaired if Rags had gone to third with no mouth. "Busher," Garl
said, "meet me in the tunnel after the game."

Rags told him, "I will." His mouth was still raw from where
Garl had clutched at him. Rags probed with a finger. He spat out a
tooth and dropped it in a handkerchief. Scarborough was horrified,
but Rags smiled behind his sleeve. "It brings you luck to give up a
tooth like that."

"You'll give up half your mouth if you meet him in the tunnel.
He learned boxing at Dartmouth."

"So what?"

The hunchback began to sway his head. "Don't you know about him and Ty Cobb? Cobb used to beat shit out of everybody in the league. He decked George Sisler. He hung a bloody lip on Babe Ruth. And Ping Bodie had to run from him. But Garl boxed him to a draw. I seen it. They both took black eyes last year in Detroit . . . now Cobb leaves him alone. Listen. Go into the other dugout after the game, and I'll get you your street pants."

"Hell no. I aint gonna hide."

"He'll murder you, Rags. He has the fists."

"Maybe," Rags said. "But don't you bring me my pants." The kid played his game. He smothered the Brownies, who couldn't break the jinx Rags put on them. The kid was everywhere. You couldn't drag bunt, or loop the ball into shallow left field. He would stagger, twist, hop, and rise off his knees with *something* in his glove. The Rooters brought their trombones to the park. They serenaded Rags before and after each catch. And they sang to him from third base.

Ragland, Ragland,
Our orphan's the best.
No one can beat us
No one at all.
With our seventh Babe.

Hearing that song must have disheartened the Browns. They left the field, losing four out of four to the lowly Red Sox. Those clowns from Boston had shot to fifth place. Scarborough kept urging Rags to sneak into the visitors' dugout. Rags stuck his fifty-cent glove into his back pocket and went down the steps of his own dugout and on into the runway. It was in this damp tunnel leading to the clubhouse that he was supposed to fight Garland James. Scarborough walked behind Rags, groaning a lot.

It was gray and windy in the tunnel. The hunchback had to sneeze. Garland stood in the middle of the tunnel with most of the

Boston club. The country boys and the Dartmouth men had come together in their hatred for Rags. The Sox couldn't win without him, but Rags took all the attention away. He was a kid with freak hands and a crazy sense of where the ball would drop; he made the whole team look like silly dogs with nothing to do.

Garl rolled up the sleeves of his jersey, waiting for Rags. Alvin Critz and Tilly Young had become his handlers. They warmed his knuckles inside their baseball shirts. Chicken Stallings glinted evilly at Rags. Garl had mocked the Chicken for two years, cackling at him, calling him an illiterate bum, but the Chicken would rather have Garland on him than play with Rags. "Close his eyes, Garl. Then we'll see how many balls he grabs away from us."

There was a sad look to Garland James. He'd gotten over the fit of having his "black beauties" destroyed. He didn't shove the kid, push him into the wet, narrow walls of the tunnel that held drainage pipes for the grandstand over their heads. The tunnel always leaked.

"Busher, do you apologize for killin' my bats?"

"No."

The Chicken was overjoyed. "Put his head on backwards, Garl. You can do it."

"Shut up," Garland said. And his voice grew sweet again. "When I knock you down, kid. I'll give you the chance to get up. But don't expect too much."

Rags made two fists, and Garland waltzed around him, his body jumping with tremendous grace between the tunnel walls. At first he hit Rags with an open paw, as if the kid were a doll that had to be punished. Rags lunged with his left fist, but he couldn't smack Garland James. His miracle arms and legs abandoned him inside the tunnel. He poked at cloudy gray air. Garl feinted, slapped, and danced in his baseball shoes. The Dartmouth men laughed at all the blue welts Garl had raised near the kid's eyes. Soon Garl began to close his fists. "Mercy," the Chicken said, "now we'll have some fun."

Garl shortened his blows; knuckles flicked out at Rags, then drew back, like a hard, muscular tongue. You heard the crush against Ragland's face before those knuckles fell out of sight. Still, Garl wouldn't spend himself on Rags. He was listless today. He toyed with the kid, but he wouldn't go about annihilating him. The Sox's admiration for Garl turned to bitterness. They remembered how ferocious he'd been with Ty Cobb. He'd knocked Cobb down with a left hook that rattled the great man's teeth. And here he was waltzing with the kid.

Garl put down his fists. It disgusted him to paw at Ragland. He was Garland James of the Red Sox. He didn't fight bushers. "You can have him," he said to his mates. "I'm through." He walked into the clubhouse with his sleeves rolled up.

Chicken Stallings conferred with Seaman Schupp and the other college men. They wanted blood out of Rags, and they didn't get any. Garl had tricked them. He'd stirred them up, given them the promise of a good fight, and there was nothing to show.

Rags had a mouse in his eye and a swollen cheek, but they didn't need Garl for that. Any of them could have accomplished the same thing. They stood around the rookie and sneered. They had to have a piece of Rags, or they'd croak. "Rookie," the Chicken said, "you'd better get down on your knees and lick our shoes."

Rags was still in his boxing stance. "I aint licking your smelly shoes."

So they tore into him, eight of the Red Sox, swinging at the kid's ears, his mouth, and his brains. But they couldn't land a blow. That frigging hunchback crept between them and Rags. He spilled five of them to the ground, bumping them with the gnarl on his back. He threw Hooks Poland into the wall. He caught Seaman Schupp in his arms, gave him a deadly hug, and dropped him on a pile of Red Sox. He seized Tilly Young, hurled him into that dumb grayness, until Tilly screamed for his life. This wasn't Scarborough, their own private brute, the middle-aged boy with undeveloped legs who delivered bats and rosin bags to them. His shirt was torn. They noticed a powerful chest they hadn't conceived before. His crooked shoulder was equipped with long bands of muscle. He had veins in his forearm that popped around like a crazy eye. They fled from Scarborough, scattering into the clubhouse.

Rags felt the cuts on his face. Then he looked at the brute. He was bewildered. With the Red Sox gone out of the tunnel, Scarborough retreated into his torn shirt. He became a bat boy again, his nose pointing into the ground. Rags could have twisted Scarborough's ear this second, and the brute would only have shrieked.

"You are twenty-three," he said. "And you lumberjacked, you really did."

The brute wouldn't answer him. He returned to the dugout to wipe the bats clean and collect old balls and rosin bags from behind the bench.

3

There was nothing in the *Globe* about any fights in a tunnel at Fenway Park. Garland wouldn't tell the journalists he was feuding with Rags. He went back to reading Homer in the dugout. He didn't need the Red Sox for company. He had his favorite books of Sophocles. He lived at the Brunswick like everybody else, but without a roommate. Garl was the highest paid member of the Sox.

He was contemptuous of all the chuggerheads he had to meet day after day, country boys who had trouble with their own signatures. He'd gone to Dartmouth on a scholarship, as the son of an impoverished lawyer from Terre Haute. His father caught a chill and died in Garland's junior year. Garl dropped out of school. He went home to the Wabash River, having to support three younger brothers, a grandfather, and a mother who was afflicted with a nervous disease; she couldn't hear, talk, or chew. He signed a contract to play professional ball. He was earning ten thousand by 1923. Half of it went to support his brothers at Dartmouth, Princeton, and Cornell medical college. But his salary wasn't enough. Garl had to play in the winter leagues. He barnstormed on the Harry Heilmann All-Stars, a loose confederation of men who would tour the South and the Far West, taking on local colleges and Black teams.

The All-Stars would end up in Cuba, going from province to province in a little red bus; they were the gringo wonders who never lost a game. The team would disperse in January. Garl drifted for a few weeks, and it would be time to head for training camp in Sackville Forest.

After he was through with the frigging Sox, Garl swore he'd go back to Dartmouth and finish his degree. Maybe he could stay on in New Hampshire, become the college coach, and teach a little

Sophocles on the side. Then he wouldn't have to live at a baseball
hotel with the likes of Scarborough, Ragland, and Chicken Stallings.

Garl was getting notes in his box at the Brunswick. They were
written in a mad scrawl. He didn't have to peek at the letterhead:
Boston, Louisburg Square. Garl recognized the bite of the ink.
That Cottonmouth woman was courting him again. Garl knew all
about the families of Beacon Hill: the Cantons, The Borgoynes, the
Beebes, and the Cottonmouths. But he had no love for the "Hill"
people. Their names could linger for a century. *His* father died an
obscure man. Garl preferred the mud of the Wabash to Louisburg
Square.

"Garland James," the woman wrote, "Garland James, Garland
James, when will you visit me?" *When the boss stops bringing you
to ball games, Marylou.* How was he supposed to truck around
with Hollis' lady friends? It was Hollis who paid him ten thousand
a year. He was indentured to his Dartmouth brother, Hollis McK-
ee. *I'm that man's slave, Marylou.*

She was the beautiful one, making a bonnet out of her own red
hair to sit high on her forehead. The woman was fond of poetry.
Hollis would invite him up to the executive office, near the roofs
of Fenway Park, and serve bathtub gin to Garl and Marylou. The
boss would grab him by the shoulder. "Garl, you're the only goddamn ballplayer on the club. I'd throw the others to the rats, but I
wouldn't trade you for half the St. Louie Browns."

He'd go on palavering like that, while the woman recited
scratches of poetry. She'd confuse Robert Browning and William
Blake, but the difference was, her palaver didn't come out silky and
smooth. She'd flirt with him right under the boss' nose. "How many
fraternities bid for you. Garland James? I'll bet you were a terrific
catch. My late husband Judah was a Dartmouth man. That's where
he and Hollis met, in a fraternity house. I'm a Bryn Mawr girl myself."

"I didn't have much time for fraternities, ma'am. I went out for the baseball team, and I had to work in the college laundry to survive."

Garl crumpled that letter he got. A perfume seemed to come off the paper and stick to his hand. Marylou's smell. The Cottonmouths weren't for him. He'd have felt out of place on the brick paths of Louisburg Square. Garl was tied to his baseball hotel.

He encountered Ragland in the hall. The kid's face hadn't healed. The marks on him were turning yellow. It was almost as if he wore a colored mask around his eyes. That's how symmetrical Garl's blows had been. They passed each other without offering the meagerest sign of hello. Garl was ashamed. He shouldn't have used his knuckles on a growing boy.

The kid was going out for a walk. He could have gone down Boylston Street to the Public Garden, where children would have begged for his autograph. Rags had a free afternoon. There was no Sunday baseball in Boston. The city fathers had declared a day of rest.

The Red Sox and the Braves would descend on the Public Garden, or the Common that was attached to it. They would arrive in their baseball caps, seek out a particular spot, and wait for widows and college girls to appear. But Rags wouldn't wait with them. He preferred that wild park, the Back Bay Fens, near his hotel. The park was overgrown with every sort of leaf; some of the leaves were taller than Rags. It was a thick, marshy land, half wet, half dry, with a snaky black pool that would often sink into the ground. This pool was called the Muddy River.

Rags enjoyed following the obscure banks of that crazy river on a Sunday afternoon. The Fens had become a lovers' lane used by clever people from the Latin School and Boston University; they enticed local girls into the marsh and undressed them as often as they could. Rags would stumble upon these creatures during his walks. He'd pardon himself and let them hide under some magnificent leaf.

On a Sunday in June he broke up a disturbance near the river bank. Two young men were annoying a woman in a light blue dress. They kept trying to drag her somewhere. They each took hold of an arm and pulled. They didn't abandon their wretched work even when they spotted Rags. They smiled at him and continued to pull.

Rags cracked one of them on the neck with his forearm. The young man tottered for a moment and fell into the river. He screamed his outrage at Rags and ran off with his friend, while the young woman took off her hat. Red hair spilled onto her eyes. She was a Cottonmouth.

"Marylou?" he said, noticing a tiny wrinkle at the corner of her chin.

"I'm Iva. Who are you?"

"Ragland. I play for the Sox. I saw you sittin' with Mr. McKee."

Iva was doubtful of him. "What happened to your eyes?"

"Had a fight. . . two weeks ago."

"Did Garland James beat you up?"

"No, no," Rags said. "He swung, I swung, and that was it."

"Don't be so proud," she told him. "Garland beats up everybody."

The daughter was beginning to anger him. "What are you doin' in the Fens?"

"Looking for my mother," she said.

"Hell, why would your mother come to a swamp?"

"Why do you think?"

Rags didn't like the way she pouted at him, as if she were lecturing a turtle in the woods, some dumb, helpless beast that could be flopped over on its back and made to writhe.

"Miz Iva, I don't care if your mother sleeps in the swamp. It's the same to me."

"Sometimes she does," Iva said. "It depends on if she can convince her beau to come back to the house."

"What beau is that?"

"Any beau she can find."

Iva wasn't making much sense. "You mean your mother comes here to meet college boys?"

"She isn't that choosy. She takes what she can get."

"And them two guys on the river bank, they weren't after you. They were after your mama. Aint that right? They thought Miz Iva was Marylou."

"Yes," she said, "but you certainly yak a lot for a baseball player. Now will you help me look?"

They began slapping at the thickets for Marylou. All they did was upset lovers in the grass. They knocked through the Fens for an hour, their faces swollen red from the heat of their work. Iva took to mumbling.

"Mama isn't in her right mind when she comes here. She gets on the trolley and she goes for a ride. It's like walking in your sleep. The madness hits her. She falls into a dream. I wouldn't care. But men take advantage of her. They steal her shoes and her purse. She brings gigolos back to the house. They live with us for weeks. They work up a bill you wouldn't believe. Mama buys them everything. Hollis has to throw them out. He was daddy's best friend."

Rags tried to listen while he searched for traces of red hair. Iva shook his arm. "Give it up, will you? When mama wants to hide, there's nothing I can do. Take me home, Mr. Ragland. I hate it in here. Mama can have her jungle. I'm soaked through and through."

Rags had never been on the far side of the Common. Iva brought him to an incredible hill of streets. He marched on cobblestones and sidewalks of burnt red brick. Iva's hill was divorced from the rest of town. It had nothing to do with baseball diamonds, Rags' hotel, or her mother's swamp. The air wasn't smelly on Iva's hill.

They turned a corner and were at a little park with statues planted on the lawn. The park had a gate around it with different kinds of spears running along the top. Someone had stuck an apple into one of these spears; the apple bled a strange pink from its open wound. Iva wouldn't let him look at apple blood for very long. He had to follow her to a row of houses on the right side of the park. The front walls swelled in and out, and Rags saw a line of undulating windows and roofs.

"What is this place?"

Iva wiggled her jaw in deep contempt. "The Red Sox must live on Mars. Every beggar in the street knows about Louisburg Square."

"Beggar yourself," Rags said. "This is the first time I'm on this hill. I've got an occupation, Miz Iva. I play ball."

"Oh, shut up, and come inside," she said, and they walked into a house near the end of the row. Things had to be snug on Louisburg Square; no one alongside that little park ever heard of robbers and thieves. Iva could come and go. The door wasn't locked.

A butler seemed to jump out of the wall. He startled Rags. Iva whispered, "That's Rhys. Don't pay any attention to him. He used to be one of mama's beaus."

"Did she lift him from the swamp?"

"Not Rhys. Rhys is too refined. Mama discovered him in a coffee shop."

Then she shouted at the poor man. "Rhys, this is Mr. Ragland of the Red Sox. He's famous. Did you see his picture in the roto-gravure?...don't forget to tell me when mama gets back. Are you listening, Rhys?"

She was a savage girl. Rags felt sorry for the butler, who had to wear a black coat all the time and take abuse from Iva. The leaves in the parlor door split apart, and a woman in red silk came through the leaves.

"Mama, you're home!"

Marylou Cottonmouth didn't have a blemish on her face. She should have been a fifteen-year-old, not Iva. Iva was an irascible witch.

"Darling, why don't you ask your friend to stay and have tea with us?"

"He's not my friend, mama. He's that infant at third base. Don't you recognize him? Babe Ragland. Look at his eyes. Garland beat him up, and he won't admit it."

Marylou was distressed. Her mouth began to jump at the corners; Rags tried to sooth her. "It wasn't much of a fight, Miz Marylou. Garl didn't hurt me at all."

Her mouth was quiet again. She smiled at Rags. He went into the parlor with Marylou and her savage daughter. There were twelve sofas in the room. You could have sat the Red Sox and Browns and still had space for most of the American League. Mother and daughter picked the same couch. Rags settled into the love seat.

He heard the butler speak into a tube that was stuck in the wall. "The best cakes, I said. Henrietta, we have a ballplayer in the house."

A horrible squeak overtook the room; it was the din of the ropes being pulled somewhere behind the wall. Rhys opened a closet, dropped his hands inside, and drew out an enormous silver tray. This ceremony of movements was for Rags. The butler knew about the kid's bastard days in Baltimore; the Evening Transcript had told him that. He figured a bastard would be unconscious of ordinary household machines. So Rhys could give the illusion of conjuring knives, spoons, napkins, and plates out of a hole in the wall.

A splotch appeared on Iva's cheek. The servant's trick had filled her with spite. She hated Rags. How could a boy be so alert with his hands and so thick in the head?

"Ragland, what's wrong? Haven't you ever seen a dumbwaiter?"

"I've seen plenty of dumbwaiters. Don't you worry."

Marylou came between their squabble and defended Rags.

"Iva, don't be such a frightful pest. Pour Mr. Ragland some tea.

Rags drank his tea from a china cup. He was careful not to slurp. Marylou offered him an apricot tart. The crust burst in his fingers after he'd nibbled off the edges of the tart. He eats like a rat, Iva noticed.

But Marylou eased him out of the discomfort of having tart slivers all over his lap.

"Do your friends call you Babe?"

"I only have one friend, Miz Marylou. He's a hunchback. And he calls me Rags.

"Don't you have a Christian name?"

"That's it, ma'am. Babe."

"Well that's the funniest Christian name I ever heard...I'm sorry Rags. I shouldn't have contradicted you."

"You don't have to be sorry. The brothers at St. Mary's always said 'Babe' to me. 'Come here, Babe.' 'Go to sleep, Babe.' Things like that. Maybe there's a different name on my birth certificate. But it's hard to tell. Because nobody knows where that certificate is. I'm a foundling, ma'am. The brothers picked me right off the front step. I was two and a half."

"It must have been dreadful."

"Not so dreadful, ma'am. Them brothers raised me good. It was like having fifty parents, instead of one or two."

Rags finished his tea. "It's getting late for batting practice," he said.

Iva rose off her couch to nudge him under the ribs. "What are you talking about? Fenway Park is closed on Sunday."

"Not for us. The skipper likes to have a Sunday drill."

But it wasn't that simple for Rags to leave the house. He still had a ruined tart in his lap. He might have been stranded on the love seat for another hour if mama Cottonmouth hadn't stooped next to him and brushed off his knees.

"Say hello to Garl for me."

"I don't know if I can, Miz Marylou. We don't talk much. But I'll ask the hunchback to give him your regards."

"Never mind," Iva said, and she walked him out of the room, opening the twin leaves of the door and shutting them behind her and Rags, so she could have him to herself. She wasn't the kind of girl who would close her eyes and wait for a ballplayer's kiss. She climbed up on Rags' shoes, thrust her tongue into his mouth, explored most of his teeth, and as he uttered a little moan, she pushed him out onto Louisburg Square. Then she strode back into the parlor and began to scream.

"Rhys, get out of here. I want to be with my mother. And Rhys, I don't like you making fun of my guests. Save your dumbwaiter tricks for the cook. Now scatter. It gives me a headache just to look at you."

That barbarous quality went out of Iva's voice soon as Rhys disappeared. But she'd already struck a terror in Marylou. Miz Iva was the mother of the house. Marylou was like a small, wayward sister who had to be chastised, pummeled, and kissed.

"Mama, why do you embarrass yourself? Does the whole world have to know you're in love with Garland James? You can't trust that Ragland boy. He's a liar. I don't believe anybody found him on the steps. The boy with no name. What a dumb story!"

Marylou had begun to sob. "But he has such a nice face."

"What's so nice about it? He never smiles. And he's always watching you. It's shrewd of him to play the dope. Then he can blabber all he wants, and nothing he says has to make sense."

The kid was glad to get out of Boston. Rags would never want to live between Miz Iva and Miz Marylou. But he couldn't stop thinking of the sweet belly Marylou had under the folds of her red silk. That belly made him wild.

The Sox were going on their Western swing, into St. Louis, Cleveland, Chicago, and Detroit. Rags welcomed the cramped runway of a Pullman car. Whatever distanced him from the Cottonmouths had to be good. But the kid was unable to sleep. As a rookie he inherited the Pullman's upper berth; uppers always rattled louder than the lower berths. Rags had nightmares while he cuddled against a jittery shelf in the wall. He would dream that Marylou's belly exploded in his face, drenching him in ripe brown blood. The explosion hurt. Marylou's blood came at him in hot pellets. He would shake himself out of the dream, spread the curtain apart, climb down from his upper, paddle along the runway in his bare feet, and sit in the washroom for the rest of the night.

He got to Cleveland with swollen red eyes. He bathed his head in the clubhouse sink, put on his uniform, and destroyed the Tribe, as he knocked down bullet-shots with his chest, picked the ball out of the rough infield grass, and made the throw to first. Rags wasn't the only one who produced for the Sox. The infield had begun to mesh. Germany Stone loosened up at first; Seaman Schupp found his niche again; Alvin Critz rediscovered the double play. They learned to live with Rags. They managed their own territories and gave the left side of the infield to him.

And then there was Garl. He punched out three hits in the opening game, and went back to the center-field wall to rob Tris Speaker of a double. The Sox, with their meager pitching staff, took three of four from the Tribe.

They jumped on Chicago and Detroit, winning nine games in a row, and found themselves in second place. You couldn't laugh at the Red Sox anymore. They were beating you with broken-bat singles and the crazy glove they had at third. Rags was frustrating the American League. What sort of book could you keep on such a kid? *Boston's seventh Babe.*

Those bad boys of baseball, the St. Louis Browns, decided they would choke off Rags and end the Boston winning streak. The Brownies weren't like the Indians and the Tigers, who kept trying to seek out a pedigree for Rags, a magical notebook that would list Ragland's weaknesses and strengths. The kid had been born in smoke and fire. He could probably field the ball when he was five or six. Who cared what teams he had or hadn't played on? The Brownies rode him from their bench. "McKee's little bastard," they said. "Orphan prick." The Brownie catcher, Hank Severeid, would twitch at Rags from behind the plate. "Bastard here, bastard here . . . bastards can't buy a hit."

They sat in the dugout, sharpening their spikes. Brownie runners would fly at Rags and aim for his throat. It was futile work. Rags would twist his body away from those oncoming spikes and tag the runner on top of his head.

The Sox took the first game, 1 to nothing, on Sheriff Smith's breaking stuff and a triple by Garland James. St. Louis journalists mourned the Browns, and admired the "new" Red Sox. Boston had come out of the American League cellar to ravage the East and the West. Briggs Josephson took a corpse and stung it to life.

Chicken Stallings scoffed at the fancy words of St. Louis journalists, repeated to him by Germany Stone, since the Chicken couldn't read or write. "Who's a frigging corpse? We're winning because Garl's got a hot bat and we're having fun. That's all. It don't take a genius to find out." The Chicken brought a few "medicine bottles" of drugstore beer up to the Buckingham Hotel, and distributed them to the players. He was celebrating the pennant in June. "Lordy Lord, we're gonna grab Mr. Babe Ruth by the balls, and squeeze 'em, until the Yanks drop out of first."

Scarborough guzzled beer with the rest. The Sox had grown a bit kinder to him after the fracas in the tunnel. They didn't want to madden the brute, or they'd have to deal with the muscles under his shirt. So they said, "Hiya, Scarborough," and gave him beer to drink.

The sixth floor had become a Red Sox station in St. Louis. Ballplayers lingered there. The Sox owned the Buckingham on their trips to Sportsman's Park. You couldn't keep bimbos, journalists, and baseball nuts out of the hotel. Everyone wanted to traffic with a team that was in second place. Scarborough trundled down the hall, his brain thick with beer. He couldn't avoid the crowds of men and women who wiggled fingers at him. "That's the mascot. He brings them luck. Say, Scarborough, will you sign your name on my handkerchief?" The ink from his pen soaked through the handkerchief, turning "Scarborough" into a meaningless blot.

The hunchback was lonely for his room. It was better when the Sox lived in eighth place. Then the halls had nothing but ghosts in them. The door to his room was open. Scarborough peeked in. Rags stood with a man in a dark brown suit. They were shouting at each other. Rags had a strange music in his voice that the hunchback had never heard.

"Tell him *this* is school for me. I don't care what he thinks. I can earn a living. Yes, I wear pajamas in front of thirty thousand people, pajamas and high socks. And I run after a ball that can knock your head off if it hits you right. But the ball feeds me. My father can go to hell."

"You'd give up your inheritance for that? Cedric, your father could have you committed if he knew."

"How? I'm eighteen, and I signed a contract with the Boston Red Sox."

"But you used a false identity."

"So what? The Sox have lawyers too. They can legalize any name I like. I'm their third baseman, Mr. Griffey. And the Sox are on a winning streak. Don't you interfere."

Rags didn't have to look up. He could feel that brute at the door and also sniff him out. The hunchback had a long shadow and his own peculiar smell.

"Goodbye, Mr. Griffey. Thanks for the advice."

The man brushed past Scarborough as if the hunchback didn't have the right to exist. Scarborough frowned at Rags. "Who was that?"

"Some duffer I used to know."

"Why'd he call you Cedric?"

"Because that's the name the brothers pinned on me at the bad boys' school. But don't you ever use it. I'm not Cedric to anybody. You understand?"

"I don't have to understand. I'm no skunk. I wouldn't call you by a name you didn't like... you said something about a father to him. Whose father is that? Orphans aint supposed to have a dad."

"It's not your business," Rags said. "Who told you to stand by the door and snoop on people?"

"You aint the king here. It's my room as much as yours."

"Maybe I should learn from Garl and get a private suite when I'm on the road."

"You can't afford it," the hunchback snarled at him. "You're stuck with me, unless your dad is rich."

Rags walked out of the room, making the hunchback scream into the hall. "What about the chocolate sodas we were gonna have?"

"Not today," Rags said. "I'm sick of you."

The secret visitor in Rags' and Scarborough's room didn't hurt the Red Sox. The Brownies were in trouble. They couldn't shake the Boston infield loose. Ragland, Critz, and Schupp kept turning over the double play. The Sox denied the Brownies their favorite weapon: the drag bunt. The infield tightened like a fist around St. Louis. Rags would lunge into the grass and begin his submarine throw, with his chin near his shoes, and the ball coming from behind one knee. The busher was eating them alive.

They were an ordinary team without their trick bunts. The Brownies couldn't lay a ball near the third-base line. But how come Rags *always* knew when they were going to bunt? Some dog of a player or coach was swiping their signals from the dugout. Who the hell could it be? The Brownies had a complex schedule of crisscrossing signs. They could have fooled the Wizard of Oz with the different monkey twitches they'd developed. But the Sox were reading their every move. Boston could pull the meaningful twitches out of all the insane nods that passed between the dugout and the coaching boxes. It was like having a snake under your own bench.

The Brownies scratched themselves and looked across the field: one man on the Sox, and only one, had an intimate sense of their dugout. It was the brute. Scarborough enjoyed special privileges as bat boy of the Sox. He was forever hovering around home plate. The brute must have carried a pair of extra eyes in his hump. He was swindling the Brownies into the American League grave.

They revised their signals after the fourth inning. Baby Doll Jacobson bunted for a base hit. Ken Williams was able to bring him across. The Browns weren't finished. They scored again in the eighth, and squeaked past the Sox, 2-1. This was the kind of baseball they admired.

With their signals protected, they took three more from the Sox, and dropped them back to third. On getaway day, the Sox crept out of their hotel and rode to Union Station without muttering a word to the people of St. Louis. They were a club whose winning streak had deserted them.

Rags put on his last clean shirt and hurried over to that swamp near the ball park, the Back Bay Fens. His heart trembled under the pocket of his shirt as he pushed through leaves and wet grass. He was like a sleepwalker on some hungry mission. Sweat poured into his eyes. The mud sucked around his shoes. Alligators could have been roosting in the swamp water. Rags wouldn't have noticed. He'd come for Miz Marylou.

He had to leave the swamp without her. Iva must have tricked him: her mother didn't take the streetcar every day. She only went looking for beaus on very special afternoons.

Thoughts of Marylou's belly swam through his mind. He forgot about baseball and his talent for choking off the bunt. The beanpole was turning into a voluptuary. He wanted to lick the juices out of Marylou's succulent navel. He'd watch for pieces of lint.

He found Scarborough sulking in their room. The hunchback was distraught. The Brownies had unmasked him. Soon the entire league would know why Mr. Briggs "brung" him into baseball. He was a frigging thief. Brutes made lousy bat boys because they called attention to themselves and slowed the game down with their temperamental walks from the dugout. You couldn't rely on them. They had a lazy character. Sometimes they could be surly. And they liked to snarl at children. But their sneakiness paid off. No one could steal an enemy's signals like a brute. They could peer into your dugout from behind their hump. Most brutes were blessed with freakish fields of vision. They could see around benches, and under a coach's shoes. Scarborough had been decoding signs—an ear twitch, nose pulls, handkerchiefs sticking out of a manager's pocket—for a season and a half. That was his value to the club.

Rags heard him sniffle. "Skipper's gonna fire me."

"No he's not."

"He is. I'm useless. I can't grab signals for him. The bastards got my number now. You think Mr. Cobb'll let me near the Tiger bench? They'll hoot at me."

"So what? They can't hide a signal from you, Scarborough. Not in their life. They can dummy things up for a while. It won't do them any good. You're the best swiper in the major leagues."

But he couldn't console the hunchback. Scarborough kept figuring his own doom. So Rags went down to the lobby, where he could watch the constant parade of men and women. People loved to be seen at a baseball hotel. Country boys like Chicken Stallings and Germany Stone would assemble in the lobby so that Red Sox fans could seek them out and pay homage to them. They would sit with bubble gum in their jaws and yap to the prettiest girls.

There was a strange perfume in the lobby, stronger than cheap cologne and the Chicken's sour breath. You could feel that special sweetness rising out of everybody's skin. It was pennant fever. It hadn't come to Boston in five years. The faithful wouldn't abandon the Red Sox. What was a four- game losing streak? The Sox had their magical infield. They were still a first-division club.

Rags had his lobby hat, an old homburg he borrowed from the hunchback and pulled down over his eyes. He didn't want pretty girls to wink at him and ask for his room number when he was crazy for Marylou. The homburg made him invisible. He could stare at the circus of people from under the brim of his hat.

He recognized Marylou's servant Rhys. The servant had just come away from the front desk. "Hey Rhys," the kid said, raising his homburg.

The servant didn't seem to know who he was. "Don't you re-member? I'm Babe Ragland. The ballplayer. I had tea at Marylou's house."

"Hiya, Mr. Ragland. How do you do?"

"You hang out at the Brunswick, huh Rhys, you old son of a gun?"

"I don't hang out anywhere," Rhys said. "I was delivering a note from the missus."

"Is that note for me?"

Rhys gave a smirk. "The missus doesn't send notes to little boys . . . it's for Garland James."

The servant fled from Rags, who pulled his homburg down again. Michaels, the house detective, caught him muttering to him-self. *She sends notes to Garl, and nothing for Rags.*

Michaels took him by the shoulder. He figured Rags was some stray dog who was trying to park his dirty bones at the Brunswick. "Say, you bum, get out of here. We don't like your kind in the lob-by."

"It's me," Rags whispered, and he had to let Michaels peek un-der the hat.

"Sorry, Babe. We have to be careful, you know, or bums come in and take a nap. What's the story with the Tigers tomorrow? I have a dollar on you boys. For God's sake, will you please murder Ty Cobb?"

"Sure I will," Rags said, to get the house detective off his back. But he had small luck with the Tigers. He pushed, scratched, ate dry brown grass to get at the ball, and the Sox could only grab one win out of five. The wounds deepened on Scarborough's face. His eyes turned a dull yellow. The brute was in mourning at Fenway Park. The Tigers jumped up and down and twittered at him from their bench, making the hand signals of deaf and dumb mutes. "Scarborough honey, read my fingers, will ya? Lookee, here's the sign for 'hit and run.' "

Briggs didn't scold the brute. It wasn't Scarborough's fault that the Brownies caught him in his act and snitched to the rest of the league. It would have happened sooner or later. Sign-swipers last a summer or two. They have a high mortality rate. Scarborough could still entertain a ball park if Briggs could pull him out of his sad sleep. But the fans didn't seem to mind. They liked a slumbering brute. It took their attention away from the scoreboard, and those big leads the Tigers were running up.

Briggs realized the bitter rule of baseball under Hollis McKee: win if you can, and give them a clown show if you can't. Scarborough would walk from the dugout with a stuttering gait. He seemed terrorstruck. His eyeballs would shrink into his head, and he had the look of a stunted child, lost in the middle of Fenway Park. The Royal Rooters composed a song for him.

> You can have your Cobb
> And your Harry Heilmann
> Manush and Hooks Dauss mean nothing to us.
> We've got Scarrrrrborough
> Scarborough, Ragland, and James.

But you couldn't please the brute. The words of the song would fall onto his back, and his hump would start to whimper. He was the most miserable hunchback in town.

Rags couldn't bear Scarborough's company. He had to get out of the hotel. And he went back to the swamp because he had nothing better to do.

He stumbled around in the grass, swamp flies attacking his nose and giant caterpillars plummeting on his head. It could have been the Amazon jungle growing across from Fenway Park, the water was so steamy and black, and the air populated with murdering bugs. The kid had to slap at himself, or have his face get eaten off. He couldn't find a single pair of lovers in the swamp grass. It was too frigging hot.

He didn't believe Marylou was in there. She'd have to be crazy to crawl through the Fens. The swamp was empty of beaus. Who could tell where the college boys were? Sailing on the Charles? Plucking a banjo in the Common? They wouldn't have gone into any Back Bay jungle in this weather, not even for Marylou.

He heard a crackle in the high leaves. Was it a swamp animal? Boston alligators? A summer fox? A hand parted the leaves in front of Rags. The leaves snapped back into place. But they couldn't hide whoever it was. Rags saw a curl of red hair. Then a woman's shoe. Mama Cottonmouth.

"Miz Marylou?"

Her face broke through the leaves. She had tiny balls of sweat on her upper lip. Hair flew over her head in a disintegrating bun that frightened Rags. He thought it was a bushel of snakes: red snakes about to uncoil. She dressed for the jungle in long skirts and a green satin belt. Her eyebrows wrinkled up for one terrible moment, and she was a madwoman with her gaze fixed on Rags. Then her eyebrows smoothed over and that brittleness went out of her face.

"I know you," she sang out in the voice of a coquette. "You're Harvard Jack."

Rags was going to shake his head and say, No, no, you have the wrong guy. I'm Babe Ragland, Miz Marylou. I came to Beacon Hill with your daughter. She has a big mouth. But he didn't want her eyebrows to knit again. He'd be her Harvard Jack.

He didn't have to coo at her, mouth little stories to make her get out of her clothes. She wasn't interested in the whereabouts of Harvard Jack. She took him into a grotto of leaves near the river bank, and she undressed, using her petticoat and her skirts as a blanket to protect them from the sharpest grass. He couldn't take his eyes off Marylou. She had beautiful freckles on her arms. Her buttocks were as perfect as a child's. Her breasts were lovely and small, the nipples pointing out at Rags in the wild leaves of the grotto. Her belly didn't have one unsightly crease.

She laughed at him. "Harvard Jack, do you always lie down in the bushes with your trousers on?"

In that fervor of watching Marylou, Rags forgot about himself. He shucked off pants, shirt, and underwear, letting these articles drop around him, in the folds of different leaves. He was embarrassed by his own erection. He'd never had such a swelling before. His glans stood like a forest onion with red and blue skin. He was amazed at all the colors the throb of blood could produce.

Marylou didn't shy away from him. She brought him down into her blanket of skirts. Her body seemed luminescent to him, as if any part of her could give off wonderful bits of light. Her cheekbones began to shine for Rags. Her fingers were in the tangle of hair at the back of his neck. She signaled her desire with scratches and strokes. He was able to enter Marylou without the slightest push. How did he get so far inside her belly? Crickets chirped in his skull. Caterpillars dropped. Flies burrowed into his shoulder. The grotto was beset with tiny animals. His body served as a frigging table for them. But he could hardly feel their bites. Who would have dreamed that he'd ever make love to Marylou?

"Harvard Jack," she said, with licks behind his ear. Her tongue was warm and delicious.

4

A blight arrived at Fenway Park. It was another plague year for the Red Sox. They lost eleven out of fourteen and fell into sixth place. Thank God Hollis McKee was preoccupied with his musical, *Eveline*. It was having its summer trial at Boston's Shubert Theatre, and Hollis would leave Fenway Park in the middle of a game and taxi over to Tremont Street, so he could bully his director and his stars hours before show time. Theatre critics worshiped his musical comedy about the sufferings of baseball wives. It didn't matter to them that Hollis' team was moving towards the cellar. The critics adored *Eveline*. Hollis had himself a hit.

That's why manager Briggs began to worry. His spies on the club told him Hollis was looking for Babe Ragland. The boss wanted Rags up in the executive suite. He only invited Dartmouth men upstairs to drink moonshine with him, unless he had some deal in his head. Then he'd grab you by the hand and give you to his "cousins" at Yankee Stadium. Briggs smelled disaster for the Sox. His infield would come apart without Ragland at third, and the plague year would be complete.

Rags climbed the great wooden stairs over the clubhouse. Secretaries passed him on the stairs and wouldn't even nod to him. He knocked on a door that had the word owner scratched into the glass. Hollis came out for him, and Rags followed the boss inside. He didn't notice one desk or file cabinet in the executive suite. They sat on upholstered chairs in what looked to Rags like a wide living room. "Congratulations," Hollis said.

Rags figured the boss had to be drunk. But where was all the whiskey?

"What's Briggs paying you, son?"

"Eight hundred, Mr. McKee."

"That's a swindle," Hollis said. "Nine hundred's the minimum on my club."

"I know that. But a hundred goes for uniforms and extra food bills on the road."

"I don't care. This isn't Paducah. It's the Boston Red Sox. We're not fly-by-nights. You're in the major leagues. Tell Briggs I'm doubling your salary."

Rags shifted around on the plush seat of his chair.

"He won't believe it, sir, if it comes from me."

"He'll have to believe it," Hollis said. So Rags settled in. What could he do? The boss had declared a raise for him.

"Don't let her talk you into eloping, son. It would break her mother's heart. She's just a schoolgirl. It will have to be a long engagement. You can't have her until she's seventeen. Otherwise the engagement is off."

Mr. McKee was starting with that crazy jabber again. The kid was a rookie in the American League. He lived at the Brunswick Hotel. He played third for Mr. Briggs. He didn't know anything about "long engagements." He figured it was smart to nod his head. He got a big raise from the boss, and he didn't want to anger him.

"You won't let me down, will you. Babe?"

"No, sir."

"I'm a single man myself. Iva and Marylou are like family to me. I won't tolerate seeing them hurt. I was at Dartmouth with Iva's pa. We were sworn to one another. Bloodbrothers. You're a foundling, and I don't expect you to understand fraternity rites. But I hope you'll appreciate this. My brother Judah is long dead, and I'm watching out for him. I consider Iva to be my own child. She's stubborn as the devil. If Iva says she's going to marry a baseball player, that's what she'll do. Only I pity the man who doesn't take my advice. No whirlwind courtships, Babe. She's fifteen and a half."

The boss stood up, so Rags did the same thing. They crossed that living room together, and Hollis opened the door and accompanied him to the edge of the stairs. Rags had been maneuvered into something, and he couldn't say what. He was in love with mama Cottonmouth, not that redheaded daughter who said goodbye to you with her tongue and then tossed you into the street.

The skipper was waiting for him at the bottom of the stairs. "Well, kid, how did it go?"

"Fine," Rags said, as if he'd just stepped out of a foolish dream.

"Is Hollis sending you to the Yanks?"

"No."

"Are you sure you won't be in a Yankee uniform next season?"

"Nobody can be sure of that, Mr. Briggs. This is the major leagues. But the boss told me to remind you that I'm getting a raise. He's giving me double money, Mr. Briggs."

Briggs couldn't grasp the mandarin ways of Hollis McKee. The skipper had been begging Hollis for months to throw the kid a few extra dollars, and Hollis had refused. He was the stingiest owner in baseball. He made Briggs "steal" a hundred dollars from all the rookies, obliging them to pay for food money that should have come out of the owner's purse. Now Hollis had decided to double the kid's salary.

The skipper said, "Good luck," and Rags went into the clubhouse to put on Boston's colors and his baseball shoes.

Rags had a miserable afternoon. He bobbled the ball twice chasing bunts, and he couldn't buy a hit. But the Sox managed to win. Garland James doubled to the left-field wall with a man on board, and they nosed out the Indians, 1-0.

It wasn't shaky arms and legs that produced the kid's errors. He couldn't concentrate on the Indians; his eyes kept wandering to the owner's box. Hollis had brought the Cottonmouths to the game. Rags watched Marylou clap after Garl had his double. She wore a pink dress, and she didn't seem like a woman who strolled in the jungle and lay down with Rags. She had precise halfmoons of powder on her cheeks: Marylou could have been a polite doll who'd come to cheer for the Red Sox and sip pink lemonade. But she had a hard time tilting the thermos jug. It was as big and clumsy as a cannon shell.

He made Scarborough deliver a note to Miz Iva. *Meet me at the corner of Ipswich and Van Ness after the game. Truly yours. Rags.*

Rags got there first. He threw a jacket over his uniform in the clubhouse, so he could hide under the lapels. The crowd was too busy flowing away from the ball-park to stop and recognize Rags. He was safe on Ipswich Street.

Iva discovered him skulking behind his lapels. "You picked a dumb place to meet. Can't we go to a little shop and have iced coffee?"

"I don't want to have an iced coffee with you," Rags muttered. His jaw was clamped so hard, a whistling noise rushed through his teeth.

"Then what is it you do want, Mr. Ragland Rags?"

She had a nest of tiny agitated wrinkles that ran under one ear. Her face couldn't shine like Marylou's. She was the most rambunctious girl Rags ever saw.

"Why'd you tell the boss we was engaged?"

She drew her head away from Rags and let her nostrils flare out. "I can tell Hollis whatever I like."

"Sure you can. He's your new pa. But I aint part of your family, Miz Iva."

"Oh, but I'll bet you'd like to be . . . you'd marry my mother in a minute."

"Your mother? Who says? I only talked to her once . . . don't you remember the tea we had?"

"I remember," Iva said. Rags thought her nostrils were going to rip. "I remember somebody who kissed me at the door and then sneaked into the swamp with Marylou. You're a disgusting liar,

Mr. Rags. I saw you down with her in the grass. You're vile when you're naked, do you know that?"

Rags' heart thumped under the jacket. His fingers had turned to lead. "Who told you to spy on us?"

"I wouldn't spy on ballplayer trash like you. My mother's a crazy woman, can't you tell? If I don't follow her, who will? I have to make sure she doesn't drown herself. You idiot, she's in love with Garland James. You could have been any man to her in that swamp. Some dumb college boy in knee-pants. Didn't you hear her call you 'Harvard Jack'?"

"Then what do you want to marry me for?"

"To punish you," she said, and she shouted other things at Rags, but he couldn't hear. His jacket fell off, and it was too late. People spotted his uniform. They milled around Rags, touching his Red Sox shirt. Their eyes were inflamed. Their mouths hung at every angle. "Babe, Babe, will you write a note to my daughter Bess? She'll be so thrilled." He was stuck inside a fence of people. He couldn't see Iva now. She'd abandoned him to all his rooters. He'd have to put his name on souvenir hats, scorecards. Red Sox flags, children's bonnets. "Awright," he said. "Here we go ... 'to darling Bess from Babe Ragland. July, 1923. Hi, Bess. Your daddy and I wish you grow up to be healthy and tall. It's good to have a tall woman in the house.'"

The kid was ruthless with the Indians in their next game. He took his wrath out on them, since those raw faces burning in the sun reminded him of Iva's red hair. He was like some weird angel who landed in the ball park to single out Tris Speaker's Indians and strike at them. The Tribe couldn't get near Rags' corner. The kid would run down men caught between second and third, stifle suicide bunts, and sidestep any jackass who hoped to barrel into him and knock the ball out of his glove. Seven Indians were stranded on second base.

Rags didn't have to dart looks at the owner's box. It was vacant this afternoon. No Hollis McKee, and no Cottonmouths to drink lemonade out of a cannon shell and clap for Dartmouth men. Hollis had gone to the Shubert with the Cottonmouths for a matinee performance of *Eveline*.

Iva and Marylou missed games three, four, and five with the Indians, who suddenly remembered how to play. They didn't have to squeeze past Babe Ragland. Doubles and triples brought their men home. The Tribe crushed Boston in the last three games of the series.

Briggs kept pulling cotton threads out of his baseball cap. The brim was nearly gone, most of it unraveled in the skipper's hand. The Sox were a game and a half out of the cellar. These men who once sat in second place, spitting on the Yankees and the Browns, had turned to spooks. They slipped away from the dugout like shadows on the run. Briggs had two live creatures left. Garland and the kid. But Garl was thinking of his retirement, when he could return to Dartmouth with his books of Sophocles; and Rags was obsessed with that jungle woman, Marylou, and her daughter who liked to breathe poison on him.

If the Cottonmouths wouldn't come to Fenway, he'd have to walk on cobblestones to find Louisburg Square. He crossed the Public Garden. He climbed Beacon Hill. And he knocked on Marylou's front door. He noticed funny things through the window. The furniture was draped with sheets. He had to knock again before that servant would open up for him. Rhys was surly with Rags. "It's an odd time for tea, old boy. We're locking up the house. Come back in October, if you like. I'll feed you dog biscuits. Don't you ever listen? We're locking up."

"Why?" Rags said.

"We're going to Tisbury town."

"Where's that?"

"My God, don't they civilize you during spring training? How can you live in Boston and be unaware of Tisbury and Edgartown?

Tisbury's on the Vineyard, you little ape. The missus always summers there."

"Martha's Vineyard?" Rags said. "Why didn't you say so? I heard of Martha's Vineyard. The governor of Massachusetts has a house on that island. I read it in the *Globe*."

"I'm glad they still teach orphans how to read," the servant told him. "Now go home to your Fenway Park. We don't like ballplayers on the Hill."

He would have shut the door in Rags' face, but Iva heard the commotion from her room, and she came downstairs to shout at Rhys. "I told you not to despise my guests."

"He's not a guest. Who invited him?"

"I did, Rhys. Get out of here."

Iva befriended Rags in front of the servant, but she didn't invite him inside. "You should have come yesterday," she said. "I could have shown you around the garden, Mr. Rags, given you the grand tour. You have special privileges now that you're my fiancé."

Rags saved his most bitter rookie smile for the girl. "I didn't sign no paper that says we're fiancéd."

"Who cares? Hollis made up a press release for me and you. It will be in all the society pages next week. *Mrs. Judah Cottonmouth of Tisbury and Beacon Hill announces the engagement of her only daughter, Iva Louise, to Mr. Babe Ragland of the Red Sox. Mr. Ragland has no family to speak for him, and no Christian name. He was educated by monks at St. Mary's reform school, where he studied baseball, shirt-mending, and Aeschylus.*"

"Aeschylus to you," Rags said, and he started to walk down the hill. Iva ran after him. She touched him softly on the sleeve. "I'm sorry. Rags. I didn't mean to poke fun at you."

"That's okay, Miz Iva. I know Aeschylus by heart. I should have told you. Garland sings it in the dugout before every game." He continued down the hill.

The kid was glad they'd gone off to Tisbury town. He had to suffer through a boring week of society columns about the Cottonmouths and him. He kept getting phone calls from an editor at the *Evening Transcript.* "No, Mr. Finnbar. No, no, no . . . the teaching brothers at St. Mary's brought me up. ... What? How can I tell you where I was born? They didn't find me until I was three. . . . Goodbye, Mr. Finnbar."

His teammates would get on his back soon as he arrived at the clubhouse. "Look who's here. The Cottonmouth Kid. How does it feel to rob the cradle. Rags? Does Miz Iva have her bleeding spells? Or do girls start bleeding these days before they're eleven?"

It was Garl who told them to shut up.

"I can't read with all this noise, you chumps. Leave the kid alone."

Chicken Stallings said, "Hell, Garl. Can't we have some fun?"

You could feel Garl about to turn mean. His eyes began to flutter in his head. "Where'd you learn about the engagement, little man? In the comic strips? Is that how retarded ballplayers get the news? Does Germany do the translating? Or can you look at the pictures by yourself?"

The Chicken slunk away from Garl and disappeared into the tunnel. Rags went over to Garl.

"You didn't have to defend me, Mr. James. I'm used to it by now. The Chicken doesn't bother me at all."

"I wasn't defending you," Garl said, lacing up his shoes. "I just wanted some quiet."

The fans must have seen the society pages, because they whistled and clapped when the kid ran down to third for fielding practice. But he didn't get any mercy from the White Sox. Their bench jockeys assembled in the dugout long before the game. They crowed at Rags. "How's the Babe? Don't you see the hair on his lip? The kid's been eatin' moon pie.

Rags stroked two singles and knocked in the run that beat Kid Gleason's Chisox. The Bosox seemed to come alive for a day or two. Then they dropped a doubleheader to Chicago, and they were still the beauties of seventh place.

The Bosox took a leap into the cellar once they got on the road. They went into Yankee Stadium and were booed for half an hour. The Yanks' hunchback, Henry Watteau, sidled up to Rags and said, "How many li'l ladies did you unflower last week, you friggin' Bluebeard?" And then he challenged Scarborough to a fight. Henry's antics were only a prelude to the games themselves. The Yanks must have had a lumberyard inside their dugout. They walloped Boston to death with their different bats. Ruth was on the bench half the time with a bad cold, but the Yanks didn't need him. They had Wally Pipp, Aaron Ward, and Henry Watteau. They took five straight from their Boston cousins.

The Sox hid out in their rooms at the Concourse Plaza. Scarborough sat with his chin on one knee. He was beginning to steal signals again from enemy clubs, but the brute lost his desire for chocolate sundaes. All he did off the field was blink his eyes and mope.

Rags screamed at him. "Damn your hide. What's the gorilla face for?"

"Who's gonna be my roommate after you go? Briggs will have to find another hunchback to stay with me. They'll say we're brothers and promote us as the Red Sox freaks."

"You're demented, Scarborough, that's what. Briggs aint hiring another hunchback. He's got you. You're enough for five teams. How can I go anywhere, huh? I'm on the road with you."

"But you'll be livin' with the Cottonmouths when the summer's gone."

"Not Babe Ragland. Not me. The papers are full of society tricks. I'm eighteen, Scarborough. They can scribble about my engagement until their noses fall off. I aint getting married until I'm fifty-three."

The brute was satisfied. He pulled on his chin, climbed off the bed, and invited Rags downstairs for sundaes at the Concourse Soda Shoppe.

Scarborough smiled with a spoon in his mouth. He had a mob of chocolate syrup between his ears. "Rags, did you watch me read the Yankee bench? You can't fool ol' Scarborough. Next time I'll knock Henry Watteau off his ass. The Yanks must have picked him up in a dog factory. Henry's retiring next year. He caught a hernia lifting them Yankee bats."

"Will you stop yakking about Henry Watteau. He's just a miserable dwarf."

The brute's eyebrows bunched along his forehead. "Who's miserabler? Henry or me? Henry's got a wife and two little girls. He owns a garage in Des Moines. What have I got? A pair of swollen balls and a big hole in my pocket."

"Well, we'll be in Philadelphia tonight. So you think about swiping plays off Connie Mack."

"That old man? I'll steal him blind."

Whatever Scarborough stole, it didn't help much. The A's devoured the Boston Red Sox. Briggs took his circus act to Washington, D.C., where the Senators proceeded to tear the Sox apart. Those funny boys, the clowns of Fenway Park, hadn't won a game on this Eastern trip. They returned to Back Bay Station and the Brunswick Hotel.

Michaels, the house detective, was barking at a kid in the lobby. The kid was in hiding. Rags couldn't see much of his face. He had a cap that came down over his ears and covered his mouth. The kid wore a wool vest in July and baggy pants that he must have found in a barrel of old clothes.

"Hey, runt," Michaels said, "I told ya to beat it. Don't come back again."

"Michaels, lay off," Rags said.

"Jesus, Babe, do ya know this runt?"

The house dick apologized. "I'm awfully sorry. I figured he was a bum who lives in garbage cans." He shook the kid's hand. It disappeared inside Michaels' paw. Rags shoved the kid along by his neck. A strand of red hair poked out of his shirt. The hunchback was watching him.

"How are you?" the kid said. "I'm Muggsy. I went to reform school with the Babe. We was on the same team. I'm a southpaw. I pitch for the Blue Sox of St. Mary's. Fella, did you notice my wing?"

"Shut up," Rags said. "And go on upstairs."

The kid took his cap off in the room. He shook his head and revealed a full scalp of red hair. The brute was mortified. "Rags, you brung a bimbo up to the room."

"What bimbo? That's my fiancée."

"Iva? She aint supposed to be up here. Michaels will have the shits. He'll say the two of us are soliciting on the sixth floor. Let her climb down the fire escape. Girl, be quick."

Rags hushed the brute. "Damn you, Scarborough, will you lemme talk to her for a second." Then he turned to Miz Iva. "What's all this playacting about? Muggsy of the Blue Sox. I'm not one of your stupid servants. You should be on that island with your mother. Tisbury town. With the governor and all the other golden men."

"I came up to Boston for a holiday. I hate the beaches and the sand. Dunes are for burying people."

"Good, but why do you need this hotel? Your mama has a place. You could sleep at home."

"The house is shut for the summer. You can't find a soul on Louisburg Square in July and August, except silly people who come looking for John Hancock's grave. I don't want to sleep in a big old house by myself. You'll have to put me up, Mr. Rags."

Scarborough paced across the room, his hump rising and falling with the lunges of his body. "All we got is one lousy bed."

"I don't mind. I can sleep in the middle."

Scarborough was muttering now. "Chase her out . . . skipper's gonna suspend us for carrying a child."

"Where am I gonna chase her to?" Rags said. "They still shang-hai girls off the street. You want her to end up in some whore's al-ley? She's practically the boss' niece. Hollis will send us to Paducah if something happens to her. She can stay for the night, and then she goes back to Martha's Vineyard. Where'd you get your cap and pants, Miz Muggsy?"

"From a ragman on Scollay Square."

"Well, he sure knows his merchandise. You look like a chump's daughter, long as you hide the red hair. I'm hungry. Let's go down and eat."

They had to skirt the house dick, who would have sniffed un-der Muggsy's disguise soon enough and yelled for the manag-er. They traveled in a line of three, Scarborough, Rags, and the girl-boy in cap and vest, moving furtively from place to place. They had mutton chops on Queensberry Street, and banana splits on Horaedan Way. They sat in a nickelodeon on Hunting-ton Avenue and watched cowboys slug Indians, prairie dogs, and white buffalo for twenty-five minutes. The cowboys didn't lose a man. Scarborough yawned but Iva wasn't taking any hints: she wouldn't rush with them to the Brunswick and go to bed. "Show me a speakeasy."

"What?"

"You know, a saloon."

"We aint got time for saloons," Rags screamed. "We're playing ball tomorrow."

Iva stopped dead on Shattuck Street. Rags whispered to the brute. "Scarborough, where's the closest saloon?"

They crossed the trolley tracks and hiked to a bluestone house on Darling Street. The brute went up the steps alone, knocked on the door, and muttered a few words. "Humpty Dumpty and his friends. Three Joes from the ball park." The door opened for Scarborough, who signaled down to Iva and Rags, and the three of them were scooped inside. They followed a man in a striped shirt through a long, narrow hall and into a half-empty bar that smelled of mahogany, beer, and nickel plate. The man said goodbye to "Humpty Dumpty" and returned to his post at the door.

Rags frowned at the brute. "How come you're Humpty Dumpty on Darling Street?"

"You can't get in here without a dummy name. That's the way it works."

It must have been a baseball saloon, because Rags spotted five of the Boston Braves: Cotton Charles, Mickey O'Neill, Hod Ford, and two utility men. They smiled at Scarborough, saying, "Hiya, Hump, how's the Sox?" They winked at Muggsy, but they refused to look at Rags. The Boston Braves didn't talk to rookies in their favorite saloon.

Rags shrugged at their insult and ordered wine and soda water for Muggsy and himself. He didn't have to watch over the brute. Scarborough was lord of the saloon. He stole a cocktail shaker from the barman and filled it with gin. He drank from the shaker, with fat Humpty Dumpty lips.

The wine and soda water loosened Iva's tongue. She growled the words of a song she remembered from Hollis' show, using the drunken voice of a man.

Eveline, Eveline, won't you wait for me?
I die on the road
Thinking of you.

Cotton Charles clapped from his table. "I know that," he said, wagging a finger at Muggsy. "That's the love song from *Eveline* ... hey, Hump, your boss Hollis laid a blue egg. His show stinks."

"There's a show that stinks worse than *Eveline,* " Rags said. "It's called the Boston Braves."

Cotton Charles leapt up in a fury. "This is a decent house. Bushers aint supposed to talk."

Rags had a fury of his own gnawing at him. His face was like a bloody hood. You could only see bits of his eyes. "I know who I am, Mr. Charles. I'm Babe Ragland, and I wear a rookie's glove. I always respect my betters. But I don't have to play a deaf mute in the company of a turd."

It was funny talk for a bastard, Scarborough figured to himself. How many orphans learned to speak like that? But the hunchback had other considerations. "Rags, there's five of them, and only two of us."

"Don't forget Muggsy. Muggsy can fight."

The barman didn't have to oversee any squabbling between the Red Sox and the Braves. He beckoned to the man in the striped shirt. The man touched Scarborough on the shoulder. "Sorry, Hump, your friend the busher will have to go."

Rags wasn't inclined to move, but Scarborough squeezed his calf under the table, and he chose not to ignore a direct signal from the brute. He got up with Muggsy and left the saloon. Scarborough came out a minute later, while Rags sulked on Darling Street.

"Why did you take that guff? I have quicker hands than any gorilla in a striped shirt."

"That gorilla happens to be from the Homicide Bureau. The saloon hires him as a sheriff once or twice a week."

"What kind of frigging world is this, where cops can become babysitters in a Boston speakeasy?"

"The same frigging world that stole Babe Ruth from us and turned the Sox into a cemetery."

"Who cares about Babe Ruth?" Muggsy said. "I'm tired. I have to get some sleep."

They brought her up to the room, but they didn't know how to arrange for Miz Iva. It baffled them to live with a girl. The toilet was out in the hall, and one of the Boston players might see her if she tried to undress in there. They would have to curtain off a little den for her in the room. Muggsy didn't need a den. She borrowed a pair of the brute's pajamas and undressed behind the window drapes. She had no trouble sleeping with the two men. Scarborough and Rags kept to the corners, and she occupied the middle zones of the bed.

Rags brooded in his pajamas. The Boston papers were swearing he had a fiancée, RAGLAND TO MARRY ICE HEIRESS' DAUGH-TER (the Cottonmouths had made their money manufacturing ice). But it wasn't an engagement worth talking about. How can you have a fiancée and not be able to touch her pajama leg? He had to squeeze over to the lumpy end of the mattress, and anchor himself somehow, so he wouldn't fall off the bed.

He was foul-eyed in the morning. His temper started to flair. He woke his bedmates at half-past six and said, "It's time for orange juice." He stuck Iva behind the drapes and told her to get dressed.

"Hold your horses," she snapped at him, but she still pinned up her garter belt and put on her shoes. Scarborough's shirttails were sticking out. Rags wouldn't give him the chance to groom himself. They went over to a coffee shop on Huntington Avenue that was a landmark now, because Babe Ruth had eaten there every morning when he first came to the Sox. Ruth would order twenty strips of bacon and ten scrambled eggs, and cover everything with ketchup. Rags didn't have Ruth's appetite. The most he could suck on were three soft-boiled eggs. The owners of the shop were careful with him. The Sox may have been a team of vagabonds, but the kid was Boston's new sensation. They wouldn't slight the seventh Babe.

"Eggs, Mr. Ragland?"

"Yeah, eggs for all of us. And orange juice."

The three of them ate their eggs in silence. Rags' foulness began to lift. "Did you sleep well, Miz Muggsy?"

"Well enough, but one of you has long toenails. My ankles are scratched."

"That's me," Scarborough confessed. "It's unlucky to cut your toes. It could put us on a losing streak."

"Cut 'em," Rags said. "We can't lose any more than we're losing now."

They walked Muggsy to the motorbus that would take her to Woods Hole, where she could catch the ferry to her mother's island. She gave Rags and Scarborough each a loud kiss and got on the bus. "See you in September or October," she said from her piece of the window. The fragrance of her kiss was lost in the fumes of the motorbus. But Rags didn't forget the impression of her teeth and the wet smack of her lips. Muggsy's lips. He wouldn't have a fiancée to think about until October. Maybe the gossip columns would leave him alone.

5

BOSTON had two dead dogs on its hands, the Braves and the Sox. But you couldn't sweep them away. Dead as they were, the dogs had real properties: groundsmen and players, dirt and yellow grass, grandstands, scoreboards, a hundred thousand frankfurters, and a legion of lemonade boys. You had to let the dogs lie still, or the frankfurters would rot and the grass would run wild, invade the stands, and throw splinters into the brick walls. The fans learned how to live with these dogs of baseball, who had their own dogs' war; they were so far down in the losing columns, they seemed to exist outside the major leagues.

The faithful still had their sport. They took bets: who would be the first to lose a hundred games, the Red Sox or the Braves? Briggs didn't care what went on at Braves Field. He wasn't a frigging bookie, and he wouldn't condone such a stupid bet. He drilled his men harder than before. He would give them no free days. They fielded among themselves in empty ball parks, while their opposition ate turkey dinners or swam in country lakes.

He invoked baseball history to inspire the Sox. "Remember the Miracle Browns of 1914? I was on that club. We were in the cellar for a hundred and sixteen days. Then we started to climb. We went from last to fifth in the month that was left. We damn near murdered the league. We should have been in the Series, not those big elephants, the A's."

"Times was different," Chicken Stallings said. "The Brownies had you, skip. You're worth ten Connie Macks."

"But Boston has the kid ... no one can wear Ragland's glove."

"He's a forkhander," the Chicken said. "Forkhanders always jinx a club. You think Connie Mack would hire a forkhander to play third?"

"He'd hire the kid faster than he'd hire you," Garl said, and he went back to his Latin and his Greek.

Pep talks and drills couldn't advance the Sox. They'd win and lose, lose and win. July leaked into August, and September landed on the Sox in eighth place. Briggs said goodbye to his men, warning them about the perils of winter baseball. "I'll kill the son of a bitch who breaks a leg in Havana. Go fishing, for God's sake, or look for a wife. Maybe I'll see you bums in Arkansas."

Then he climbed upstairs to the owner's suite. He expected the boss to fire him. The Sox were exactly where he'd found them two years ago: at the bottom of the well.

He couldn't understand what Hollis was smiling about. "Briggs, how much did you steal from me this summer?"

"I didn't steal one bloody dime."

"I'd say you stole six or seven thousand. Isn't that what I'm paying you? I'll have to check."

"You've been paying me six, Hollis. I ought to know my salary."

"That's what I said. *Six.* Well, what if I raised you to six and a half?"

Briggs had been with baseball too long to trust an owner's word on the last day of the season. "Are you asking me to come back next spring?"

"Of course I am. I know the rubes you've had to work with. We collect fodder from the rest of the league. You did the best you could."

Briggs told himself Hollis was a lunatic. *He sells his players and then blames the team.* But the skipper understood— Hollis' mind wasn't on baseball. The boss was dreaming of *Eveline.*

Briggs shook the boss' hand, but he'd forget baseball until a contract arrived in the mail. You couldn't tell what would happen in 1924. Some wise developer might turn Fenway into a skating rink. The Sox would disappear from baseball, and Boston would be a one-team town. Briggs scratched his jaw. God help a city that had to depend on the Boston Braves.

The Sox could have lost ten more games, and Hollis wouldn't have cared. Owning a ballclub was a fool's occupation. But he enjoyed seeing himself on the metal plate in Fenway's front wall, BOSTON AMERICAN LEAGUE BASEBALL COMPANY. HOLLIS McKEE, PRESIDENT. Who else had twenty-five dummies in red and white suits that he could barter with, buy or sell any day of the week? It was like swapping toy soldiers. Hollis paid them, and they had to bite their tongues. He picked up as many Dartmouth men as he could. He was loyal to his college. But it wasn't only that. He didn't want to shame Boston with a band of shoeless country boys.

Besides, Hollis was an impresario, a man who created musical comedies. He'd have sold his Sox if the chance came along. It never did. No one would have the Red Sox. He offered them to the governor of Massachusetts, a friend of his. "Bob, let the Commonwealth take my boys. You can bicker over who to buy and who to sell at the Old State House."

The governor laughed, but he didn't want the Sox. Hollis winked at him. The president of the Red Sox was in a playful mood. He was bringing *Eveline* to Broadway. *Eveline* would arrive at the Morosco in another week. It couldn't miss. It would make up for the half million he'd lost on his last two shows. He hired a special train to deliver him and ninety-five guests to Manhattan. There would be congressmen on board and the governor himself They could close one eye when the whiskey went around. Hollis invited Garland James, Rags, and the Cottonmouths, who'd just come home from Tisbury. He didn't like ballplayers to mix with his theatrical friends. Garl and Rags were the only two Red Sox on the train.

Rags had to buy monkey clothes for the launching of *Eveline*. He sat in a boiled shirt, with a collar that pinched his neck, and a tie that nearly strangled him. A servant (it was Rhys) traveled down the aisles of the car, ladling quantities of hot rum with a golden spoon that he would dip into a great wooden vat on wheels. A flame sputtered in the middle of the vat, and filled the car with a sulfurous smell. Rags had to sneeze. He wiped his nose with a towel that he lifted from the servant's pocket. He kept sneaking looks at Marylou. She wore a marvelous black cape that only covered half her body. Capes were getting shorter and shorter that year.

She couldn't have noticed Rags. All she did was stare at Garl. "Garland James, why don't you ever come to see us on Beacon Hill?"

"It's not that simple, ma'am. It's hard to visit when you're playing ball."

"But the season's over."

"Not for me, Miz Marylou. I go barnstorming next week with the Heilmann All-Stars."

"That's not the reason," she exclaimed. She was getting bolder with Garl. "You always have a good story."

"I'll try to come, ma'am. I will. I'll pack a day early if I can." Then he excused himself and went into the washroom. Rags followed him in there. Something bothered the kid. He hadn't received a single invitation to join a barnstorming club. What was wrong with him? He had better hands than most third basemen, and nobody wanted him. Even Chicken Stallings had gotten a bid. The Chicken was going to play with Bob Meusel and Babe Ruth.

He unwound that death knot of a tie, dipped his fingers in the water basin, and said to Garl, "Can Harry Heilmann use another hand at third, Mr. James?"

"I don't think so, kid, but I'll ask."

Garl noticed Ragland's sullen eyes.

"You didn't get a bid, did you?"

"I guess I could play winter ball in some outlaw league."

"That would be dumb. You could get fined for doing that. Keep away from the outlaws."

The outlaw leagues were made up of professionals who had been suspended for life by the commissioner of baseball, Judge Kenesaw Mountain Landis. The Judge declared that whoever played with them, or was seen in their presence, would be subject to a hundred-dollar fine. The fines were impossible to revoke, since the owners themselves had little power over the Judge.

"Don't worry," Garl said. "You'll get your bid. But you'll have to sit out a year. Heilmann won't take on a rookie, no matter how spectacular he is. That's the rule."

"Funny rule, if it keeps a man from playing."

"I didn't invent baseball, kid. It happens to everybody. Don't bitch. Harry Heilmann wouldn't even look at me until I was in my third year."

Rags shrugged his shoulders in the gloomy light. "What am I gonna do all winter if I can't play?"

"Run around the Public Garden ... I don't know." They walked out of the washroom together and rejoined the Cottonmouths. Iva was peculiar with him. She'd lost that playfulness she had when she'd come to the Brunswick in men's pants. He called her "Miz Muggsy," and she didn't say a thing.

A row of private cabs met Hollis' train in New York. The cabs crawled up Seventh Avenue like a funeral procession and dropped Hollis' ninety-five guests outside the Morosco Theatre. Rags had a seat up front with other members of the "Boston party." The governor of Massachusetts clapped hands with anyone who came his way. Rags failed to see how the governor could gather votes in New York. But politics was a crazy business.

A woman sitting behind Rags touched him on the shoulder. "Oh, my God, aren't you Babe Ragland of the Red Sox?"

There was no use denying who he was in a public theatre. "Yes, ma'am. I'm the Babe."

"Haven't the Yankees gotten around to buying you yet?"

"I'd rather play for the Sox, ma'am. Does New York City have a wild park like the Fens? A park with alligators and rats that can fly? I'll stay in Boston and live near the swamp."

Rags felt the point of a shoe attack him on the shin. It was Iva's doing. She had the seat next to him. She shouted into his ear. "Do you flirt with any old witch who recognizes your face?"

"I wasn't flirting," Rags said. "Just being polite." But he hunched down in his seat, so other women would find it difficult to tap him on the shoulder. The lights gave three flickers of warning and went out. Ushers barred the aisles to latecomers. The theatre grew still. Rags heard a couple of bassoons. The band was striking up the overture to *Eveline*.

The kid didn't have an ear for music. The fiddlers in the band could have scratched on wooden boards, and it would have been the same to him. He was thinking about the stupid winter he'd have to spend playing pepper ball with Scarborough in the room. He wondered if the hotel would let him swing a bat in the halls.

It could have been a hundred years of overtures. The fiddlers scratched and scratched. He'd have sworn his hair was turning gray inside the Morosco. Had Hollis rigged the thing? Were you supposed to collapse and die before the end of *Eveline?*

The fiddlers stopped. The curtains spread apart with the sound of rattling wind. Nine men in Red Sox uniforms pranced onto the stage. No one could ever believe they were from the majors. Their chests were much too puny. Rags could see the paint on their lips from the third row. Nothing was rumpled about them. Their hands looked soft; they should have been gnarled, with broken knuckle joints. Their uniforms had been pressed before the show.

They were a frigging chorus line that danced and chattered into song. Rags cocked his head, but he couldn't unravel the words. The dancing was too loud. Skinny men in baseball hats pushed themselves and shouted gibberish that only a cossack could have understood. It made no sense, the Red Sox singing Russian songs.

Then the hero arrived. He was fatter than the rest.

Eveline, Eveline, won't you wait for me?
I die on the road
Thinking of you.

There were sniggers behind Rags. The theatre began to empty, and it was still the first act. Hollis was stuck with a fat man who swooned a lot.

The second act was devoted to Eveline and her gang of baseball wives. They could have been hens out of the Boston poultry markets; the red kerchiefs they wore shivered like chicken necks. Their shrill voices brought no sympathy for them. They complained about husbands who took to the road and left them to lie in an idle bed. People hissed openly now.

The third act united Eveline and the fat hero. They performed their duet, kissing, touching, singing with the chorus of men and wives. It was much too late. The charm had gone out of *Eveline*. They were singing in a graveyard. Hollis' own guests had deserted him. There were under twenty spooks in the theatre for the final kiss. Hollis had a stubborn actress playing Eveline's part. She insisted on her curtain calls. She came through the curtain with her eyebrows twitching like the devil. Rags clapped for her. What else could he do?

It was the first and last performance of *Eveline* in New York. Hollis had sunk a fortune into the show. His backers were ready to sue. Hollis had been precipitous with their money, they said. *Eveline* should never have gone to the Morosco. It would have died in Boston if Hollis hadn't paid certain newspapermen to puff the show. Hollis swore it was a lie. "I don't tamper with the critics." He hadn't lost faith in *Eveline*. It needed more work, that's all.

His actors quit. Hollis assembled a new cast. He went into rehearsal at Boston's Colonial Theatre. The papers stood behind him. "A little patching here and there, and *Evy* will be a wonderful show." No backers came forth with additional money. Hollis sank another fifty thousand into *Eveline*. and then he had to tell his actors and actresses to go home.

He consoled himself with a piece of undeniable truth: he still had his Red Sox. "I'm president of a baseball company. Those moneylenders can't grab the Sox away from me."

But it didn't cheer him up. Hollis had nothing but turkeys in his yard: a bum show about the Red Sox and the bums themselves. He was the town fool. Men he didn't even know sang snatches of *Eveline* to him on the street.

> Evy, Evy, stay with me.
> It's hell in Chicago
> Grief in Detroit
> Without my darlin' wife.

The boss went into seclusion. He exchanged no words with his employees. He locked his door at Fenway and retired to his rooms at the Ritz-Carlton Hotel. Hollis cast aside the small dignities of his station. He wouldn't put on a robe for the busboy who brought in his afternoon paper, his coffee, and his rye toast. He would stand in his underwear and look out at the Public Garden. Hollis' rooms were on the twelfth floor, and he could see all the way to Charlestown from his window.

Those heartless bastards in New York. I'll rewrite Eveline *myself. I'll play Ferdie Wills. I can sing.* Ferdie Wills was the ballplayer-husband and hero of the show.

The busboy would watch over Hollis while he was in a stupor at the window. "More coffee, Mr. McKee?"

Hollis turned his head. "Rory, can you dance?"

"Dance, sir? No."

"It's a pity. I could have used you in *Eveline.* "

He ate his suppers in his room. He didn't go near any of the five Boston clubs that had him on their membership lists. He would have been bored to death discussing the ups and downs of baseball with merchants and vestrymen who'd never been on the road with the Sox, and hadn't endured spring training at Sackville Forest. He could visit one of the bordellos on Gloucester Street. But whores were a chatty lot. Hollis was a little more anonymous without his clothes. Yet the girls always recognized him by the incision he had across his belly, where his appendix had been removed as a child. They called him the man with the scar. The man with the scar was rich. He owned the Boston Red Sox. The whores would only ask him about Garland James if he went to Gloucester Street. They loved his dark handsomeness. "Why don't you bring your center fielder, Mr. McKee? We'll play catch with him. We'll be careful he doesn't bend his thing."

Sometimes, in a panic, he would pray that Judah Cottonmouth was still alive. Judah had been his one good friend. They'd survived the snobberies of Old Boston together, became mavericks, choosing Dartmouth over Harvard, Amherst, and Williams. Judah could make him laugh. He'd throw spinach under the table at the Algonquin Club. He'd piss in the same urinal with Hollis' ballplayers.

They'd lie with a single whore half the night, ravage her, grow bored, ravage her again, drop cigar ashes on her belly, stuff a hundred dollars in her quim. He'd go on mourning Judah. How many bloodbrothers could a man have?

Hollis went walking after dark. He'd climb down the back stairs, so he wouldn't have to nod like a monkey on the elevator, and he'd exit from the hotel on Newbury Street. It was past the shopping hour. Bostonians had gone home to have their baked beans. Hollis could travel on foot without being sneered at. He was forty-one years old. He'd had three hits on Broadway. An American League franchise belonged to him. He was the man who sold Babe Ruth. Money turned to clay in his fists, kindergarten clay, red, blue, and yellow.

He could twirl a million dollars out of that clay, and then lose it all. His existence seemed poisoned to him. *Eveline* was his only passion.

Foolishly, his walk had taken him near the Brunswick Hotel. He couldn't avoid Babe Ragland. The kid had gone out for an ice-cream soda. He was crossing Brookline Avenue. "Ragland, hello."

Rags hadn't seen the boss in a month. Hollis had deep gray circles under his eyes. He could have been a wax man who decided to wiggle his arms and talk.

"Have you been laying in for winter, Ragland, or what?"

"They wouldn't let me barnstorm, Mr. McKee. I'm stuck in Boston."

"So am I," Hollis said. "Here, I'll sign my name on a card, and you can play billiards at my club. Stay with billiards, and the winter will go fast."

Rags took the little card that was offered him. "Thank you, Mr. McKee, but I don't play billiards. Baseball's what I like. Me and Scarborough have been throwing the ball around. The hotel empties in November. So there's lots of room for us."

"How's your fiancée?"

"Miz Iva? She don't have much time for me now. She's studying poetry at school."

"Well, you wouldn't want to marry a girl who didn't get good grades, would you, Ragland?"

"I guess not," Rags said.

"Good boy. Don't you catch the sniffles. Winter colds are hard to get rid of, and I'll need you at third. You're not a rookie anymore. Remember that. Briggs isn't the only expert in this town. I can measure what a man is worth." He pumped Rags' hand, said, "See you in Arkansas, son," and went right on with his walk.

It was a dog's winter in town. The hunchback would go to speakeasies and tank up as often as he liked, but Rags didn't have the urge to drink. He would arrive at Fenway in battered cleats, shout until the gatekeeper let him in, and he'd run on frozen dirt. That was his occupation, except for pepper games with the hunchback. He figured cotton would start to grow in his head if the calendar didn't shake loose and come to February, so he could pack for Arkansas.

Once, in deep November, Miz Iva came looking for him at the hotel. She wasn't Muggsy now. She wore a green blazer and long woolen socks. The green showed well with her hair. She was a day student at Miss Drabble's School for Girls on Chestnut Street.

"Funny you should remember me," Rags said. "I thought the engagement is off."

"That's a lie. Miss Drabble works us like donkeys, or I'd make you court me every night."

"How'd you get up to the room? Didn't the house dick notice you was a girl?"

"Oh, him? He's blind. Where's your roommate?"

"Drinking whiskey somewheres."

She stood Rags against the wall and kissed him with the full resources of her mouth. Rags couldn't say why his hands began to crawl. They were inside the blazer and under her blouse. Her breasts hardened to Rags' touch. They were much more swollen than Marylou's.

"My leg hurts," she bawled at him. "Are you going to undress me standing up?"

Rags grew aware of his fingers and he pulled them away from Iva's blouse. "What if Scarborough comes back?"

"We'll give him a few nickels and tell him to blow."

Iva shed everything she had and went under the covers with Rags. He sat on her, chewing her back, his erection jumping up her spine. "You'd better not go in, Rags. Mama will kill me if I'm not a virgin when I get to the house." The blood twisted in Rags' ears, and his penis turned profoundly blue, but he didn't penetrate Miz Iva. All that touching in bed seemed like torture to Rags. Iva began to dress in half an hour. "I'll visit you, sweetheart, soon as I can. And don't you ever think we're not engaged."

Rags had to walk around with a blue penis; thank God the swelling went down, or he couldn't have played pepper ball in the room. The snows had come to Boston when Iva knocked on his door again. She met Rags in a pair of filthy boots. He had to crouch in front of her and tug at the heels before her boots would come off. He sweated in the cold from all the pulling he had to do (steam at the Brunswick was an irregular affair). They accomplished the ritual of undressing themselves. They had their rigid play under the covers, kissing and a scrape of hands. Rags' knees shivered with lust. He had the same blue prick. "Couldn't we get married tonight?"

"Don't be a silly boy. Miss Drabble doesn't take wives into her school. And we'd need a home. I'm not living at the Brunswick Hotel."

"What kind of home can you get on a Red Sox salary?"

Iva stared at him as if he were the Boston idiot. "Hollis makes allowances for married men."

"He's already paying me double," Rags said.

"Who cares? Mama and him will provide for us."

But there was no more talk of houses and stipends for married players. It was the last he saw of Iva in the winter of 1923. Rags hiked up and down the halls for exercise. It was much too bitter outside to run in Fenway Park. He was more of a bachelor now than somebody's fiancée. He dined in soup kitchens with bums from the railroad yards. The brute had his speakeasies. Iva had her school. Rags went into winter shock. He could invent the sound of a ball rushing through dry yellow grass. That sound preserved whatever sanity he had left.

By February he was a frozen stick. He stuttered and blinked. The house detective would have hurled him into the street if he didn't know it was Rags under all that stubble on his chin. "Mr. Ragland, you look sorrowful, if you ask me. You have to prepare your mind for the Boston winter. It takes some disciplining. You crawl under your own skin like the grizzly bear, and one eye sleeps while the other's awake. That's the trick. You can die in Boston if you don't follow the grizzly bear."

"You should have told me that in October. I might have learned from it. But that's okay. We're going to Arkansas."

"Best of luck. I hope you boys get to the top. I'd like to make a pile on you. Only Hollis McKee'd have to disappear before that happens. That man's ruined us all."

Scarborough and Rags were the first scrubs to arrive at Sackville Forest. Icicles hung from their window at the team's boardinghouse. The hammock on the front porch was stiff as a dead man's arm. The playing field sat under a curtain of ice. "Where the hell are the Red Sox?" Rags groaned. "Aint this the month of February?"

Rags had insulted the brute. "Mister, I know what month I'm living in. Skipper's smarter than us, that's all. He can sniff the air in these parts. He'll open camp when the weather's right."

The Sox began to dribble into town, one by one, with red eyes, long beards, and shaggy tails. Since when did Arkansas pirates break into the major leagues? They could have been hill people come down from the Ozarks for a look at the civilized life of a baseball camp. But there was no baseball camp. Nothing but red eyes and shaggy tails. Chicken Stallings still had the trace of a sunburn on his nose. He blabbered about his times with Babe Ruth.

"Me and the Babe socked hell out of them Blacks in Havana. The Babe won't bat against a Black boy until he crosses himself. They're devils on the mound. All you can see is them black eyes. The Babe asked for an extra thousand in Havana, and he got it. I didn't have trouble swinging against the Blacks. I hit three triples one day, off the blackest man on this earth. I figured how to get to him. I just didn't look at his eyes."

"You must have paid that Black to sweeten the ball," Tilly Young said. "You never hit a triple in your life."

But you couldn't train on Chicken's stories, or Tilly's rebukes. Then, as the boys grew surly feasting eyes on each other, Briggs appeared. He was a fox about the weather: the ice had begun to crack on the playing field. He stood quiet for a few days and wouldn't stir from the boardinghouse; then he ordered the Sox to get into their practice suits. They didn't play ball. They chopped through the ice with their bats, and that was the opening of Briggs' camp at Sackville Forest in 1924.

One man was late: Garl missed the ice-chopping ceremonies. He didn't play pepper on the muddy field. The "A" and "B" squad games began without him. Rookies were invading Sackville Forest. Rags was insufferable to them. He'd developed a mean sophomore streak. His own bitterness surprised him. Why was he so quick to jump on those rooks? "Hey, busher, tie your shoes. This aint Paducah. It's the Red Sox training grounds."

The hunchback would scowl when he saw Rags join up with the Chicken or Germany Stone to taunt a new kid.

"You sure have a lean memory, brother Rags. Those country boys stuck you in the ribs during your rookie days."

"That's baseball," Rags said. "That's how it goes."

"Who says you have to keep up that shit?"

"I do. Ask Briggs. You'd rot to hell in Arkansas if you didn't have a few rookies to make you laugh... hey, where's Garl?"

"Garl knows how to find us. He'll get here when it's ripe for him to come."

So Rags went to the boardinghouse and picked the icicles off his window; the hunchback had ruined his taste for rookie-busting. The Sox looked scruffier than last year's team. Rags was waiting for Garl. Garl would pull these bushers together, create the Bosox of 1924.

He arrived in camp the first week of March, having walked out of some Nicaraguan jungle. The clothes were peeling on his back. His hands were scarred. But he didn't have winter fat on him. Garl came ready to play. The Chicken could brag about Babe Ruth. But it was kid stuff. The Babe would go wherever he was adored. His suite of followers lived at the best hotels in Havana and San Juan. He didn't hack out baseball diamonds with a machete and field a team of mestizos, convicts, and Nicaraguan Indians, like Garland James. Ruth barnstormed in white pants, with golf clubs and his own personal caddie, and enough ketchup and mustard to last him through the winter. Grown men and women would pay a dollar a head to watch him swing from his ankles. He was the most beloved giant in the world.

Garl was just a center fielder with a last-place team. He had seventeen triples in 1923 and batted .311, but he didn't hit more than five home runs. He wasn't beautiful when he struck out, like the Babe could be, his ankles hooked, and his body twisting into an incredible corkscrew machine. Garl only struck out eleven times.

His barnstorming was a different thing. Reporters didn't follow him. No one kept a record of his hits. He didn't have mustard raids and ketchup fights. He started in October with the Heilmann All-Stars, snaking down to Florida, leapfrogging across the provinces of Cuba, and ended winter baseball on his own. Who could be sure how many mestizos he converted to the game?

It didn't matter now. The Sox had him in short center field. The other outfielders wouldn't bump around, or crack a tooth with Garl there, signaling them away from the ball.

The ice lifted off Sackville Forest that week of Garl's arrival; tiny green stubs broke out of the muddy earth, as if Garl had come onto the playing field at midnight and put them in the ground. The Sox had a miraculous planter on their club. The rookies idolized him. "Can you show me how to grab the bat, Mr. James? I'm not getting any wood."

"Take a wider grip. You're not Babe Ruth."

The rookies kept away from Ragland, who guarded his terrain at third. You couldn't field with Rags. He ate up every grounder that fell within twenty yards of him. "Hey, you bushers, get out of my friggin' territory." The Sox didn't need a left fielder in Arkansas. Rags could chase down any fly that got to the left-field wall. But he wouldn't move into Garland's spot. He avoided center field.

He began drinking moonshine with the country boys. The Chicken took him into their irascible club. He wasn't a "kid" on the Bosox anymore. He was Babe Ragland. The country boys made room for him on the porch. They needed a strong ally against the Dartmouth men, who still dominated the Red Sox. Rags was replacing Germany Stone as their leader. They didn't bring up his obscure birth. Suppose he was an orphan. A bastard couldn't hurt, and who else among them would stand up to Garl? Something made them uneasy. They couldn't have Rags without the brute, and they detested Scarborough. "I can swallow as many bastards as you can find," the Chicken muttered to himself. "A freak of nature is something else. That has to be the unluckiest son of a bitch in the United States."

But Scarborough didn't intend to join their pack. He wouldn't run with bullies and practical jokers, who victimized cats, dogs, and any poor kid who came for a tryout with the Sox. The hunchback roomed with Rags, but otherwise he was alone.

That same mysterious man, a certain Mr. Griffey, who'd argued with Rags in St. Louis and called him "Cedric," showed up at camp. He was a persistent bird, this Mr. Griffey. He kept stalking Rags. He would drink soda pop, rent a chair from the boardinghouse, and watch Ragland play. He wasn't living in Sackville Forest. He'd come every morning from someplace else. Maybe the bird had a bungalow at Hot Springs.

The brute wouldn't spy on Rags, but he couldn't help hearing them scream.

"You've had your fun, your little immersion in baseball," the man said to Rags. "Now it's got to end. Your father won't tolerate much more of this."

"He'll have to tolerate it, Mr. Griffey. I'm not grubbing here. I'm on salary. I'd rather be a third-stringer than have to shine my father's shoes."

"Who said anything about shoes? Cedric, your father doesn't want you to beg. But his patience is being used up. I'm warning you. Get out of this wretched mud hole, resign on your own, or else . . ."

Rags must have had some moonshine in him. He grabbed ol' Griffey by the bottom of his coat, twisted all that material, and threw him down the boardinghouse steps. Griffey stopped haunting Sackville Forest. And Rags continued to laze on the porch with the dumbest part of the team.

Then the lord of the Red Sox came to town. Hollis had two show-girls with him, Nancy and Edna Mae. He was breaking them into the musical business, he said. They sat on his lap, took mousy bites out of his eyebrows, and spoke in baby language, but these girls had a feeling for the hierarchy of a baseball club. They would only flirt with Dartmouth men and the seventh Babe. Hollis punished them with a slap on their knuckles soon as they went near Rags. "That boy's engaged. He's going to marry my dead friend's little girl."

"But he's a honey, Mr. McKee. I'll bet he's wild as hell."

"It's not for you, Edna Mae. He has to save all that wildness for his wife."

The girls were only a decoration for Hollis. He hadn't come to Arkansas to philander with Nancy and Edna Mae. He was looking to arrange an exhibition series for his Red Sox.

"Hollis," Briggs said. "I know Emma Raines. She'd tour with us."

"Who's this Emma?"

"She owns the Cincinnati Black Giants with her husband Carl."

"You must be out of your skull," Hollis said. "Mix my boys with a black outfit? Those Giants play too rough."

"It's only a tour, Hollis. I could advise Emma to take it slow."

"Slow, huh? I heard what they did to the Cardinals the year before last. Crippled half their men. You can keep your Black Giants. We'll stick to the college circuit."

"Excuse me, Hollis, but we won't draw shit."

"We'll draw," Hollis said. "Just you wait awhile."

The boss was right. His Sox went to Fayetteville for a five-game series with the U. of Arkansas and sold out the park. The fans had heard of Briggs' sophomore wonder, and they wanted to see him catch and throw. What other team had a lefty at third? They weren't disappointed in Rags. They saw a whirlwind cover third base. That body would leap out of nowhere to untwist a line drive and turn the double play.

The Sox were on fire in all the college towns. They sold out wherever Hollis could book a game. But a band of crows was following them around. Rags saw these crows. They had a Buick with an open top. The Buick's sides were made of mahogany. The crows would rest on this mahogany and watch Briggs' team. They never paid admission. They would park their Buick across from the playing field and eat out of paper bags. They had the pinkest gums in Kentucky, where the Sox were right now. They could have been Black undertakers. All the crows wore dark suits.

Rags went to Scarborough. "Who are these guys?"

"Sockamayocks."

"Talk plain, will you? What's a sockamayock?"

"They're scrubs from the Cincinnati Black Giants."

"Why the hell are they following us?"

"It's an honor, Rags. They must be scouting you."

"You crazy? I'm with the Red Sox. I aint signing with no Black Giants. Are they figuring to steal me away?"

Scarborough smiled at Rags' stupidity. "That's how sockamayocks make their living. Sometimes they act as scouts. It means you aint a kid anymore. The Black Giants have heard of you, and they're aiming to copy your style. They do that with everybody in the big leagues who's more than a little good. They got a man who plays like Hornsby, a man who plays like Heilmann, and a man who plays like Garl. It's an act with them. They stop a game after five innings and pretend they're Heilmann and Cobb. There's a Black on the Giants that you'd swear was Babe Ruth."

"How come you're such an expert on the Cincinnati Giants?"

"Skipper took us to see them play, that's how come." "Well, if they're imitating people, they must be clowns."

"They have to clown to stay alive," Scarborough said. "The Cincinnati Giants are the best team in baseball. Ask Mr. Briggs. Even the sockamayocks in that car could tear hell out of us."

"Undertakers couldn't beat the Red Sox. If you're so cushy with them, why don't you ask the sockamayocks if they want to play?"

The brute slouched in front of Rags. "I wish I could. The boss wouldn't let us into a game with them. He says it'll hurt our image if the Sox are caught on the same field with the Cincinnati Giants."

They didn't have to argue about it. The crows disappeared. Rags didn't need sockamayocks around him to play. He dazzled every little town and humiliated all the college babies.

Boston and the Copper Kid:

BOOK TWO

6

The Sox opened in Philadelphia that year. They'd feasted on college pitching for over a month, and they expected the A's to lie down for them like the U. of Arkansas had done. The A's trimmed them, 5-2. Hollis was still in a cheerful mood. The Sox made a bundle for him on their spring tour. He could lose one to the A's. So what? His men turned around and buried the Athletics, 13-3. Garl homered into the roof, and Rags had a pair of doubles. The Sox split four games and got out of Philadelphia.

They didn't come home to an empty house. The Royal Rooters were at Back Bay Station to welcome Rags and the Red Sox. They brought xylophones and straw hats that their wives had painted red. Briggs had never seen the station so packed. *They're forgetting Babe Ruth, they're forgetting Babe Ruth.* Hollis dreamed of turnstiles. The idea of dollars at the gate got him to quit brooding over the failure of *Eveline.* He planned on thirty thousand for Opening Day at Fenway Park.

Those red-hatted Boston zealots serenaded Rags with a song, beating out the music on their xylophones with little wooden claws.

> You can keep your Yankees and your Browns
> We have the true boy
> He can hop and skip
> Our Babe's a grownup now
> Red Sox, Red Sox, 1924

The Royal Rooters would have carried Rags to his hotel, but he wouldn't allow it. "Thanks," he said. "I've got my own two feet." He kept giving his autograph away as he proceeded through the station.

There was a party for the Sox at the Brunswick Hotel. The manager had ordered wieners and a tub of sauerkraut from Jacob Worth & Co. Rags nibbled on a wiener and announced he was going to bed. The dark hadn't come to Boston yet. It was two o'clock in the afternoon, and Rags had a troubled sleep. Lizards crawled on his body. His toes were in muddy water. He must have stepped into the Boston swamp. Only Rags would dream of the Fens on his first day back. What was he trying to do? Walk across the swamp? He could hear sobbing in the Fens. The sobbing grew louder. It wrenched inside his head. Were the lizards crying for him? The sobs had a tremor that didn't seem strange. Rags opened his eyes.

The brute was sitting on the bed. His face was wet. A shudder went through the hump on his back. He was holding a newspaper. But he didn't look down at the words. He mewled something to Rags.

Rags couldn't understand him because of the sobs the brute was making. "What are you crying about?"

"You aint nothin' but a two-star fake. Talking to me like you come out of an orphanage when you're a college baby, like the rest."

Rags spread open the front page of the *Evening Transcript*. A headline barked out at him from the top. RICHES TO RAGS. "Who wrote that shit?"

There was no name under the headline, just a photograph of Rags wearing his freshman beanie at Amherst College. And a caption that said he was Cedric Tannehill, the son of a copper millionaire.

The sight of that hump moving up and down on Scarborough's back filled Rags with a loathing for himself. "You must think I'm the dumbest man in America," Scarborough said.

"Scarborough, I had to lie... it was the only way I could get on the team."

"I'm your roommate. You didn't have to lie to me."

"I would have told you, I swear."

But the brute turned his back on him. Rags got into his clothes and crept out the door. He barreled through the lobby with such a hard look that no one dared yell "Cedric" at him. He invaded the *Transcript's* offices on Washington Street. He stood in the ancient city room, with slow-eyed reporters and copyboys snoring behind a multitude of desks. Rags woke them with a frightful scream. "I'm Babe Ragland. Who wrote this about me?"

The reporters stared up at him while the copyboys ducked out of the room.

"Take me to the son of a bitch."

The reporters rubbed their eyes and began to have a faint recollection of Rags.

"Will you answer me? Where's the yellow bastard who's been monkeying with my life?"

The reporter closest to Ragland gave a shrug.

"Hell, Babe. The story came to us. We don't know how."

"You'd better start remembering," Rags said, "or I'll finish this place. I'm pretty good at throwing desks out the window."

Two night watchmen arrived. They had gigantic billy clubs, and badges pinned to their chest. They couldn't grit their teeth at Rags. They were Irishmen from Columbus Park, and the loyalest of Red Sox fans. "For the love of God, Babe, will you go home now? The rat who says you're Tannehill will stew in Hell. Let one lad desert you at the ball park, and we'll chop off his nose."

Rags grumbled out a smile. The watchmen wouldn't let him depart until he scratched "Babe Ragland" on their billies. The copyboys had come back. Rags waved goodbye and left the *Evening Transcript*.

Babe Ruth was in town. He'd come for Opening Day with the hunchback, Henry Watteau, and all the other Yanks. There wasn't a seat to buy. Hollis stuck the overflow crowd in "Duffy's Cliff," that sharp embankment in left field named for Duffy Lewis. The great Duff didn't need a piece of leather on his hand. He carried an extra shoe. He climbed that crazy hill from 1910 to 1917 and chased fly balls under the tongue of his third shoe. Not even Garl could equal that.

You couldn't find a Yankee fan in the overflow on "Duffy's Cliff'." The Boston faithful wouldn't have allowed mongrels and halfwits among them. They didn't sing a word about Babe Ruth. They had a Babe of their own, and it wasn't important now if he was a bastard, or the son of a millionaire. The *Globe* could scream whatever it liked this morning. Copper magnate? Marcus Tannehill? King of the Southwest? What did the faithful know about copper and the Southwest?

They mocked Ruth during Yankee batting practice. And they were furious at Henry Watteau. The Yankee hunchback was going to retire at the end of the month. Henry had a weak heart. He crouched in the dugout as much as he could. But a mascot has to do more than hide. Henry had to go onto the field and face those Boston lunatics. They called him "Babe Ruth's little man," because he would bring out bicarbonate of soda in a tall glass whenever the Bambino had one of his monster bellyaches.

It frightened him to be on Boston land. Henry could feel the pounding of his heart. He thought it would break through his ribs and leave him with a bloody wound inside his jersey. Baseball had never been kind to its brutes. It would pit one hunchback against the other. Henry could see an evil glint from the Boston dugout. Scarborough's eyes were burning into him. He didn't have the energy this year to frighten little girls and make a fist at Scarborough. Damn the Boston brute!

Scarborough wasn't thinking of Henry Watteau. *Tannehill* was in his head. The Sox had planted a college baby in his room. They'd stuck him with a rich boy, a rich boy who tells lies. The hunchback looked around: there wasn't any furor in the dugout. No one seemed disturbed by Rags' masquerade. The Dartmouth men snubbed him as much as they ever did. Could Rags talk Sophocles, like Garland James? He was still a fresh kid who had bumped their own man, Snake Attreau, off third base. And what about the country boys? They didn't shy away from Rags. The country boys were in awe of him; their new leader had gone to college. They didn't have to take guff from ol' Garl. Amherst was as fine a place as Dartmouth and Cornell.

Scarborough couldn't accomplish much on his own silly steam. Who would side with him? He didn't catch the skipper scolding Rags. He was one man against his roommate, Cedric, the copper kid. He felt a pair of baseball knickers brush past him. The knickers belonged to Rags.

"Aint you gonna talk to me ever again?"

The brute was furious. "Don't give me that rookie palaver. Orphans can use *aint*. Not you. Nobody says aint at Amherst anymore."

Rags had to take the field with the rest of the Sox. There was a maddening roar soon as his head emerged from the dugout. "Rags, Rags, Rags." He trotted alongside the Red Sox announcer, Bull Weingarten, who was carrying his megaphone up to home plate. He had to shout at Bull to make himself heard over that constant roaring of his pet name.

"Listen, Bull, I'm still Babe Ragland. If you call me Cedric in front of everybody, I'll jam that foghorn down your throat."

Bull's eyelashes fluttered in the Boston wind. "We'll settle this in the tunnel," he told Rags. Bull was sixty-three. He had the strongest tonsils in baseball, but he couldn't have danced in the tunnel with an eighteen-year-old kid.

Rags could tell the stupid thing he'd done. Bull wouldn't scorn a Red Sox player. He wasn't disloyal to Rags. The kid said, "I'm sorry. I shouldn't have . . ."

He went to third base with his shoulders hanging down. "Rags, Rags, Rags. We love Rags." That roaring couldn't revive him. Who was he? Cedric Tannehill, or the seventh Babe? His roomie slept on a little hump at the edge of the mattress, as far from Rags as it was humanly possible to be.

Bull Weingarten startled Rags out of his dreamy condition. Bull stood near home plate with his feet spread apart and spit into that leather funnel. He was the only announcer on this earth who could quiet a Boston crowd. Even "Duffy's Cliff" stopped quacking and listened to the Bull. He went through the Yankee batting order without much of a stir from the boys and girls of Fenway Park. The fans had lost interest in jeering Babe Ruth.

Bull took the Boston names out of his vest pocket. "Batting first for Boston and playing second base is Seaman Schupp, our kid from Notre Dame." He knew how to string out a man's title. Bull did. The crowd was going crazy.

"Batting second and playing shortstop is Old Reliable, Alvin Critz." Then it was Tilly Young and his Phi Beta Kappa key; Garland James of Dartmouth, the clean-up man. "Batting fifth and playing first base is the boy from Ronkonkoma. New York, Germany Stone."

Bull had the park in his grip. He wiped his mouth with a handkerchief and raised his funnel again. "Batting sixth and playing third is the sophomore sensation. Babe Ragland out of Baltimore and the St. Mary's orphan school league."

A peculiar bedlam broke out in "Duffy's Cliff." You could see the snaky rhythm of six thousand shoulders, as the men and women on that hill began to scream like demented cats. "We got an orphan here." The whole stadium picked it up. "Orphan, orphan, we got an orphan here."

The fans had defied the newspaper stories. They believed in their little bastard. Rags' shoulders straightened. He began to smile. *I'm Ragland. I play third.*

Bull called out the tail end of the lineup and trotted away with his leather funnel. Rags went into his familiar crouch at third, swinging on his knees, his head low, his knuckles in the dirt. The Yankees hooted at him from the dugout steps. "Talk to us, Cedric baby. How's the copper market? Can you buy us some shares? Tell us, do orphans like to play with copper shit?"

Rags didn't care. He had "Duffy's Cliff" behind him. He went to his left for a mean chopper and threw out the Yankee's first man, Whitey Witt. He turned to look into the owner's box. The Cotton-mouths weren't there. Hollis sat by himself this afternoon.

He wished Miz Iva and Miz Marylou had come to smile at him and scream *orphan* with his other fans. But he could hit without his fiancée. He socked the ball into "Duffy's Cliff" in the fourth inning. It was a ground-rule double that drove in Alvin and Garl, and put the Sox ahead, 2-0.

Babe Ruth tripled in the seventh with none away. "Kid," he yelled to Rags. "Fuck the newspapers. They're out to get orphans like us."

Kinship with Rags couldn't help the Babe. The Yankees left him stranded on third. When he came up to bat in the ninth, he grimaced and touched his belly. It was a signal for Henry Watteau to arrive with a glass of bicarb. The Babe drank it and belched to the crowd. He was still Babe Ruth, and you could afford to love him a little when your team was two runs ahead. But that love didn't include Henry Watteau. The fans took out their hatred for the Yanks on poor Henry.

"Drink poison, you shrimp."

Popcorn boxes rained down on the brute. Those that thumped against his back did him no harm. But when the sharp edge of a box landed in his face, Henry would go down on his knees. He had a gash along his nose, and different cuts on his ears. Blood trickled onto his Yankee blouse. None of the Yanks jumped off the dugout steps to shield the brute and bring him to safety. He wobbled into the dugout on his own and collapsed against the water fountain. He had a gray froth on his tongue. The Yanks forgot to notice him. He was their brute, that's all. They were watching the Babe.

He slapped the ball into the sky over third. It was heading for "Duffy's Cliff." Rags waved off his left fielder, Steve Dubec, and began to chase the ball. He ran on stubble and grass, his elbows pumping at his sides. His knickers were like long white leaping stones in the sun. He got to "Duffy's Cliff," reached in with his hand, and pulled that ball out of the overflow.

Ruth said "shit" to Boston. The kid had robbed him of a double. He crossed the infield on his famous pigeon toes, muttering to himself. He didn't see Henry lying near the water fountain. The Bambino was in a rage. He'd lost to the fucking Red Sox in Fenway Park.

7

THE Yankee brute woke with his own sad image staring into his face. He wanted to scream for his life. Scarborough was in the same room with him, sitting near his bed. The Boston brute had discovered Henry Watteau in the Yankee dugout and got the Red Sox trainer to call an ambulance. That was three days ago. Henry had gone from the emergency ward to the only private room at Boston City Hospital. The room overlooked a tiny yard where chickenpluckers worked on a mountain of feathers. But Henry hadn't noticed the view. He'd been delirious, moaning, spitting, crying, and begging Red Sox fans to leave him in peace. Now he had Scarborough with him. And it was like a horrible sore, having a fellow brute to look at up close.

"Where's my wife?"

"I called her," Scarborough said. "She's coming on the bus."

Henry sat up in bed, scowling at his double. "You make me sick, you know that? It gives me chest pains just to look at you."

"You aint such a pleasant sight yourself, little man." Henry began to chuckle. "How long have we been goin' at each other in the ball parks? Two summers? Did I ever bite you on the ear? Lemme see? I'd have bitten them flappers off by now if I didn't have a bad heart. Get out of the game. I'm telling you. Go live in a circus. It's better than being a baseball freak."

"Ah, it aint so bad with the Red Sox . . . hey, Watteau, don't you worry about this room. The Babe is paying for it."

"Ragland is paying for this room?"

"Your Babe," Scarborough said. "Not mine. He'd be here with you, only the Yanks have gone to Cleveland. I heard him say to the hospital, 'Put it on my tab. Henry gets the works.' "

Henry seemed a little miffed. "Didn't he say, 'Sky's the limit'?"

"Yeah, I think so. 'Sky's the limit for Henry Watteau.'"

"That's the Babe, all right. He's always saying, 'Sky's the limit.' A heart of gold that man has. Heart of gold." Scarborough stood up. "Hey, Watteau, I better get out before the nurses find me with you. I aint supposed to be here more than a minute."

"Did you really call my wife?"

"She's coming on the bus."

The Boston brute met Ragland in the hall. The kid was carrying a wand of pink and yellow flowers for Henry Watteau. "Gimme them daisies," Scarborough said. "Visitors aint allowed." He snatched the flowers away with a mean swipe of his fist. And he went back into Henry's room, shutting the door on Rags.

The kid wandered up Commonwealth Avenue to the Brunswick Hotel. He had to wear a cap over his eyes, or he would have been mobbed in the street. It might have been Ruth, Ruth, Ruth, everywhere else in the civilized world, but Rags was the beloved kid of Boston.

He had a guest in his room: Miz Iva had sneaked upstairs in her uniform from Miss Drabble's School for Girls. "Why didn't you come over to the house?"

"Nobody invited me," Rags said.

"They don't have to. You're my fiancé."

"I can't come over. Your mother must hate my guts for telling her I was an orphan without a Christian name."

"Oh, I never believed that hogwash. Mama knew it was a lie."

She shed her blazer and her high green socks. Her hips had broadened over the winter, and her breasts seemed rounder to Rags. Iva was turning into Marylou. Rags had such a swollen penis, he could hardly get out of his pants. But she continued that same peculiar lovemaking of last fall. They weren't allowed to touch each other below their bellybuttons. It exhausted Rags to lie with her and pet, while his glans tightened like a powerful bolt and his own erection became unbearable to him.

"How come you didn't write to me from Arkansas?" she said.

"I can't spell."

"Hogwash. They wouldn't let a nonspeller into Amherst."

The veins pulsed and pulsed on Rags' prick.

"Cedric, what's the matter?"

"Don't call me that. I'm Cedric to my father, and nobody else."

"Well, whoever you are, you have a green face."

"It's part of my complexion," Rags said, grabbing for his clothes. Iva squeezed into Rags' double bed. "I want to hug some more."

Too bad. Hugging you makes my prick stand up and whistle blood. "I can't, Miz Iva. You see, it's lousy for my batting eye."

"What is?"

"This staying in bed so long. I start looking at the ceiling, and I notice crazy blue spots, and the skipper says it can kill your eyes."

"He's a bigger idiot than you are," Iva said, but she got into her green socks. "I'm not going back to Miss Drabble's in the fall. I'm tired of her silly school. Rags, let's get married in July."

"Yeah, sure, July," Rags said, making her dress in a hurry. Iva wouldn't leave off kissing him. The kid had to shove her out the door. Then he dropped his pants, waddled over to the sink, and poured cold water on his burning blue prick. Petting was for dogs, he told himself. But he had to admit that Miz Iva was developing a beautiful bust.

The Sox went on the road mired in seventh place. They couldn't move up or down. The White Sox were the new Blacks of the American League. Boston stomped on them and did nothing else. There was a hole everywhere you looked. Sheriff Smith destroyed the Yankees and the Browns with his fireball and his wicked change of pace. But the rest of the staff was composed of knuckleheads like Frank Howe and Chicken Stallings, who had no pepper in their arms. Seaman Schupp was going stale at second base; Alvin Critz dragged his toes at short; Steve Dubec mumbled to himself in the outfield and missed ordinary fly balls; and Tilly's knees began to wobble behind the plate. The skipper could rely on four men: his fireballer, Sheriff Smith, his center fielder, Garland James, his third baseman. Rags, and Scarborough, his clown. Enemy fans loved to hiss at the Boston brute. Scarborough would climb the dugout wall and howl back at them. The brute enjoyed himself. He was the last surviving hunchback in the major leagues.

But he worried about the kid.

He wouldn't talk to Ragland. Ragland had broken the rules. Only a busher would be reckless enough to deceive his roommate. A roomie was as sacred as a wife. Still, Scarborough couldn't ignore what was true: the kid's lies had gotten him into trouble.

It was all right for visiting teams to call you the millionaire's boy. You could suffer through the worst sort of ridicule at home. Rags had the Boston faithful behind him. They sang to him from the stands and "Duffy's Cliff." He was the orphan they loved.

But who would sing for him on the road? The crowd paid its money to see Boston's left-handed wonder at third, the kid who liked to invent fables about himself. These fans weren't kind to him. They'd watch Ragland, but they wouldn't clap. Sometimes they'd clap for Garl, because they admired his footwork in center field; Garl didn't turn his body into a pretzel to come up with the ball; Garl didn't tell orphan's tales.

Christ, why did he have to copy off Babe Ruth?

Scarborough wished Rags had stolen another man's history. If he'd come into camp as a simple rookie called Rags, a millionaire father wouldn't have caused him so much grief. Who would have cared about the piles of copper in a kid's past? Now he couldn't outrun his own lies.

The bench jockeys feasted on him whenever Boston came to town. They razzed him in Chicago, they razzed him in St. Louis, they razzed him in Detroit. The Chisox were the worst offenders, because they were a bitter, frustrated team, stuck in the cellar, with the Red Sox sitting just on top of them, a game and a half away. They couldn't dislodge Boston. The Red Sox would bump them around. So they took their revenge on the kid.

The Chisox had a special party of buffoons, utility men who warmed the bench and could go at Rags all game. They were a party of four: Bibb Wallace, Shano Roth, Harvey Leonard, and Mike Welch. They would swagger on the dugout steps and yell across the infield at Rags. They'd heard somewhere that the kid's father had a limp, so Harvey Leonard came onto the field dragging his right foot and shouted, "Gimme copper, gimme copper," until the first-base ump chased him back into the dugout. Then Bibb Wallace began his routine. He swiped the announcer's megaphone and serenaded Rags. "Cedric Tannehill, son of Marcus the millionaire, tell us who your mama is. Aint she the Queen of Sheba?"

"My mother's dead," Rags repeated to himself and charged across the infield to get at Bibb. Tilly, Alvin, and Seaman Schupp had to take him by the belt and hurl him to the ground. The umpire seized the megaphone and tossed Bibb out of the game. Rags sent Chicken Stallings into the Chicago dugout with a message for the buffoons; he would meet with them in their own tunnel after the game and settle his accounts.

The White Sox chortled over the message. If the buffoons could break one of Ragland's legs, Chicago might climb out of the cellar. But those Chisox should have thought about the game. The Boston Sox whipped them, 5-2, and Chicago was a whole foot deeper in the cellar after nine innings of play.

The Red Sox were chortling now. They drank warm beer smuggled in from a speakeasy at the Wentworth Street corner of Comiskey Park. It was getaway day and Scarborough was collecting all the bats and the team's traveling bags. He couldn't find the kid. "Where's Ragland?"

"You talking to me?" the Chicken said. "Rags has a date in the Chicago tunnel."

"What kind of date?"

"He went in to knock shit out of the White Sox and he said he didn't need no help from us."

Scarborough ran out of the clubhouse. *Some team I'm on. It sucks up beer and won't protect a man.* He had to go through the visitors' tunnel to get back onto the playing field. Mice scuttled around his shoes. *It's a lively ball park.* The players' tunnels in Chicago were as foul and windy as the tunnels at Fenway Park. Each tunnel had a urinal on its south side, so the men wouldn't have to hike to the clubhouse in the middle of a game to relieve their bladders. Scarborough wondered who cleaned the urinals here: the wind carried the smell of piss straight to his nose.

He went from the tunnel into the visitors' dugout, climbed the steps and crossed the infield with its balding grass, sneaked into the Chicago dugout, littered with old tobacco pouches and peanut shells, and ducked his head into the home tunnel with its familiar smell of stale piss. He pulled out the two bats he was carrying in his baseball knickers. But the Chicken had been right. Rags didn't need help from a hunchback. He was boxing the four buffoons. It was a curious match. They could land eight blows to his two. But they were the bloody ones, not the kid. They tried to hit him with their windmill rights and lefts. The kid would waltz around and jab each of them on the nose.

"Hiya, Scarborough," he laughed, winking at the brute.

"Jesus, don't turn your head," Scarborough shouted into the tunnel. But it was too late. Bibb Wallace had clipped Rags in the ear. That ear began to bleed, and the kid's eyes were going blurry. Scarborough moved closer with his bats. The kid wouldn't let him into the fight. He danced until his head cleared, and then he finished the buffoons with punches that seemed to arrive from no place the buffoons could tell.

He didn't learn that boxing in the street.

The kid had science on his side; Rags laid out the buffoons on the tunnel floor. The rest of the White Sox had to bite their rage, watching him from the clubhouse stairs. They were still determined to break one of the kid's legs. They came down the stairs in a fighter's crouch.

Scarborough twirled his bats. "Don't get cute. You Chisox are gonna have a hard time fielding a club what's got dents in their skulls."

They wouldn't attack a moron with a bat in each hand. The Chisox dragged off the four buffoons and withdrew to their clubhouse.

"Lemme see that ear?" Scarborough said to the kid. "The ear's all right. It stopped whistling on me."

"You sure are God's gift to the Red Sox," Scarborough told him. "You lied about the boxing too. Pretending to fight Garl last year like you didn't know the first thing about closing a fist."

"Hell," Rags said. "Boxing was the rage at Amherst. Everybody did it."

"I'll bet you did it a lot better than most. Mister, you could fight with Ty Cobb and win."

Scarborough wasn't angry anymore. Standing against the whole Chicago team had made them roomies again. They would have gone to the nearest drug store for a honeymoon of chocolate sodas, but they had to rush back to the clubhouse and make the sleeper to Boston.

Rags went from furor to furor.

His wedding banns had been published in the *Evening Transcript*. He was supposed to marry Miz Iva at Salem Street's Old North Church on the last Sunday in July. The wedding banns sounded like a goddamn batting order. He could imagine Bull Weingarten croaking it out through his leather funnel. "Cedric Tannehill, known as Babe Ragland to his Red Sox fans, and Iva Cottonmouth, daughter of Marylou Wilks Cottonmouth and Judah Cottonmouth, deceased . . .

He went to Iva's house on the Hill. That servant, Rhys, was short with him, but Rags pushed his way through. Iva's mama opened her parlor door to see what the tumult was about. She looked confused. "Harvard Jack?" she said.

"No, it's Babe Ragland, your intended son-in-law. Where's Miz Iva?"

"I'm here," she said, coming out from behind her mother's wing.

"I'd like to have a talk with you in private."

Marylou gave over the parlor to them, and Rags prowled that room of sofas, drapes, and chairs.

"I wish I didn't have to read about my life all the time in the Boston *Transcript*. Who says we're getting married in July?"

"We agreed on it, you dope."

"When?"

"Last month ... in your room at the baseball hotel."

"I don't remember that."

Rags sat down on a sofa, far from the girl. "Are you moving in with us at the Brunswick?"

"Don't be silly. We'll live with mama. In this house."

"I can't," Rags said. "I have a roommate, and I'm not going to desert him."

"You want to bring a bat boy into this house?"

"He's sensitive," Rags said. "He'll die if he has to live alone."

Iva's nose began to twitch; she was unbelievably pretty in her schoolgirl's blouse. "All right. He can live downstairs. Mama has an extra room in back of the kitchen."

Rags hadn't expected her to give in so easily. "Shouldn't you ask your mother first?"

"No!" she screamed at him. "A bargain is a bargain. But he can't be your best man."

"Best man?" Rags said. "What best man?"

"At the wedding, you silly goose. Mama won't stand for it. She wants Garl."

"Garl's no friend of mine. Who's getting married, anyway? Why should Garl be my best man?"

"Take it or leave it," Iva said. You couldn't outtalk this girl. Rags was only a kid who stepped on yellow grass in front of third base. "If your hunchback is going to live in this house, then Garland has to be best man. Hollis has already straightened it out with him."

"How did the boss get into this frigging pie? He's the one who told me I couldn't marry you until you were seventeen."

"Hollis changed his mind."

"That's swell of him," Rags said, moving to a different sofa. "Does Hollis own a piece of the *Transcript?* How come they picked the beginning of the season to swear I had a father, unless Hollis wanted to build a crowd for Opening Day? ... is that why you're marrying me? Because my pa is rich?"

Iva stood up and began to swing at Rags. He bobbed away from her fists without having to shuffle his feet. A girl couldn't hit Rags. He'd knocked out four men at Comiskey Park. She was crying now, and he pitied her girlish swings. So he let her smack him once.

"You can go to the devil with your father and his copper fields. My father was twice as rich. His people used to manufacture all the ice in Massachusetts."

"That's what they'll say," Rags muttered. "Copper is marrying ice."

The two leaves of the parlor door began to shake. The leaves split and Miz Marylou walked in. "Children, what's going on?" She came over to Iva and whispered in her ear. Then she walked out, shutting the leaves behind her.

"Mama's writing invitations," Iva said, her cheeks flushed with embarrassment and a purple rage. "How many guests do you figure your pa will bring?"

"He won't bring a soul. There's no use inviting him. He won't come to my wedding. My father thinks I'm a bum."

"We can survive without him." She took Rags by the hand and led him behind a sofa. Iva undid all her buttons. "Suppose your mother comes in again?"

"What if she does. Fiancées are allowed to kiss."

Rags shivered inside himself. *Oh, Lord, lemme marry this girl so we can end the petting stuff. I can't take too much more of it.* He wouldn't refuse Miz Iva. He kissed her behind the sofa and felt that bursting in his pants.

The Sox were on the road again through the first half of July. Rags caught it in every big-league town. Dugouts devoted themselves to mocking the kid. The jabber never ceased. They had a new item to torture him about: Cedric's bride. "Where you having the honeymoon, Cedric? In a dollhouse?" A sucking noise would rise off the dugout steps and grow shrill as it carried across the infield and got to Rags. But he smiled at the monkeys on the steps. Scarborough had given him good advice.

"They'll eat you to death if you have rabbit ears. You gotta learn to ignore them dodobirds. If they see you stutter and blink, they'll ride on you and ride, until your hands are jelly and you've got nothin' in your knees. Then the dodos will really start to peck. They can pick out your eyes with their songs. So you play your position and give them the old horse laugh. That can aggravate a dodo. They'll start dropping off their bench."

The kid put a knuckle in his mouth. "Where the hell did you get all this? You've only been with the Sox three years."

"A bat boy gets to see a lot. He's like a second catcher on the field. You ask Mr. Briggs."

The kid didn't have to ask. He smiled at the dodos in the dugout, hugged the line at third, and made himself deaf to their twittering. You could find more gruesome things than dodobirds on a bench. The Sox had come to St. Louis in the middle of a heat wave. The temperature climbed to a hundred and six. The grass burned under your feet at Sportsman's Park. You played with a dry mouth. Your shirt clung to your back. The fans begged for shade. They deserted the open pavilion in right field, walked along the roof, and settled in the upper decks somewhere, shouting at the lemonade boys to hurry. But the park was out of lemonade. The Brownies couldn't satisfy their fans' lust for a cold drink.

They were listless on the field, those Browns, a team that had dropped to fifth place. Their bark and their swagger meant little in the heat. Sheriff Smith struck out Baby Doll Jacobson four times in a single afternoon. Urban Shocker, the Brownies' thirty-three-year-old ace, kept firing up doubles to Garl. Rags hit one of his few home runs. The Sox bombed St. Louis, 12-6.

But they had no relief outside Sportsman's Park. You could have fried a whole hog on the ceiling of Rags' and Scarborough's room at the Buckingham Hotel. The wallpaper crackled and spit an ugly brown glue. When the shutters were open, the heat scorched everything in sight. The kid's bat case turned blond in St. Louis. The hair fell out of his shoe brush. The buttons to the coat he left out of the closet yellowed on him. And the room sealed up like a coffin, with the shutters closed.

The Red Sox weren't going to sleep at the Buckingham in that bloody weather. They soaked all their sheets in the bathtub and went downstairs in their underpants, with the sheets draped over themselves, like outriders of the Ku Klux Klan. They got to the park across from the Buckingham, curled into a bench, and tried to sleep.

There was a constant traffic from the park to the hotel, as the sheets began to dry. The manager, the house detective, and the St. Louis police didn't interfere with this pilgrimage of the Sox. It was an old baseball practice to wear wet sheets in the park.

Rags and the brute found a quiet bench near a duck pond. The ducks were too lazy to move; they rested at the side of the pond, with their necks out of the water. They looked at the white sheets of the two Red Sox without disturbing themselves. One small duck slapped its head around to take a drink of water. And the pond was still again.

The brute slowly fell into a dream. His hump twitched under the sheet, and his eyes rolled back into his head. Rags didn't know if he should wake the brute or not. *What's it hurting him to dream?*

But the kid himself couldn't get to sleep. The Brownies and their dodobirds didn't stick. His mind went off St. Louis. He was thinking of his wedding march and the church on Salem Street. The kid would take a wife in seven days. Iva was down in Martha's Vineyard with her mama and Rhys. They'd have to cut their summer short and open the house on Louisburg Square for the wedding party. He could kiss that baseball hotel goodbye. Rags and his roomie were going to live on Beacon Hill.

His petting days were over. She couldn't tell a husband where to touch. He'd have that girl, only Miz Iva would be Mrs. Ragland now. Wife of the seventh Babe. He was nineteen years old. His mother had died of pneumonia when he was six. He'd had nurses, aunts, and tutors to watch over him. And his own servant, a Black boy named Charles. Charles ran away once, and he was whipped for it. His father's handymen whipped him in front of Cedric. Then they held his mouth open, took a razor, and slashed his gums. That was a lesson for runaways. Black boys didn't disappear after their gums were slashed. Rags couldn't forget that long zip of blood where the razor had gone into Charles' mouth. But Charles did run away again. They found him dead. A few miles from his father's properties, outside Abilene. He didn't have a mark on him. Do Black boys die of fright?

Cedric Tannehill.

Rags poked his head out from under the sheet. The brute was snoring, that hump riding low on his back. Were the Brownies in the park, trying to plague the kid?

Cedric Tannehill.

He didn't spot Baby Doll Jacobson behind a tree. He looked down into the pond. Could a sleeping duck quack the name of Rags' birthright?

Cedric Tannehill.

Was it the Black boy, Charles, come back to haunt him for his father's misdeeds?

"Charlie, is that you? I'm Ragland now. Cedric died at Amherst College."

He saw a cane beat in the grass. The cane was as deliberate as a man's shoe. Rags couldn't be wrong about its swish.

"Pa?"

His father wore a bowler and a dark brown suit in the boiling night. He didn't have his factotum with him, Griffey the lawyer. Marcus Tannehill, the copper millionaire, had come alone to St. Louis.

"Pa, should I run upstairs and get you a sheet? You'll roast in your winter suit."

Marcus had Rags' bony jaw. Except for his limp, which he'd gotten twenty years ago in a mining accident and gave his body an uncertain thrust, he could have been a slightly older brother to

Rags, another third baseman for the Red Sox. He was left-handed, like the kid.

"Pa, did Griffey get our schedule for you? How did you know the Sox were in St. Louis? I hit one off Urban Shocker this afternoon. The dope challenged me with his sinkerball. I got it with the sweet end of my bat."

Marcus jabbed the hunchback with his cane. It made a little twist in the sheet. But Scarborough didn't give up his snoring.

"Pa, I'm getting married! At the Old North Church. On Sunday. Did the Cottonmouths write to you? Pa, will you come?"

Marcus hopped away on the end of his cane. He passed bench after bench of ballplayers in wet sheets. You'd think it was Rags who was chugging along on a stiff leg.

The brute woke up.

"My pa was here."

Scarborough rubbed his eyes. "Your pa? What did he say?"

"He wouldn't talk to me, but he touched you with his cane."

"I didn't feel it," Scarborough said.

"Well, he touched you. I can show you the spot."

Rags pointed to the little twist in Scarborough's sheet. It could have been the impression that a finger would make. "That don't look like no cane mark to me. I aint a man of cotton. You think I wouldn't feel a stick goin' in? You dreamed it."

"No, he was in the park with both of us."

"It's hot, you're scared of getting married, and you dreamed it. Good night." And Scarborough went under his sheet.

8

JUDAH Cottonmouth was dead, and his little girl had no man to give her away. So Hollis McKee had to become the "father" of the bride. He ran the wedding like a baseball club. He scolded ushers and vestrymen and the four schoolgirls from Miss Drabble's who attended to the bride. Miss Drabble herself wouldn't come to a schoolgirl's wedding. She was always furious when one of her girls ran off to church with a man. It finished your career at Miss Drabble's. She wouldn't allow married women to corrupt her school with the mark of sexual intercourse upon them.

Hollis was glad the crazy old witch had decided not to come. It gave him one less person to worry about. The church was packed, and Hollis had to find pews for everybody. The governor was there. His Excellency couldn't afford to boycott the wedding of the most popular kid in Massachusetts, even though this Ragland had a tainted history. He was an orphan with a millionaire father in his past. His Excellency had to side with the rabble. They could vote him out of office if he didn't swear allegiance to the seventh Babe, like any Royal Rooter. His kissed the little missus, Iva Ragland Tannehill Cottonmouth (the girl would be heavy with names), posed for photographers from the society pages, but he couldn't locate the president of the Red Sox. Hollis was in the sacristy, crying for his dead college brother, who hadn't lived long enough to see his little girl marry the Babe.

"Ah, Judah boy, we'd have put some team together. I wouldn't have sold that big baboon to the Yankees if you'd been there to shout at me. But I got us another Babe. Jesus, can he go to his left. And I made him your son-in-law." Two churchwardens stumbled into the sacristy. They didn't give Hollis a chance to wipe his eyes. He scowled at them. "What's wrong?"

"We'll have to close the doors, Mr. McKee. There's five thousand people out on Salem Street. The church will fall down on them. We can't hold that many people."

"Those are Red Sox fans," Hollis said. "They've come to the Babe's wedding. They won't break into your precious church. Let them have the sidewalk. I don't want any doors shut in their face."

The two wardens had to slip out of the sacristy on their toes and let the Babe's fans mill in front of the Old North Church, while Hollis composed himself and went into the chapel. Most of the wedding party could leave through a side door. A fleet of Chryslers waited for them on top of Snowhill. But Rags wouldn't sneak out of church. His fans had stood for three hours on Salem Street. So he walked to the front of the chapel with his bride, his roommate, and his best man.

The crowd yelled and jumped at the first sight of Rags. Iva was alarmed. She'd never experienced the crush of so many people. But they adored the kid. And they allowed a small hollow to exist between Rags and themselves. "God bless you. Babe. We hope you and the little woman live to be a hundred."

Rags felt ridiculous in the opera hat Hollis made him wear at his own wedding. He sallied into the crowd, smiled at babies, shook hands, and returned to his bride. The brute had to step behind her and hold up all the trains of her wedding gown. Garland acted as a local magistrate for the bride and groom. He would grab an elbow here and there, give a gentle tug, and get his people through.

They traveled out of the North End, with hundreds sticking to them. It had the look of a sacred hike. They picked up stragglers, bums, and half the Quincy baseball team at New Sudbury Street. These pilgrims arrived on Louisburg Square, which was already mobbed with curiosity seekers, Harvard men, followers of the Babe, and bohemians from the bottom of the Hill.

Garl managed to sheriff the four of them into the house. The bridesmaids fell on Miz Iva and began to devour her neck. They occupied a whole corner of the house and took to giggling with obscene smirks on their faces. Rags threw his opera hat into the closet.

The governor collared Scarborough and tried to feel him out on the possibility of Republican strongholds at Fenway Park. Would His Excellency be booed by the fanatics of South Boston if he appeared in Hollis' box? Scarborough wouldn't commit himself. Bat boys didn't tinker with politics.

Marylou kept staring at Garl. A kind of hysteria crept up in her and colored her throat because of his nearness to her. She wished it had been a double wedding. Rags and Iva. Garl and Marylou. The center fielder was quiet, beautiful, and lean.

"Would you care for some fruit punch, Mr. James?" Garl wouldn't flirt. He had all the reticence of an Indiana man. He wasn't stupid about the qualities she had: hips and ankles and a slow, silvery speech. But Marylou was linked with the boss in a way that was difficult to tell. She was half daughter, half mistress and companion to Hollis McKee. "Thank you, ma'am, but I don't drink punch."

Garl would have run from this house. But he was sworn to protect Ragland on his wedding day. He had squired Rags in and out of the Old North Church. He purchased the opera hat. He'd carried the wedding ring. Now the Sox had a legitimate husband on the roster. He was beginning to like this kid from Amherst, St. Mary's, and who knows where. He caught Rags mumbling to himself.

"Ragland, it's your party and you're supposed to smile."

"Who's the little man with Hollis?"

"Finnbar of the *Evening Transcript*. Noel's in charge of the society page."

"I figured that," Rags said.

Noel Finnbar wore a blue vest. His hands darted in and out of his cuffs as he talked to Hollis McKee. Rags waited until Hollis went into another room before he descended upon the society editor. Noel jumped. Rags had a frown line in the middle of his face.

"Where'd you get that picture of me in my freshman college hat?"

"What picture, Babe?" Noel Finnbar said, as if Rags had a chump's voice.

"The one you printed in your rotten paper...on the goddamn front page."

"You'll have to ask our features man."

"You can take your features man and chew on his foot," Rags said. "Listen, Finnbar, if you start in on me again, I'll find you at the *Transcript* and show you what it means to have a bloody head."

The kid waltzed away from Noel Finnbar. But he couldn't have any peace. Marylou's servant patted him on the shoulder.

"You're booked in at the Ritz-Carlton. The missus reserved the bridal suite."

The kid had to ask him, "What for?"

"For your honeymoon, Mr. Rags."

"Ballplayers don't get a honeymoon, Rhys. The Tigers'll be in Fenway tomorrow."

"The rooms are for tonight."

The bridesmaids wept as Miz Iva packed her pajamas in a small overnight bag. Rags wouldn't take a thing. They were five minutes from the Ritz-Carlton. He could always come back for extra underwear.

Scarborough had already moved in. His quarters were downstairs, in an alcove off the kitchen. It would be the first night in over a year that the two of them had slept apart. Rags could say goodbye to Hollis and Garl and the governor of Massachusetts, but it seemed silly to shake hands with his own roommate. So he shrugged to the brute, that's all, and left the house with Iva and her long wedding train. The skirts trailed on the cobblestones, because she didn't have Scarborough to hang on to them and hold them up. The bride and groom walked down Chestnut Street, entered the Public Garden, people shouting, "Babe and Iva...Iva and Babe," crossed the footbridge, came out on Arlington Street, with Rags shaking the dust and bits of grass off Iva's skirts, and checked into the Ritz-Carlton Hotel as Mr. and Mrs. Babe Ragland of the Boston Red Sox and Beacon Hill.

It was the only place in Boston where people didn't make a fuss over him. Pashas and kings had stayed at the Ritz. The kid wasn't even batting .300 this year. He was a sophomore with a crazy glove.

No one laughed at his wedding tie, or the girl's incredible train. The elevator boys were dressed in the Carlton shade of blue. They wore white gloves. And they drove their cars up and down. The motors purred for them. Iva didn't feel any jolts.

Rags was put on the fifteenth floor. You couldn't find a loose tack in the carpeting. The doorknobs were made of green glass. Rags did a reckoning of the bridal suite. "It's bigger than the club-house. And it's got a view."

They could see the dome of the State House, half of Beacon Hill, and the bend in the Charles from the windows of their sitting room. A magnum of champagne stood in a large silver bell near one window. "Did mama do that?" Iva wanted to know.

"Na, it comes with the place."

"Who says?"

Rags picked a little card out of the ice in the silver bell.

The card had the hotel's emblem on it, embossed in blue: a lion looking sideways, with its tongue sticking out.

"See, it's from the Ritz!"

Iva looked in all the closets. Rags had a difficult time opening the champagne. "Son of a bitch." The cork shot up to the ceiling, and a blue smoke emerged from the bottle. Rags filled two long-stemmed champagne glasses, but Iva refused to drink.

"You have to make a toast."

The kid scratched his head.

"I drink to love and no more petting."

Iva was chagrined. "I want something better than that."

"Well, what about a life together in your mama's house, with Scarborough under the stairs?"

"Stop joking," she said, but she took a sip and started to laugh. The bowl of the champagne glass was too big for Iva's mouth; she had to clamp her teeth into the glass and suck up champagne. Bubbles got into her nose. Iva had a spell of hiccups. Rags frightened her with a horrible face, and the girl was cured.

They decided to have their honeymoon meal right in the sitting room. Rags pressed a buzzer in the wall, and a waiter arrived. "We'll have this and this . . . and this," they said, shoving their fingers along the menu. The waiter returned with a tray that could have come off a battleship. Bride and groom sampled sturgeon and roe, a *crudité* of carrots, broccoli, and blood tomatoes, sweetbreads under glass, lobster in whiskey sauce, grasshopper pie, and cherries jubilee. The kid rang for a second bottle of champagne.

"Me and my pa always used to eat like this," Rags said. "He took me everywhere."

"He's a louse," Iva said. "He never answered mama's invitation."

"I told you he wouldn't come... and don't call pa a louse. I disappointed him and left college like a bum."

"He should be proud of you. The Sox wouldn't keep a bum on third base. Where the hell did you grow up? In a monk's house?"

"Tucson and Texas," Rags said, his tongue growing heavier and heavier with each gulp of champagne. "I learned baseball from the Blacks on my father's ranch. They didn't have any uniforms. Just neckerchiefs. It was the blue neckerchiefs against the red. But they sure could play. And they didn't have the big leagues sitting on their backs, teaching them how to hit and field the ball. If a lefty took a liking to third, nobody stopped you. They had lefty catchers, lefty shortstops, and everything. Those red and blue neckerchiefs could have pissed on the Sox."

"Don't you say a bad word about Hollis' team. Hollis is my goduncle."

Rags blinked at her. "What's a goduncle?"

"It's like a godfather, but not so sticky and tight."

"Well, those neckerchiefs were all goduncles to me."

"It's not the same," Iva said. "Hollis raised me and my mother after my father dropped dead."

"How could he raise your mother when she's already a woman?"

"Mama's less than a child."

The kid was too bewildered to answer her right away. He drank champagne, and drizzled all over his wedding pants. "Didn't your mother go to Bryn Mawr?"

"Mama couldn't spell Bryn Mawr if her life depended on it. She was my father's servant wench."

Rags sat in his wet pants and blinked at Miz Iva.

"Mama's a po' girl from Jackson, Mississip, who ran away from home. She landed in New England, a kitchen maid at my father's fraternity. She was Hollis' wench too. They shared her with five or six more fraternity brothers."

"Why did your father marry her then?"

"He wanted to shock the Cottonmouths, I guess. He brought his own whore to Beacon Hill and made her his wife."

"It's a dumb lie," Rags said. "Who told you this cock and bull story?"

"Mama did." Iva was sniffling now. "We're famous for the peculiar weddings in our family."

"What's so peculiar about us?"

"Nothing, nothing at all. A girl who can't finish high school and a boy who's ashamed to let his father know he's on the Red Sox."

Rags felt a ringing in his head. He was sick of so much blab. "Let's go into the other room."

The kid didn't leer at his wife. He took her sweetly by the hand and they both wobbled into the bedroom in a duckfooted walk. The blue drapes had been pulled for them. Only a magician could solve the honeymoon bed. It seemed to have a hundred coverlets and feather pillows on its summer quilt.

Rags couldn't undress the wife.

He grappled with Iva's wedding gown, leaning on her in his woozy condition. His fingers slipped off her buttons and her stays. "Lemme do it," she croaked, falling onto the bed.

The kid watched her unravel herself. *I won't have a blue prick tonight.* He tore at his wedding clothes, imprisoned in his cuffs. Iva had to come to him naked and unbutton the poor kid. Her body was smooth against his gruff ballplayer's skin. The back of his neck was freckled and dark where the sun beat down upon him behind third base. His thighs were bruised. His hands were gnarled from the smack of so many balls. He felt like a tortoise next to the wife.

They flung off the pillows, pulled away the coverlets, and got the bed down to its basic quilt. They crept inside and started to kiss. *Cedric's dead. Cedric's dead. I'm Babe Ragland. I have a wife.* He explored between her legs with his bumpy wrist. Iva sang her delight with a gentle moaning that tasted like silk in Rag's mouth. He went into her and moved against her hips with the slow, contented rhythm of a rocking horse. Then he pulled out.

She looked up at him, her cheeks swollen with raw animal surprise. "Where's the blood?" he said.

Rags wasn't a dope. He spent six months at Amherst, where he studied the laws of male and female anatomy. "A virgin's supposed to bleed."

"I did my bleeding." Iva sat up, her nose flaring out at Rags.

"Who was it that made you bleed?"

"None of your business."

A rage caught hold of him; he took her by the arms and squeezed. "Who was it?"

"Rhys," she said, as if to bite him with a single word.

"You put me off for a goddamn year, you lie to me with your virgin stories, and that bum is crawling into your bed."

"I didn't lie. It happened last week...at Martha's Vineyard. He was drunk with mama, and I was getting curious ...I thought you wouldn't like me if I didn't know what to do. So I asked him to teach me, and he did. . . ."

Rags got into his clothes; his collar was rumpled, his shirttails stuck out, and his wedding tie lay on him like an evil tongue.

"Where are you going?"

"For a walk. Some husband I am. I have to wait on line for sloppy seconds with my own wife ... Rags gets in after Rhys."

And she couldn't keep him from marching out the door. He was rude to the elevator boy. "Take me downstairs," Rags shouted in the boy's face.

He galloped across the Public Garden with his tails wrapped around one leg. He wore a jackal's grin when he arrived on Louisburg Square. He stood outside his new home, remembering that the Cottonmouths didn't bother to lock up at night. Rags let himself in.

Was the servant downstairs with Scarborough, or upstairs with Marylou? He climbed up to the bedrooms on the second floor. He knocked and knocked until he found Rhys hiding in Marylou's bed. The kid dragged him out of the pillows. He'd ruined their sleep. He could smell their lovemaking on the two of them.

"Mister, you shouldn't have monkeyed with my wife."

He wasn't out to murder Rhys. He smashed the servant around the kidneys with no more than half his might. But he didn't know how to stop. He punched and kicked, and the servant began to swallow his own blood. Marylou's wailing couldn't get him off Rhys. He felt a hand go under his crotch.

He was lifted off the ground like a common potato sack and hurled into a chair. No ordinary man could have done that to him. It was the brute. Scarborough came upstairs in his pajamas to see what the noise was about. He had Marylou fetch a basin of water and a towel, and he administered to Rhys. He washed the blood away, inspecting all the marks Rags had put on him. Rhys curled his head behind Scarborough's knee.

"You know what that bum did?" Rags said. "He taught my wife how to screw."

"You just got married today. So he couldn't have taught her when she was your wife."

Rags didn't like the way a hunchback reasoned. Scarborough should have been kinder to him.

"Who cares when it was. She was still my fiancée. I ought to twist his neck."

He couldn't get the brute to look at him straight. Then Scarborough gave him the old familiar scowl that one roommate reserves for another.

"Raggsy, you're on your honeymoon. Go back to the Ritz."

Winter Ball with the Harrys:

BOOK THREE

9

IT was a dog's life.

A bride who'd been punctured by another man; a mother- in-law who lay down with boys in the swamp because she loved Garland James and couldn't have him; a roommate who lived in a rat's hole two floors under Rags. And all the kid ever wanted to do was play ball.

He had a father who was richer than the whole American League. *Who's your pa, little boy? My pa is copper and beef. Copper and beef.* Marcus Tannehill mined copper in Arizona and Colorado and had a ranch in Texas to amuse himself with. The ranch could have swallowed up ten Boston swamps and twenty Beacon Hills. The kid developed a dinosaur's eye for open spaces. And a coyote's ear. Baseball seized hold of his senses. It wasn't a series of rituals between men in flannel suits. It was wild play. Rags defined himself against the territory of an infield and the smack of horsehide on wood like a prairie animal. His instinct was to lunge for that ball, grit his teeth, and throw.

At fifteen he played Texas baseball behind his father's back, pretending he was a bullrider's boy from Abilene who did everything with his left hand. But Griffey, his father's lawyer-toad, was on to him, and he had to give it up after a month. Marcus tutored him at home and sent him East to Amherst College, thinking to cure him of his baseball habits and his coyote smells. The kid stayed long enough to learn how to box, and study a little Greek, then he jumped to Arkansas.

It wasn't a silly act. The Red Sox were the most desperate team in baseball, and he knew he could get into their tryout camp. *I'm Babe Ragland.* Why couldn't the kid be an orphan like Mr. Ruth?

He'd read so many stories about the bad boys' school in Baltimore, he could mutter *St. Mary's* by heart.

Now he wished somebody would put him in that bad boys' school and hide him from reporters, baseball owners, and the Cottonmouths. He was the most miserable husband on earth.

He searched for Garl in the clubhouse, with that dog's look on his face. His gums seemed bitter yellow inside his mouth. Garl was astonished over the change in Rags. He'd heard of recent bridegrooms falling apart, but yellow gums were new to him.

"Mr. James, is Harry Heilmann going to treat me like a rookie again? . . . can I play on his winter team?"

Garl didn't bother to ask what was putting winter into Ragland's mind. He told him outright about Harry. "I've inherited the Heilmann All-Stars. Harry's given up barnstorming as a winter career. He's got a sick shoulder. He'll go to California to hunt and fish."

The kid suddenly went shy. His back hunched over like the brute's, and he said in a low voice, "Will you carry me, Mr. James?"

Garl intended to offer third base to Homer Ezzell of the Browns, but he couldn't refuse a kid who had the dirty gray eyes of an injured wolf. "I'll carry you."

The kid's mouth curled up into a narrow grin. "What about Scarborough?"

"Yeah," Garl said, "I can always use a bat boy. I'll carry him too. But his expenses will have to come out of your own pocket."

"Sure thing," the kid said, and he was less of a hunchback now. It was the first time in Garl's life that a major leaguer looked so happy about the prospects of a barnstorming trip. You had to play in chickencoops all over the countryside and eat every sort of shit. He felt sorry for the Babe. Garl wouldn't live in that house on Louisburg Square. It was filled with Cottonmouth spooks. Rags shouldn't have moved in with that crazy mama. Why didn't he push the girl out and bring her someplace else? The Brunswick had plenty of bridal suites.

Rags was in a gay mood crossing Commonwealth Avenue. He'd solved his winter for himself. He was going to barnstorm with an all-star team.

He met the brute walking on Acorn Street. Scarborough was wearing Rags' opera hat. A Russian seamstress had fixed up a swallow-tailed coat for him that softened the lines of his hump. These were his Beacon Hill clothes.

"You're with the Red Sox," Rags muttered, "not a team of cockatoos. You can throw your new duds in the closet. We won't be here in October."

"We going around the world, Raggsy?"

"Better than that. We're playing in the winter leagues." The swallow-tailed coat must have had a miraculous seam because Scarborough's hump swelled out from under the lining. "Why do we have to step in dirt when we got Beacon Hill to climb?"

"I had to beg Garl to take us on, and you want to wear your fancy hat and smile at all the swell people . . . don't come."

"I didn't say I wasn't coming . . . when do we pack?"

"Soon as the season's over."

He went in to have a talk with the wife. Mrs. Ragland was quiet as he delivered his song on winter baseball. "Give me a chance to play with a decent infield. Garl wouldn't carry fools like Alvin Critz. My wing gets frozen if I lay still from October to February. I have to catch the ball."

She was a baseball wife like the girls in *Eveline*. Only sixteen, and her husband was ready to crawl away.

"Can I go with you. Rags?"

"Wives don't barnstorm," the kid said. "We'll be living in dirt-water towns, playing Blacks and all. We'll probably have to sleep on the grass."

"Will you come home for Christmas?"

"I'll try."

September dribbled out for the kid. Boston was still locked in seventh place. The kid held back; he wasn't going to burn his legs completely for the Sox. He had to save a little stuff for the Heilmann All-Stars.

He was disappointed when he saw the actual team. Garl had Topper Rigney of Detroit to play short, and ancient Zack Wheat in the outfield, but the rest of the All-Stars was a skunk's list: third-stringers, like Chappie Gruel and Steve Bumpo, who would have had a hard time making the Red Sox. Garl couldn't afford to carry more than two or three front-line men on the All-Stars. Come October and November, the country was deluged with all-star teams. There was the Rogers Hornsby All-Stars, the George Sisler Americans, the Babe Ruth All-Stars, the Rabbit Maranville Kings, and the Harry Heilmann All-Stars who had to go without Harry this year.

But the kid would have played for a circus, rather than spend another winter in Boston. He fled his Beacon Hill bride in a yellow and green barnstorming bus. Garl had rented this old bus for the team. He was manager, player, and entrepreneur, and his own booking agent. It wasn't so easy to book behind Rabbit Maranville and Babe Ruth. The Harry Heilmann All-Stars had to grab whatever they could. Bookings were slight until the Cincinnati Black Giants rescued them.

Garl got the Cincinnati Giants by default: no other all-star team would barnstorm with them. The Giants were too rough. Rabbit Maranville always kept a hundred miles between himself and "them Cincinnatis." The Giants were known to chew up baseball men. They were like a wrecking company. They'd fight a whole town if you insulted them on the field, and ride off, leaving you to sit in the debris.

But those crazyheads could draw a crowd. People came to hiss at the Black Giants. Garl didn't have much of a choice. He had to connect with the Giants, or get out of winter baseball. So he gambled with the bones of his men. Garl was the eldest son; and the burden of his family fell upon him. He had a disabled grandfather, a brood of maiden aunts, a sick mom, and three brothers who hadn't finished their schooling yet.

He pointed his bus driver towards Maryland, where he was supposed to rendezvous with the Black Giants. Rags was confused about the wanderings of the bus. "Didn't we make the wrong turn? This isn't the road to Cincinnati?" "Not so loud," the brute said. "You'll set the men to thinking. And they'll all start to twitch."

"Let them twitch. Shouldn't we head for the Giants' home park?"

"Raggsy, we aint hooking up with the St. Louis Browns. This is Black baseball. The Cincinnati Giants don't have a park. Black boys have to sneak onto a field if they expect to play."

"Then why call yourself the Cincinnati Giants?"

"Because that's built into their name. They have to pretend to people that they have some kind of home."

"Do the Cincinnati Giants ever play in Cincinnati?"

"Probably not. The Philadelphia Black Eagles don't even know where Philadelphia is. You'll learn."

"There's nothing to learn," Rags said. "It's crazy, that's all."

The bus hit upon a fleet of Buicks outside Annapolis, seven autocars with wooden hulls and no roofs. It was a baseball caravan: the players and worldly goods of the Cincinnati Black Giants. Their boss, Carl Raines, stood at the front of the caravan with his arms akimbo and frowned at the yellow and green bus. He was a small man with a wizened face.

"We're in trouble," Scarborough whispered to Rags.

"How come?"

"His wife Emma aint with the team. She must have run off with the local milkman. Carl's gonna give us hell."

The All-Stars clambered out of the bus, stretching their knees after the ride down from Boston. The Giants stuck to their auto-cars. They were the most aristocratic Blacks Rags had ever met. Where were the sockamayocks, those second-stringers who had scouted Rags in Arkansas? Rags couldn't find one sockamayock among the Black Giants. They ignored the All-Stars with their ill-tempered eyes, as if a team of worthless fellows had come to play with them.

"Don't you pick an argument with these sassy Blacks," Scar-borough said. "Just smile, or they'll scowl you into the grave. They practice voodoo, Carl and his Black sons of a bitch."

Raines shook his head at Garland. "Looks like we'll have to car-ry you on the road, young fella. You aint got much of a drawing card without ol' Harry Heilmann. Harry take sick?"

"No, he went fishing in California."

The little man produced a bitter, raucous laugh for the Black Giants. "You hear that? Harry went fishing in California. He left his All-Stars to try and feed themselves. Mister, without Harry you a pile of shit."

"We have enough," Garl said.

"Who you got? Topper and Zack and little Steve Bumpo. They couldn't bring out the horseflies."

"We have the kid, Babe Ragland."

Raines laughed so hard, a shiver went through his body. "Fella, I got four lefty third basemen sitting in my hind car. I use them to sweep up after the games."

"The kid can play his spot," Garl said. Raines and seven cars of Giants couldn't irritate him.

"Pharaoh'll eat him up," the little man said. "He'll cry and beg for lessons after he watches the Pharaoh do his tricks. But I aint sure Pharaoh Yarbull will come onto the field with you. White folks make him sneeze a lot."

"Who's this Pharaoh guy?" the kid asked the brute.

"Their top dog."

"Does he pitch?"

"He plays anywhere the Giants need him."

"Point him out to me."

"Never point at a Black. It means you want to fight."

"Am I allowed to scratch my ass without insulting the Cincinnati Giants? I won't disturb Mr. Yarbull. He can talk to me with his bat and glove."

"He'll talk you into the bleachers," Scarborough said. "If he could put on some whiteface and pitch and field for the Sox, we'd have took the pennant this year."

"That's good to know. When do we get to play these miracle boys?"

"Soon," Scarborough said. His mournful looks disgusted Rags. The brute was all curled up. Rags had played with Blacks on his father's ranch. He understood the flamboyances of their game. Blacks liked to shave a ball with a piece of emery cloth, or nick it with the tooth on a belt buckle, so the ball would hop at you out of the corner in ways you couldn't predict. You had to stare back at the Black on the mound and swing under the crooked eye of the ball with one tiny flick of the bat. You could use their own stuff against them; the ball would carom off the bat with the same peculiar hop. Otherwise you'd be swinging all day, and you couldn't go near that Black pitch.

The seven Buicks began to make sense: little Carl was carrying a small country of men. He had an umpire, a witch doctor, wandering carpenters and groundkeepers, and fourteen Giants. The groundkeepers set up a baseball diamond in a field across from the bus. They labored like fools with their trowels and their scythes, while the carpenters built a grandstand near first base. They'd

turned a stinking field into a diamond in forty-five minutes. That
little man had magicians on his side.

The Buicks became a dressing room for the Giants. They ventured out in uniforms of snug gold and white. The All- Stars wore
a dumpy gray that seemed like woolen underwear next to the Cincinnati colors.

The little man chided Garl. "Lord alive. I'm ashamed to be
around you scruffy boys."

"I forgot to bring my washerwoman along," Garl told him. "I
picked the darkest uniforms I could find."

The little man said something about "mud pies," and he sent
his pretty Giants into the neighboring villages to drum up business for both teams. The Giants brought placards with them
that announced "A Colossal Baseball Match Between the World
Champion Cincinnati Giants and those Great Contenders, the
Harry Heilmann All-Stars of the White American League." The
witch doctor, a sickly man called Samuel Sham, blessed their
trip. Rags couldn't say what kind of mumbo jumbo this Samuel
used on the Giants. But it worked. Five thousand Marylanders
followed Carl's gold-clad pitchmen back to that temporary diamond in the field.

The Giants didn't have to go to their emery boards. They walloped the All-Stars, 15-1, without doctoring a single pitch. Yam
Murray was on the mound for them, and he got to the Harry
Heilmanns with his cunning and his smoke. But it wasn't bats
and pitching arms that really interested the kid. He didn't care
how many Black Walter Johnsons and George Sislers the Giants
had. It was their fielding that stupefied Rags. The Giants were like
rubbery extensions of the ball. Those bodies must have been made
of liquid and glue. There were no false jumps, no extra moves to
satisfy the crowd. The Giants wouldn't shimmy on their diamond.

Pharaoh Yarbull was at third for them. The Pharaoh threw with
his left hand. He went into the hole deeper and faster than Rags

ever could. And he skewered line drives out of the air with a whirling motion that would have been impossible to see if he hadn't worn a gold stripe.

The fans expected a baseball circus, and all they got was black magic. The Giants would clown for an inning, as Muley Jones mimicked the patter of Babe Ruth's little feet, and the Pharaoh charged a suicide bunt like Ragland himself might do, with his elbows pumping hard, and then they'd return to their natural game of destroying the Harry Heilmanns. They didn't chortle once. They took their win without much glee. It was almost a secret among themselves how good they were.

The Marylanders still enjoyed the show. "Them Blacks sure can dance." And they pitied the All-Stars who had to take on Blacks without Harry to enliven their attack. The fans returned to their villages resigned to the reality of an evil world, where Black devils couldn't lose.

Even the Harry Heilmanns weren't disgruntled about what had happened in the field. The Harrys went their nine innings. They drove in a run. They didn't shout at the Blacks. They swung their bats and stayed polite. Rags was the only one who seemed upset. The kid walked over to Chappie Gruel and snarled at him.

"You fell asleep on us."

"I didn't sleep," Chappie said. "I played. Ask anybody."

"I don't have to ask. The next time you snore in the middle of a game, I'll kick your teeth in."

Garl stepped between Chappie and the kid. "I do the managing here, Mr. Ragland. You'd better apologize to Chappie."

If the kid wrestled with his manager, and kicked Chappie in the mouth, he could say goodbye to the Harrys and go back to Boston and the wife. It would be a winter of Beacon Hill. He'd have to count the blue shutters on Acorn Street to get some exercise.

"Didn't mean it about kicking your teeth," he mumbled, looking at his shoes.

"That's okay," Chappie said. "Hell, they aint nothin' but a bunch of crazy Blacks. You can't beat them, so why kill yourself? But I don't snore when I'm in a game."

"Yes you do," Garl said. "The kid was right. You lie down on us again, Chappie, and I swear I'll strap you to the bus. The Harry Heilmanns aren't a juggling act. I play to win."

Garl had to find a boardinghouse to hold his men for the night. But he didn't see the Giants go scrambling for accommodations. They pitched their hotel under that grandstand the team's carpenters had made.

"You're welcome to bunk with us," the boss of the Giants said. "We got plenty of room."

It would have been like sleeping in a cave for Garl. "Thanks, but we'll try the boardinghouses."

"Suit yourself. Only mind this. The punkies are mean in these parts. Maryland's got the worst bedbugs and flies in America."

Garl should have listened to that little man. The boardinghouse he picked for the Harrys was overloaded with lice. They lived in the wallpaper, loving all the glue, but when Garl brought his men around, the lice ate through the walls to feast on Harry Heilmanns. The sound of ballplayers scratching themselves invaded the boardinghouse. The Harrys crawled out of their blankets and spent the night in sitting chairs.

The Giants were ready for them in the morning. Their pitchmen had assembled another big crowd from the next group of villages. These Marylanders heard about the whipping the "Black team" delivered to the white Harrys. And they'd come to watch the slaughter all over again. They didn't have to hoot at the Blacks, since it wasn't a legitimate series in their eyes. Any Black diamond was perfect for a carnival.

Chappie Gruel stroked his knees and hopped around in left field. No one could accuse him of snoring now. But a sockamayock like Chappie couldn't change the complexion of a baseball war. Pharaoh Yarbull stationed himself in center field and brought down whatever the Harrys could sock over the pitcher's head. He went into the trees for a long fly ball off Garland's bat. And he was like a fifth infielder who could guard the blind spots in back of second base. The Pharaoh doubled twice, and smashed a wicked ball through the fingers of Rags' glove. The Giants took the Harry Heilmanns, 17-2.

They also played in the afternoon. The pitchmen had already located a different crowd. Yarbull must have been restless; he moved to first base. He grabbed pop flies for his catcher, and stretched his body for throws that should have gone into the grandstand. There was no one person in the white leagues to compare with him. He was Garland James in the morning, George Sisler in the afternoon. In addition to that, he was Pharaoh the enchanter, who could step out of the ordinary workings of time, and appear to float while he was making the most savage and impossible leap; the Pharaoh could trim down his moves and translate them into absolute energy. It came with a price. He forced his body beyond what other men could do. But that terrifying tension he induced in the field had aged him. The Pharaoh was old at twenty-five. The muscles around his knees had begun to knot. He would have spasms in his thighs as he slept with his mates under the grandstand. The witch doctor had to unknot his legs every morning, or the Pharaoh couldn't have walked to first base. The skin near his eyes was pinched back, as if the Pharaoh wore a mask to cover that pain of his, and deaden it to the crowd.

The Giants won the afternoon game, 12-2. It was turning into a ritual for the kid, where the Giants would score at will and allow the Harrys a run or two. Their owner must have reckoned that a shutout might humiliate the boys in the stands. It wasn't good business to make the whites look like complete monkeys. The Harrys had to have some little streak, back-to-back hits in an early inning, so the Marylanders wouldn't start to yawn.

The kid brooded over this. He wasn't going to be a hankie in Pharaoh Yarbull's back pocket that you could mop your head with and stuff away whenever you liked. The Harrys were becoming invisible. The Giants blew on them, and plotted the course of each game. Rags felt like the negligible partner in a slow, killing dance. He intended to stop the Black Giants.

He cornered Garl near the bus and begged him for a decent crop of men. "We can't win with the ginks you hired."

"Should I telegraph George Sisler to come rescue us? I can barely meet the payroll as it is."

"Who said anything about George? You could wire Tilly and Sheriff Smith."

"The Sheriff won't play with Black boys, and Tilly has bad knees. Any more suggestions?"

The kid went to Scarborough, who'd become coach and trainer to the Harrys, bandaging this man and that, and signaling for a suicide squeeze from his foot of grass behind first base.

"Scarborough, you have to try some voodoo on them, or we can forget about winning a game."

"I can't voodoo them. I don't know how."

"Then learn," Rags said. "Steal from their witch doctor, that guy they call Sam."

So the hunchback set out to voodoo the Cincinnati Giants. He would strut alongside their team, throwing up his hump at them. He would mumble incantations over their drinking water. He would crook his pinkie at the Pharaoh, wherever the Pharaoh happened to play.

The Giants laughed at his silly work. But Samuel Sham was outraged. The witch doctor shuffled near the brute's tiny coaching box. "Don't you fuck with me. I'll put boils on Mr. Garland's ass. I'll bring the plague to you Harrys. You'll be shitting frogs out of your guts."

Samuel couldn't frighten the brute. Scarborough still displayed his hump to the Cincinnati Giants, and he would hex the Pharaoh as often as he could. The witch doctor wasn't conspicuous about his retaliation rites. He had no flagrant magic to offer up. He was a sickly man who didn't carry devils in his socks. But the plague did arrive. The Harry Heilmanns began to hog the little outhouse the carpenters had erected behind the stands. The whole team came down with the flux. The Harrys would rush from the diamond to the outhouse, from the outhouse to home plate. Chappie Gruel was too weak to hold a bat. Steve Bumpo quit the Harrys, traveled down to Cape Charles, and jumped into the Chesapeake, hoping a swim would cure him of his stomach fever. Zack Wheat went home to Missouri.

Garl was left with eight men. He had to put the brute on first base. Scarborough was agile enough. He gave up his voodoo to concentrate on trapping the ball in his mitt. It amused the villagers for a day to have a hunchback struggle on the diamond, but the war between the Giants and the Harrys had begun to lose its shine. The carpenters dismantled their benches in the field, the groundkeepers destroyed the diamond they had landscaped out of ordinary dirt and grass, and the caravan crossed over to Virginia. Garl tagged along.

The Harrys dropped nineteen games in a row; they hadn't crept within five runs of the Giants. Their lot didn't improve once they reached the Virginia line. The Cincinnatis camped outside Fredericksburg, creating a new diamond and putting up a pile of seats. The pitchmen gandered about with their placards, hauling in fresh villagers to watch a baseball war that had become a bloodless affair. The Harrys seemed shackled to the Giants and their movable diamond. They lost another dozen games, with lopsided scores. It was like a theatre piece performed over and over again, with innings instead of acts. Rags was stuck inside a drama the Giants had prepared for him. Yarbull went from position to position, and Rags chewed lima beans and dust.

Garl couldn't dwell on the scores. He had to produce beds for the Harrys without too many lice. The kid got to live with bugs in his pants. Someone had tracked him to the team's Virginia boardinghouse. He had a caller on the telephone. His wife. He could hear her sniffle all the way from Beacon Hill.

"I miss you, Rags. Will you come for Christmas?"

"I'll try."

He knocked on the manager's door. "Excuse me. Skipper Garl. Have you been telling certain folks where we are?"

"Our schedule isn't a secret, kid. I promised Hollis I'd keep in touch."

"Have you changed your mind about Sheriff Smith?"

"I told you. The Sheriff doesn't play with Black boys."

"Then we'll lose and lose and lose. The Cincinnatis own us, skip. We're more than cousins to them. We're a team of babies for the Giants."

Rags shouldn't have despaired so much. A peculiar fate caught up with the Giants at Fredericksburg. Emma, the boss' wife, had left her milkman, whoever it was, and come back to the Giants. She was a high yellow woman of thirty or so, with reddish brown hair and a soft neck that reminded you of the dents and veins in a dish of cream. Her scowls were prettier than most people's smiles. She had long fingers, a fine back, and her hips held close to the denims she wore. She was half owner of the Cincinnati Giants.

She could turn Carl into a crazy man. The boss jumped up and down. He raged at her for abandoning him, and then he started to blubber. He was helpless around his wife, who could disappear as often as she pleased. His body became a gnarled thing with Emma in the caravan. His love for her twisted into a hatred that he tore out of his own skin.

It demoralized the team to watch Carl suffer like that. Yarbull made his first error in forty games. Yam Murray's sinkerball didn't come forking down at the batter with its usual breeze.

"Call the Sheriff," Rags shouted in Garl's ear. "I'll pay for his goddamn trip. He can tolerate Blacks for half a day. We'll send him back to sweet Georgia after nine innings. Garland, I'd like to win one game . . ."

The Sheriff arrived on a Monday in November. His forehead puckered when Rags kissed him on the cheek, to show what a joy it was to have Sheriff Smith on the Harry Heilmanns. The Sheriff wiped off that kiss with the length of his sleeve. "Shit, Garland, I said I'd strike out Blacks for you, but I didn't agree to getting kissed ... show me those Cincinnatis."

The Giants were aware of Sheriff Smith. They knew all about his smoke. The Sheriff had twenty-five wins for the seventh-place Sox. They snorted at him from the wooden hulls of their Buicks, pretending to shiver over his size. Then they scrambled onto the diamond. Their criers had already declared the pitching duel of the century, between Yam Murray of the Giants and Sheriff Smith. They lured nine or ten thousand to the field. Carl had to put the overflow near the foul lines. Pharaoh was the shortstop this afternoon.

The Harrys looked pathetic in their dirty grays. The Sheriff gave them an extra man, so Garl could pull the brute off first base. Rags told him not to. "He'll bring us luck, skip. Leave him there."

"When did Scar'bruh win for us?"

"He'll win today."

Rags mustered whatever totems he could think of. He wore his socks inside out. He twisted his belt around, so the buckle was over his arse. He ate pieces of thread off his unwashed blouse. And he had a brute on first to protect the Harrys from Samuel Sham. He reckoned that Scarborough's hump would behave like a lightning rod and drink up the Giants' voodoo.

The kid could feel that black logic after four weeks of bedbugs and lice. The blood they took from Rags enlightened him. It was no haphazard, scrambling war between the teams, with independent fight-outs in all the different villages. Carl the bossman was stingy as hell. He told his Giants not to give a game to the Harry Heilmanns. Beat them, beat them, beat them, from Maryland to Floridy. Walk like Babe Ruth, diddle a bit, let the Pharaoh have his nine positions, but never, never lose.

The kid made his stand outside Fredericksburg, with Scarborough, Sheriff Smith, Topper Rigney, Garland James, and the sockamayocks. The Giants weren't alarmed. Emma had bitten into their playing style, because of the hold she had on Carl. But you could bust the seams on their golden baseball pajamas and tie one of Pharaoh's hands, and they'd still devour the Harrys.

The game began as a replica of all the others. Yam hid his smoke for an inning and allowed the Harrys a string of hits. Topper doubled into the grass behind first. Ragland squeezed him over to third with a bunt to the pitcher's box that he ran out for a chump's single. Garland homered to put the Harrys three ahead. The Giants did nothing but smile. They enjoyed this little rally that Yam provoked with a lazy thumb. He tightened his fist and struck out the next three batters, using his sinkerball.

The Sheriff whistled on his strut to the mound. "Where's my pillow, Garland? No gang of Blacks can slap this ol' Sheriff for three runs."

Pharaoh was the leadoff man. The Giants didn't share the white leagues' theory of a "balanced" attack. They wouldn't save their sluggers for the middle of the batting order. The heaviest hitters came at you first.

But this was Sheriff Smith, who had made war on Cobb, Sisler, Heilmann, and Ruth. He wouldn't concede an inch of batting room to any man. He dusted Yarbull for trying to crowd home plate. Then he leaned back and threw his fireball. Yarbull socked it into the trees. Fast as he was, Garl didn't have the chance to spear that ball. It traveled over fences and stray cows, into a neighboring pasture, five hundred feet away, and then fell out of sight.

The Sheriff shrugged his right wing. "That's the last ball them Blacks will touch with a bat." He laid his smoke on the Giants and put them out, one, two, three.

The game went another five innings without a hit. Then the Pharaoh strung a frozen rope that knocked off the bill of Scarborough's cap and continued on into right field for a stand-up triple. Muley Jones came up to bat. The Sheriff had struck him out twice with fireballs and slow curves. He was convinced that no Black in the world could solve his change of pace. The Sheriff spun a drop pitch and Muley drilled it into the hole. Rags hadn't watched and watched the Pharaoh out of idleness. He leapt with both feet, his torso acting like a javelin, and snared that ball as it sank around his shoestrings. The Pharaoh had committed himself, lunging for home, and he couldn't get back to third.

Carl stood near the overflow with his wife. Emma had to smile for any kid who could catch Pharaoh Yarbull running to the wrong base. Carl had an attack of bitterness. "That aint no white man out there. He plays like a Black." Bossman Carl went to his witch doctor. "What's the matter with you, Sam'l? We two runs behind, and them sisters are standing on their feet."

"Mr. Carl, the hunchback is in my way."

"Lay him low with the measles, I don't care."

"Lord, I tried. But I can't work around the pimple on his back. He's got Satan someplace in his shoulder."

"Forget the hunchback and you bring a storm down on the Harrys. Aint you got your root?"

"Yes sir, Mr. Carl."

"Then go to it. I want them Harrys to play in mud." Samuel Sham had manufactured rain dozens of times with the root he kept in a jar. It was his grandmother's root and it had never failed him.

Samuel was the number one root- worker in the Black leagues. He walked behind the grandstand, sneaked into the outhouse, closed the door, and worked that root, shaking and shaking the jar until the sky turned black. But the storm didn't break over the Harry Heilmanns. None of the Harrys got wet. It rained everywhere except on that baseball diamond. The grandstand flooded and people began to disappear. The Giants had the Harrys and themselves and no more paying customers. They finished out their innings in an isolated field. The boss cursed the witch doctor and his temperamental root that rained on him but wouldn't rain on the Harry Heilmanns. His wife was beautiful with wet brown hair. She stood in Samuel's rain and licked at it with her mouth. The boss had a miserable pinch in his groin.

He put his hope in Yarbull. The Pharaoh had one more at bat coming to him. You couldn't fool him with any goddamn fireball. The Pharaoh could murder slow stuff too.

Garland crouched near a stone wall at the end of the field and waited for the pitch. The Sheriff threw a junk ball at the Pharaoh that came in knee-high. Yarbull didn't have to look at it. He whipped his bat around, swinging from the heels, and clubbed that ball. The rain slowed it down, Samuel's rain, the rain that should have wrecked the Harrys. Garl didn't wander more than a dozen feet from the stone wall. "Goodbye, Pharaoh." He ran towards the diamond, signaling to the other Harrys. He had the victory ball in his glove.

10

THE kid arrived on Beacon Hill two days after Christmas. He missed the candlelighting ceremony and the caroling that marked every Christmas eve at Louisburg Square. The first thing he did was throw Marylou's servant down into the kitchen area. "I'll ring you when I want you, Rhys. This is your home while I'm in the house. Stay out of the bedrooms, you understand?" Then he kissed Iva and said hello to his mother-in-law.

Iva was huffy with him. "You have a fine sense of Christmas, don't you, Rags? Mama and I had to light candles for you. There's supposed to be a man in the house on Christmas eve."

"You had your mama's servant," Rags said, with spittle on his tongue.

"Don't you talk about him . . . where's Scarborough?"

"He went to Cuba with the team. Garl wouldn't give him Christmas off. He's too valuable to us. He breaks Black voodoo spells."

"Don't you talk about voodoo in this house. It brings bad luck."

Her body was hard when Rags took her to bed. It was as if he hadn't gotten out from under Samuel's root. Iva could have been some votive creature. Her hips moved, but her presence seemed to have vanished from him. Iva girl wasn't there with Rags.

"Are you finished?" she said, with her eyes on the wall. He got up, feeling a rage against the Cottonmouths. He grabbed Iva by the wrist and flung her out of the room. He couldn't bring a terror into her eyes.

"Are we going for a walk without our clothes? It's too late for caroling."

"You'll carol in your mama's bed."

He could see the imprint of a smile on the wife. "Is that what you want, Rags?"

They went naked into her mama's bedroom. Mother and daughter looked at each other without the slightest blush. Rags had his way with them. Marylou didn't complain. She whispered "Harvard Jack" in his ear.

Iva watched.

Ballplayers have such sharp hands and feet. Rags could cut you with his body, claw between mama and the girl. The bride was thinking to herself: my mother's insane. Mama and her Harvard Jacks! Iva had a husband who was late for Christmas. He'd rather play ball than live with her. *Baseball, baseball.* She'd married a glove and a pair of flannel pants. The kid dug a home for himself around third base. He wouldn't take Iva on the road. She was dumb "Eveline," the baseball wife. Raggsy could have been a sailor. He went from port to port with his winter and summer teams. Was she supposed to do needlework while the hero was away? Or join a lending library? He shouldn't have brought her into her mama's room. Oh, she'd do his bidding. She could be Raggsy's little doll. But dolls can scratch too. And she'd find a way to scratch that kid.

Rags was lonelier than he'd ever been, lonelier than Tucson, lonelier than Abilene, where his companions were bulls and Black cowboys with neckerchiefs, gloves, and splintered bats. He couldn't make his bed with the Cottonmouths. Their love screams tormented him, their breath was like a killer perfume; he listened to the pounding of their hearts with a chill in his entrails. He got dressed while the Cottonmouths were asleep.

He ran to South Station with his equipment bag, shirts and underpants rolled between his bats. He was a ballplayer, not a husband with two redheaded wives. His desire froze in him. Curled against mama and daughter only half an hour ago, he couldn't reach into their vitals. It was like touching the dead. The kid had too many selves in that house. Ragland, Cedric, Harvard Jack. Everybody and nobody all at once. Would someone tell the kid who he was? He could catch a baseball in either fist. That's as much as he knew.

He was recognized on the "Beeline Express" to Miami. It comforted him to play Ragland again. To talk baseball with businessmen and honeymooners. To sing about the Red Sox and the Harry Heilmanns. To declare how the Harrys had beaten the Black Giants on a rainy Monday in November with a hunchback at first. "They couldn't live with that one defeat. Sure, they whipped us plenty after that. We didn't come close. But it wasn't the same thing. We scratched the Giants, 3-1, on their own diamond, and they couldn't forgive themselves."

He got to Key West and took the mail boat to Havana. There was nothing unfamiliar about the bottle-shaped harbor he landed in. The old Spanish town was crazy for *beisbol* Twelve American teams, Black and white, had been working Cuba for a month. They had a World Series in Havana, Camaguey, and on the Isle of Pines. But there was a major disappointment among the fans. The Cubans loved the Yanquis, and what did they get? Rabbit Maranville, Rogers Hornsby, and a team that borrowed Harry Heilmann's name. Babe Ruth was in Puerto Rico that year. His winter contract didn't have Cuba in it. He was fat and muddy-eyed, but he still pulled in a thousand dollars a game, because the Juanitos adored his strikeouts as much as his home runs.

Rags couldn't locate his own team. The Harrys had dispersed throughout the provinces, and were playing in various winter leagues. He found Chappie Gruel in an American bar on the Calle O'Reilly. Chappie had a broken foot. He and the kid didn't get along, but Chappie was glad to see another Harry Heilmann. They drank rum all afternoon.

"Chappie, what happened to the foot?"

"Christ, they don't have grass in this country. You have to run on hard red clay. It's a miracle I didn't break my neck."

"Where's Garl?"

"In Camaguey, fielding a team of Black farmers."

"Did he take Scarborough along?"

"Na . . . your roomie's out of baseball."

Rags figured the rum had gone to Chappie's broken foot and was feeding him with lies. "He's given it up, I'm telling you. The brute got married."

"That's impossible. I've only been away two and a half weeks."

"Well, he took the vows. Married a mulatto woman, I think. Nobody's seen the bride, but I'm told he discovered her while she was working on her back."

"Chappie, what's his address?"

Chappie sucked up more rum and gargled his throat with a grin on his face. "Can't tell you, kid. The brute swore me to silence. He's afraid of you. Says you'd scream at him for picking out a wife."

"Can't you give me a hint, or do I have to walk the whole island?"

"He's in the sailors' district," Chappie said. "You'd better wear your uniform. It's a rotten part of town, but they might have pity on a baseball man."

So Rags put on his filthy grays with HARRY HEILMANN sewn across the chest, and he wandered into the *barrio marino,* near the Havana seawall. It was a district of whores, sailors, pirates, Turks, male prostitutes, and starving old men. The *calles* looked as if they'd been eaten by a pack of wild boars. He passed wine cellars that could have housed coffins too. The smell of piss and old men's pants was everywhere. A bride and groom couldn't have walked abreast in those alley streets. But no one ruffled the kid. A gringo baseball player could go wherever he liked, as long as he wore a suit of magical pajamas.

He met a colonel on horseback, galloping through the narrow, crooked *calles*. The colonel saluted Rags and yelled *Yanqui boy* at him. He saw two infants leading a turtle around on a leash. He mumbled the choppy pidgin Spanish he could remember from his days in Old Tucson. *"Beisbol Hunchyback. Jorobado. Bruto. Monstrosamente. "*

The infants neglected their turtle to go with Rags. They led him to an alleyway stuck between two streets and left him there. Rags looked up at a building that had a few brittle balconies and line after line of hollowed-out floors. A tribe of bats collected on one window and slept with their noses pointing down. Rags woke the bats with a shout.

"Hey, roomie, show yourself."

The bats flew onto another window but couldn't settle into any permanent sleep.

"Scarborough, do I have to come up for you?"

The brute appeared on the topmost balcony. He wore his baseball knickers and nothing else. His hump rose like a marvelous welt out of his shoulder blades. Sweat gleamed from the muscles on his arms.

"Raggsy, go away."

Six or seven brats accompanied him on the balcony. Two were blond, and the rest were dark-skinned. They clutched Scarborough's hands and thighs and screamed "Papa, papa." Then the bride came out. She was a Black woman with delicate bones in her face. She could have been twenty-five or forty. How could Rags tell the age of a woman on a balcony wall?

The brute seemed to have a murderous temper now.

"It's all right for you to get married, aint it. Rags? What about me? ... go away. You're scaring my kids."

Rags followed the seawall out of the sailors' district. He returned to the Calle O'Reilly. He had nowhere else to go. He sat at the American bar two days and two nights. Chappie Gruel must have fled to one of the bars across the street. Rags shaved in the toilet and lived on plantain milk and rum. He would have waited out the winter on O'Reilly Street if Garl hadn't come for him.

"Chappie says all you do is shit and eat."

"You paying him to spy on me?"

"No. That little skunk feels sorry for you."

"I brought my equipment bag. Who are we playing next?"

"The season's over, kid. You'll have to swing your bat in a dead park. It's January, and I'm going on my vacation."

Rags wiped the rum off his mouth with a finger. "Take me with you, Garl."

"I don't need a partner where I'm going."

The kid seemed tied to that bar stool with some terrible loss of spirit. Garl couldn't abandon him to the tourists and the bar-flies. He held Rags under the shoulder and lifted him off the stool. "Okay, sockamayock, you can come with me."

Rags was like a helpless baby who had to be spun through the streets. He found himself near the seawall again, in another part of sailor town. Garl had put him on a fishing boat. The kid heard rough talk between Garl and the tillerman. But the tillerman stayed on the boat. Rags reached down with a tin can and tried to taste the sea water. Garl twisted his head back and threw the can away. They broke out of the harbor, with the tillerman grumbling at them.

The kid had lost his sense of time and place. He knew they were on the water. His cuffs were growing wet. He wanted to play fungo in the boat, but Garl ordered him to keep quiet.

"Garland, do we have to sail around the pirate coves?"

Piratas, he told the tillerman, and the tillerman laughed at the crazy gringo in the *beisbol* suit.

He took them into the half-deserted territory of Quintana Roo. It was a dumping ground for undesirables and political prisoners from Honduras, Mexico, and Guatemala. The tillerman was happy to get rid of his cargo of two baseball idiots.

Garl didn't pull Rags inland. They lived on the beach. It was a funny idea of a vacation for the kid. You couldn't even find a lizard in that dumb gray sand. Zombies walked the beach, men with eyes that didn't jut from the middle of their heads. They went up the beach and down, in a line that never varied. One of the zombies had a little scar under both ears.

"Who is that gink?"

"Shut up," Garl said. "He's a friend of mine. He used to be the governor of a goddamn state in Honduras until his party ruined itself. They forgot to steal some miserable election."

"If he's such a friend, how come he doesn't talk?"

Garl shook his head in disgust. Rags had to be the most ignorant boy in the territory.

"Governor Hermosa can't talk. The opposition ripped out his tongue and put him on Quintana Roo. They couldn't kill the old man. He had too many relatives around."

"How do you know the history of Honduras?" Rags said.

"If you come every winter you learn what it's like."

Garl left the beach for an hour and came back with stores of food and three handsome women. He couldn't have rented these women if they hadn't been in disgrace with their own village. They were fornicators, drunkards, and foulmouths whose husbands had deserted them and taken other brides. But the kid didn't find them wanting in any way. They jabbered in their native tongue, cooked a splendid turtle soup, and hugged the three men (Rags, Garl, and the silent governor), with absolute devotion.

The *beisbol* began to drift out of Rags. He could have wintered at Quintana Roo for the whole twelve months of the year. February was coming, and Garl touched the kid on the shoulder while he was sleeping with one of the disgraced wives. "We have to go. It's time for Arkansas."

"Hell, Garl, why don't we fuck baseball camp and stay right here?"

"I have a family to support. . . and if I don't bring you to Sackville Forest, Hollis will stick my pay envelope in his mouth and chew on it."

They said goodbye to the governor with a wave of the hand, and Garl returned the three women, who cried at the loss of such stupendous and agreeable men. The village took the wives back and waited for other beachcombers and ballplayers to rent these foulmouthed women.

The players' camp was in a shamble when Garl and the kid arrived at Sackville Forest. The Sox were without a manager. Briggs Josephson had jumped the club. Hollis never sent him a contract, thinking to whittle down his salary for 1925. The Brownies hired him away. Hollis swore to blackball him and sue the American League if he couldn't get satisfaction. He was readying an appeal to Kenesaw Mountain Landis, the high commissioner of baseball. But he dropped the subject of Briggs' piracy the minute he saw Garland.

"Mercy on us. I don't have to bring in a new man. You're my player-manager, Garl. That's three thousand extra in your pocket."

How could Garl refuse? He'd rather manage the Sox, and be their tyrant, than play under someone else. But he had no illusions about where the Sox would go. He'd have to fight like a crazed horse to keep them out of the cellar in 1925.

Meanwhile, Hollis frowned at the kid, who still wore his winter grays. "Get out of those stinking pants. You're with the Red Sox, or did you forget?"

He was down on Ragland this year. He knew about the troubles between Iva and the kid. And he blamed Rags.

The kid dragged himself to the Red Sox boardinghouse. There was another man's trousers in his room. And a baseball cap. The brute had beat Rags to Arkansas.

"Son of a bitch," Rags said, with his first smile in Sackville Forest. "I thought you were finished with us. Chappie told me that."

"He's a liar," Scarborough said. "I'm the Boston bat boy. I never miss a training camp."

"What about that woman on the balcony?"

Scarborough began to hide his chin. "She's my winter wife."

"We ought to celebrate," Rags said. "It's an event, isn't it, when roomies meet after a month? Let's see if we can dig up chocolate sundaes in this rabbit town."

The kid's wife showed up on the bus from Hot Springs. Hollis had arranged for the trip. He was the girl's "goduncle," and he had the right to mend her marriage. He found a separate bungalow for Iva and Rags, away from the boardinghouse.

The reconciliation didn't work. The girl had come for revenge on the husband who took her mama and her into bed, had his fill, and disappeared. She waited until Rags went with Hollis and Garl and Sheriff Smith to talk baseball in Hollis' private bungalow. Then she strolled up to the boardinghouse in her spring coat. The country boys were sitting on the porch. Chicken Stallings sensed that she had nothing on under the coat. He watched the play of her calves on the porch steps. The outline of her buttocks was clear and true under the green of her coat. "Your man aint in this house," the Chicken said. "He's with the boss ... in the far shack."

"I know," Iva said, and she continued into the boardinghouse. The country boys whistled to themselves. "Somebody's getting some poontail," the Chicken muttered. And he sneaked behind the girl.

She'd gone up to the hunchback's room. She didn't shut the door. She began to unbutton her coat. Scarborough couldn't take his eyes off those fingers twirling around the buttons. He wanted to scream his head off, so the blood would break in him and turn him blind. How could he miss the red patch between her legs?

Iva walked over to the brute. She remembered lying next to him and Rags in their room at the baseball hotel, when she came up from Tisbury town the summer before last. The brute had shivered all night, his erection putting a tent in their mutual blanket. He wouldn't disobey her now.

His tongue grew into a fat toad. He was an imbecile with hot hands pulling on his baseball shirt. She undid his belt, kneeled, and suddenly his knickers were on the floor.

The brute was making love to Raggsy's wife. Her body glowed under him. She had a cat's eyes. The hump on his back had gone away. He bent perfectly into the wife. She didn't rush the brute. Iva stayed with his frenzy, held him while he moaned and fell weak against her side. He'd come out of her. He moved off the bed and sat hunched in the corner.

The Chicken had been watching from the door. He'd seen the ripples on Scarborough's back, the muscles that snaked down from his neck while he was stuck to Miz Iva. But the girl was free, waiting on the bed, with lots of room between her thighs. The Chicken let his suspenders drop. Rags wasn't his leader anymore. The kid stopped fighting for the country boys. Hadn't he come into camp with their enemy, Garland James? Rags had jumped over to the Dartmouth crowd. So why couldn't the Chicken enjoy his wife?

Iva ruffled her forehead when he climbed on top of her, but she didn't refuse. Then it was Germany Stone at the door, with one or two Dartmouth men, Hooks Poland, and a full array of country boys. They stood on line for the girl. The Chicken had her twice.

The brute was muttering in the corner when Garl came in. He slapped at his own players, punched all the Red Sox in the room until he was near the bed. Iva had a deep glaze on her throat. She didn't recognize Garland. She thought he was another country boy who would get on top. He began to shove her into her coat. The brute stared up from his corner. His eyes touched on Garl for one terrible moment. He could have been in Egypt. All his sensibility had fled from the room.

Garl noticed that shriveled body, but he couldn't attend to the brute. He'd have a civil war on his hands if he didn't get Iva out of there. He gathered her belongings and drove the girl to Hot Springs. He didn't tell Hollis. Garl was manager of the Sox, and he understood the laws of training camp; a team fell apart every time a player's wife began serving other men.

It didn't take the kid very long to discover what went on in the boardinghouse. The boy who took care of the linen was fond of Rags and he ratted on the country boys. "Sorry, Mr. Ragland, but half the club had your missus."

Rags didn't ask about his wife. "Where's Scarborough?"

"Dunno," the boy said. "He run off somewheres. She took him first. I saw them from the window."

The country boys locked themselves inside their rooms. Rags didn't bang on the doors and challenge them to a boxing duel. He went searching for the brute.

He looked in all the little shacks around the playing field. He broke into deserted bungalows. Then he walked into the woods of Sackville Forest. It was a few acres of short, twisted trees and ancient bear dens. The kid went from tree to tree, calling "Scarborough, Scarborough."

The brute was there. He couldn't have heard Raggsy's calls. He had smoke in his head. The smoke licked at him with a hot tongue. He stumbled in and out of bear dens, thinking of ways to destroy himself. He might have been a collector of mushrooms, with a finger on his back that twitched in the presence of hyenas and poisonous toadstools. But there was hardly a mushroom in these woods, or a hyena. That hump twitched with a sense of its own disaster. A roomie shouldn't fuck a wife. *I had Miz Iva. Sin. sin.*

The brute stepped out of his pants. He carried them in one arm and began to sock at trees. *Shitface. Whoreboy. Fuck. Fuck. Fuck.*

The kid spotted two naked legs dangling near the ground. Rags charged for those legs like an uncurled snake. The brute had tried to hang himself with his own baseball knickers, knotting them to the branch of a tree. His hump had saved him. His neck was too strong. It wouldn't break on a stunted tree in Sackville Forest. He was gagging, with slime on his tongue, when Rags pulled him down.

The kid tried to stroke his ear, comfort him, but Scarborough let out a shriek. It could have been an orphan wailing, or a lunatic.

"Don't cry," Rags said. "It wasn't your fault. She was only getting back at me. I got crazy in that house. I put Iva and her mama in the same bed."

Slowly the brute got onto his feet and followed Rags out of the woods, but he wouldn't let the kid touch him, steer him, or hold him around the waist.

The Bad Boy of Baseball:

BOOK FOUR

11

THE kid got his old room back at the Brunswick Hotel. He and Scarborough slept under the same summer quilt. Beacon Hill fell out of their vocabulary. But it's a fickle thing to discard a baseball wife. The Royal Rooters had been fond of the kid's bride. They brought xylophones to the park, and beat out little tunes on their pieces of wood. The devotion of 1924 was gone. They'd turned cool to Rags.

He wasn't that familiar bastard, who'd stop a ball with his kidneys or his head to accomplish the double play. He was a mean kid now. He didn't acknowledge their songs. He seemed removed from the Boston infield. He never spoke a word to Alvin Critz. He growled at umpires. He'd have shoving wars with enemy catchers near home plate. He knocked down Muddy Ruel of the Washington Senators. The fans sided with Muddy in this war. Muddy was two inches shorter than Rags. And he had a rotten leg.

Garl fined the kid thirty bucks. He couldn't allow rhubarbs like that to happen. He wasn't raising bandits on the field. He had to hold a team together. But his Sox were pathetic without the kid. Whatever spirit they had burst out of his crazy glove.

He yelled at Rags in front of the team. "I don't care whose tongue you bite after a game. You don't attack a man when people are around. Save your feuding for the tunnel. Is that clear?"

The kid nodded in a perfunctory way. Garl had the mind to pull on Rags' nose. That might wake him up. Yet he had to go soft with him. He understood the kid's torment. Rags was a veteran at nineteen, a bastard with a live dad, a baseball tramp, and a husband who'd returned to bacheloring.

Garl whispered to the brute behind the kid's back. "Scarb-'ruh, he can't fight everybody in the American League. His brains will be rolling around in the dirt. We haven't seen Detroit. What if he starts with Ty Cobb?"

"Cobb's an old man," the brute said, with a thin smile. "Rags can bust his face."

"Cobb's not *that* old, Mr. Scarb'ruh. Anyway, if the kid hurts a finger, he's useless to me. Calm him down, for Christ's sake. Take him to the picture show. Introduce him to a couple of whores. I'd rather he come down with the clap, than have to hear about his fights."

"I'm his roomie, skip. I aint no sorcery man. I can't stick his anger in a bottle and drown it in the Charles."

Garl thought of hiring a detective to watch over Rags. What's the good? He'd hit the detective in the jaw, and Garl would have to beg the local magistrate not to impound his third baseman. This time, when he received a note from Marylou in his hotel box, he decided not to ignore it. Maybe she could help him with the kid. He wouldn't march to her house on the Hill, because it was spooked with Cottonmouths, but he asked the bellboys at the Brunswick to show her up to his room.

She wouldn't discuss the kid. "I don't have any influence over my daughter, Mr. James. You'll have to ask her about the marriage."

"I'm in a pickle, Miz Marylou. I wouldn't want Rags to say I'm tinkering with his life. You see, ma'am, he's not surviving too well on his own, and..."

"Doesn't he have a roommate?"

"Sure, but Scarb'ruh isn't the same as a wife."

The skipper was too involved in the running of his team to notice any signs of agitation in Marylou. Why was she shivering in Garl's sunny room? The hair whipped around her head like a serpent's rod. Her eyes went a bitter color as she stood close to Garl. He had Ragland in his mind. How could he tame the kid? He never heard the muttering in his ear.

"What, Miz Marylou?"

The words came like small intense bites from her mouth. "Would you like to undress me, Mr. James?"

She was beautiful with the sunlight burning in every hollow of her cheek. Garl couldn't place his own desire. He should have kissed her on the mouth, and spent the afternoon with the lady of Beacon Hill. Baseball strategy had turned him into an invalid and a fool. He didn't call out to her when she left him there, with his infield problems and his concern about the Tigers who were arriving tomorrow.

She'd had small luck with her men, Miz Marylou. A husband who died on her almost out of spite. That Judah. He felt her ass when she was a kitchen maid at his fraternity house. Judah got down on his knees in front of his brothers and proposed to her. They laughed and laughed, the Dartmouth boys and Judah dragged her to Beacon Hill to show off his kitchen maid-wife. His slut, he said. But she had a child with him. Hollis was more of a father than Judah was. Hollis taught Iva how to ice-skate. And Judah went and strangled on a chicken bone.

Marylou was in love with a baseball man. Quiet Garl. So serious. With three brothers in college. How many times could she offer herself? She might as well hear the frogs croak in the Fens. She'd find herself a frog lover if she could. Frogs were reliable. They didn't plead baseball. They croaked their songs and shook the mud off their backs. But she couldn't be sure. Maybe frogs had their own baseball league in the swamp. And they sang about their batting averages, just the way some men did.

I'll marry the frog in center field.

Garl didn't give another thought to Marylou. His team dropped three in a row to Detroit. Ragland challenged half the Tiger bench.

He almost pushed Ty Cobb into the dugout wall. The great man was ready to fight. Cobb had lost his old handsomeness. He no longer had the look of a hawk. That sharp face of his was a matter of history. He developed jowls, and his ears were two puffy twists of flesh from all the knuckles he'd taken in his life.

Rags spit on the ground, near the great man's feet. "I don't fight grandfathers," he said, and he walked away from Ty Cobb. The great man threw himself at Rags, but the kid spun around and pushed Cobb off with an elbow.

The golden days were finished. Fans had stopped booing Ty Cobb. The American League had a new battler: Ragland of the Red Sox. He didn't have to struggle with a thirty-eight-year-old man. He added to his reputation by spurning Cobb's offer to fight.

He did go into the tunnel with Heinie Manush and Frank O'Rourke. He knocked Heinie senseless and chipped O'Rourke's teeth. He was the bad boy of baseball.

Christ, Garl figured to himself. I should have bloodied his head when I had him in the tunnel two years ago. Then he might have given up the habit of using his fists on other people.

Garl's telephone rang. It was Hollis McKee who wanted him. "Garland, have you heard from Marylou?"

"I talked to her last week . . . about Ragland."

"Well, she's missing, Garl."

"Missing? I don't understand."

"What's wrong with you? The woman disappeared."

Boston's fire companies worked with the police to find Marylou. Boats from the harbor patrol were raised onto fire trucks and shuttled over to the Fens. A dredging operation was begun in that wild park. The police had up to fifty boats in the water, dragging the marshland and the different pieces of the Muddy River for Marylou's corpse. They discovered an armada of sunken bottles, strangled cats and dogs, the bones of certain prehistoric fish, but nothing that resembled a woman or any of her clothes.

"I'll bet my thirty years in politics that the missus aint at the bottom of that lake," the mayor of Boston declared. The Republicans at the State House weren't so sure.

The police slapped and slapped at the water, while the Sox went on the road. Rags climbed on the dugout roof at Yankee Stadium and offered to take on twenty thousand fans. Altogether, or one at a time. He'd slug the women too, he said. Scarborough had to pull him down.

Rags fought with the A's and the Washington Senators. Fans assumed the practice of bombing him with soda pop while he was at third. It became routine for the ump to call time-out, so the bottles could be carted off the field. The booing didn't discourage Rags. He was batting .328. His mother-in-law was still missing from Boston and the rest of the world.

Two days after the police removed all their materiel from the Fens, Marylou rose to the top of that marshy water. She had weeds on her and cuts along her face. Her body was bloated with gas. But she wasn't unbeautiful. Nothing could damage that red hair.

The Boston papers screamed about Marylou:

HEIR TO ICE FORTUNE FOUND DEAD
POLICE EXPLORE POSSIBILITY OF FOUL PLAY
MURDER, SUICIDE, OR BIZARRE ACCIDENT?
WHAT WAS RAGLAND'S MOTHER-IN-LAW DOING IN A
SWAMP?

The Sox returned to Boston with all that crazy news. Rags didn't stop off at his hotel. He rushed from South Station to Louisburg Square. The front door wasn't locked. He stood in the main hall and started to yell.

"Iva? It's me . . . I'm sorry about your ma."

She came halfway down the stairs with her mother's servant. Rhys was carrying a blunderbuss, a pistol with a long snout. He couldn't keep it still. It wavered in his hand, like a frozen squirrel come alive. "You, get out of here."

"I'm talking to my wife," Rags said, starting up the stairs.

"So help me. I'll shoot."

The servant's teeth were chattering. Rags walked up to the blunderbuss, and pushed into it with his chest.

"Iva, I've come home... Scarborough doesn't have to live with us . . . maybe I could find a house . . ."

Iva didn't lunge for the pistol. She wouldn't splatter Rags against her wall. She pulled back her arm and brought him down to the bottom of the stairs. It took five hard slaps.

"Don't you ever come to this house again, Mr. Rags. You're not my husband anymore."

"Iva, I. . ."

She locked the door on him, and the kid stood on the salmon-colored bricks of Louisburg Square with bumps on his face. *That girl knows how to slap.*

12

THE bad boy of baseball only got worse. He broke Pinky Hargrave's mouth under the grandstands of Sportsman's Park. He would have gone through the Brownies' roster and destroyed that team, with his Amherst boxing style. You couldn't gang up on the kid, trap him at the players' exit, and teach him a lesson with bats, fists, and spikes on a shoe, because the hunchback would get behind Rags and cover for him. And no bat or shoe in the world could penetrate that boil of armored skin and bone on Scarborough's shoulder.

Briggs Josephson had helped the Brownies climb to second place, but they wouldn't last the season if Ragland tore apart their infield, their outfield, and all their battery mates. Rags' old skipper left a message for the kid to come to a speakeasy opposite Sportsman's Park. It could have been a ploy to finish off Rags before he got out of St. Louis. The kid wouldn't bring Scarborough along. He went into the speakeasy by himself.

It must have been a haven for Brownie addicts, hoodlums, and gambling men. They scowled at Rags from the tables and the bar. He wasn't surprised. It was an enemy camp wherever he walked in St. Louis. Briggs ushered him into a private room. You had to be careful with Kenesaw Mountain Landis. The high commissioner had informers in each baseball town. And Briggs didn't like to be accused of tampering with another team's third baseman.

"Hiya, kid."

They drank soapy beer. Rags' old skipper smiled at him. "I won't be able to field a team pretty soon. Do me a favor, huh? Leave me nine men who can stand on their feet."

"It's not my fault," Rags said. "Tell your bench to lay off ... I'll make them silly in the head if they go on riding me."

"Ah, what's a few goddamn words."

"Briggsy, they can spread shit about me. I don't care. But tell them not to mention my wife, my pa, and my mother-in- law who drowned. You don't hit a guy's family. It's dirty business."

"Rags, you owe me one."

"How's that?"

"I brought you into the league, remember? I found you in Arkansas, a lefty third baseman, and I carried you right away."

"Then you ran to St. Louis, and you forgot to take me with you."

Briggs looked into the beer mug. "You bonehead, I didn't forget. I'm dealing for you. I offered Gene Robertson and Baby Doll. Your skipper has to clear it with Hollis McKee."

"I won't walk without Scarborough. He has to be included in the deal."

Briggs swirled his beer, until it foamed up like a mug of warm piss. "Heck, I could have had Scarborough ages ago. But he dropped the same damn story. "You take my roomie, or you can't have me."

They shook hands over the cloudy beer. "Stop causing trouble. I can't use a prizefighter on the Browns. And don't breathe a word until you get to Fenway, or you'll queer it for us."

Rags kept his mouth shut on the sleeper to Boston, but he had to spill *something* to his roommate. "Scarborough, we're going to live right near the Mississippi. Garl's trading for me and you. He's giving us away to the Browns."

"Don't be so sure," Scarborough whispered.

"I'm sure," Rags whispered back. "When did Briggsy ever lie?"

Garland didn't approach him after batting practice. Rags winked, but the skipper kept a stone face. The kid had to corner Garl in the dugout, while the rest of the Sox had gone up the stairs to shed their practice uniforms.

"Skip, don't you have some news for me?"

"What about?"

"I thought Baby Doll was coming to Boston, and I was heading for the Browns."

There wasn't a stir in that stone face.

"I thought so too. I tried to deal you. That's a fact. You're ruining my club with those fists of yours. Baby Doll was just a throw-in. He's thirty-four. I wanted Gene Robertson. He'll give me the glove I need at third."

Garl stopped talking, and Rags followed him around the dugout. "Well, what happened?"

"Hollis killed it... I can't say why. The deal made sense. Robertson's a ballplayer. You're a frigging shark. But Hollis isn't letting you out of the bag."

Rags strode through the tunnel in a fury and took those four flights to the executive suite. He knocked on Hollis' door, the glass rattling against his list. "It's me. Ragland. The kid."

Hollis chased his secretary out, and Rags had that giant office for the president of Boston baseball and himself. "Trade me to the Browns," he said.

"No."

"I hate it here."

"Good."

"I'll split your fucking club. Believe me. I'll punch every man you got."

"That's fine."

"Why won't you give me to St. Louis? Robertson can play third."

"I know that. He hit .319 last year. He's got the hands. And he isn't a lefty freak. But I want you in this graveyard. You're going to die with the Red Sox. You son of a bitch, you murdered Marylou."

Rags jumped across the room and grabbed Hollis by the lapels. "I don't give a shit whose boss you are. You didn't buy my tongue, Mr. McKee. Marylou drowned. So don't say murderer to me."

"You broke her heart when you abandoned little Iva."

The kid dropped Hollis into a chair.

"Mister, her heart was broken long before that. I'd swear Dartmouth was the place. When you and Iva's pa grabbed her for yourselves. Play with the country girl. Eat her up. Tell me, boss, how did you and that Judah Cottonmouth decide which one would marry her? Did you cut the deck for Marylou?"

"Get out of my sight," Hollis said, his body sinking into the chair. His lips were a ghostly color.

"I'm not finished with you."

The kid seized the armrests of the chair and dragged Hollis up close to him. "Have you been touching pinkies with my father's lawyer? It's funny, isn't it, that the *Transcript* should shout Tannehill, Tannehill, last year, just before Opening Day. Griffey got to you, didn't he?"

"Yes," Hollis spit from the middle of his chair.

"You held on to the story, and you leaked it to Noel Finnbar. You got pictures of me at Amherst, the ones I sent to my pa, and you made Noel promise not to print them until you gave the word . . . lovely bastard that you are."

"I did what any owner would do."

"Mister, you don't have to trade little Cedric. I'll play for you. But if you ever come near me, on the field, and off the field. I'll wring your miserable neck . . ."

Rags turned aside from his enemies in the American League. He wouldn't fight with the Browns, or hurl insults at the Cleveland bench. He began to make war on the Sox. He didn't single out those bumpkins who had enjoyed the pleasures of his wife. That was a forgotten part of his war games. He took retribution on the whole roster of Hollis McKee. He bent Chicken Stallings' thumb, so the sockamayock couldn't pitch for a week. He insulted his own catcher, saying that Tilly Young ought to have a rocking chair. Tilly came from the U. of Alabama, where insults could fire a man's blood.

He offered the kid a chance to apologize. Rags said no, and Tilly went to box the kid's ears back. He couldn't find the kid's ears. Rags dropped him with two vicious blows to the cheek. The catcher's tongue was split.

Garl had to put a stop to this crazy bloodbath. Who was next? Would the kid chirp at Seaman Schupp, or go after Alvin Critz? Garl suspended him for twenty-five days. Rags couldn't wear his glove on the field. He couldn't swing a bat. He had to warm the bench.

"Touch one more man, Ragland, and you're finished for the year."

The words came bitter to Garland's mouth. He'd butchered the Red Sox by suspending Rags. The guts were torn out of the Boston infield. He had to try a busher at third, a boy from Michigan named Mark Travers. A rookie glove couldn't improve the Sox. Boston was so busy snoring in the cellar, it might fall out of the American League.

The brute became an emissary for Garl. "Skipper says he'll reinstate you if you promise to keep your knuckles inside your pocket."

"Tell him to blow."

And Rags sat on the Boston bench, with a wide girth between him and the other players. He wouldn't give any tips to Mark Travers. The fans were pulling for the new boy. But Travers seemed a bit shy of those pellets that were aimed for his skull. He would duck under a line drive, and he didn't have that third baseman's instinct to throw his chest into the path of an oncoming ball.

"You could sure use Gene Robertson," Rags would say to Garl. "Can't you twist Hollis' arm a little? The Sox are gonna be in baboonville in another month. Trade me to the Browns."

"I'd resign before I did that. You have your bench, Mr. Ragland. That's where you belong."

Rags stuck his knee out and tripped the fireballer. Sheriff Smith. Garl helped the Sheriff to his feet and then he looked at Babe Ragland. "You've been crying for this, haven't you? . . . meet me in the tunnel."

Rags shrugged off Garl's invitation. "I won't fight with my skipper. It's rotten baseball."

"Well, you'll have to pass over my body if you want to get to the clubhouse. I'm tired of your shit."

"Garl, you haven't punched a soul in two years. You're out of practice. You aim at my nose, and you'll be hitting wind."

"Try me, you arrogant prick."

The hunchback threw his hands over his eyes. But he couldn't get his sorrow to go down. He knew all along it would come to this. Sophocles and the bad boy of baseball. He wasn't sure who to pity, Garl or Rags? He'd have a pair of losers in the tunnel, that much he understood.

He appealed to Rags. "You can still back off. Make believe he's Mr. Cobb."

"How? Garl doesn't have bushy ears. He's the best outfielder in the East."

The Sox were exuberant. They'd have their revenge. No man could survive the skipper's combinations. His left was as wicked as his right. Scarborough had a different sense of things. He wanted to run from Boston and hide in some dark well.

The Sox lost to Cleveland, 7-2, and the players scrambled down the dugout steps and through the tunnel door. Rags stayed on the bench. He held his jaw in one fist. He liked Garland James. Garl had sailed with him to Quintana Roo. He couldn't have had his winter vacation without the skip. It was Hollis he was after, not Garl. Hollis McKee, who bought and sold players and country girls. Rags didn't have any desire to punch the skip.

"You can wait here until they dress."

It was Scarborough standing over him.

"That's no good. Garl means what he says ... come on."

They walked into the tunnel, past the water fountain and the urinal, felt the dampness and the wind, and Rags began to warm his knuckles. Garl stood alone, midway up the tunnel. He wouldn't let the Sox hover close to him. They had to crouch on the clubhouse stairs.

Garl went into his boxing stance. Rags would have smirked at any other man. The Dartmouth position was a silly way to box. It followed the rules of 1905, that declared you had to display as little of yourself as possible. Narrow the target. Give your man nothing to hit. But the Dartmouth position cramped up your body. It couldn't induce that lightning in your elbow. It belonged to the grandfathers of a New Hampshire college town.

Amherst boxing was much less orthodox. It allowed you to spin off from the heel, and to lower and raise your center of gravity. You couldn't absorb a punch as well as any Dartmouth man. But you didn't have to. The Amherst style was to hit and run.

"Are you ready, kid?"

The first blow was off Garland's fist. It struck Ragland on the left nostril. The force of it threw the kid into the tunnel wall. The edge of his nose was pushed in. Rags pawed at the nostril, wiping the blood away. "Pretty, Garl. Going to my blind side."

The skipper snarled at him. "I didn't ask you for a commentary. *Fight.*"

Six short blows landed on Garl. For a minute Scarborough believed the kid was using different pairs of fists. Garl shortened his own punches. He knew how to flick at a man. But he couldn't land with Rags' frequency.

Humping Jesus! In all his misery, Scarborough was amazed. A fist would shoot out and die in the murky wind. There was so much weaving of bodies, you couldn't be sure where Amherst ended and Dartmouth began. Rags' head seemed disconnected from his feet. It was like watching two skeletons in baseball pajamas who had some missing joints. But their dance was starting to kill.

Garl wouldn't surrender to a boy. He could have taken all the cuffs to his eyebrows and his ears, only his knees twisted out from under him. He gave back whatever he could. Flurries of blows would pass between Garl and the kid. He couldn't get around that Amherst defense. Rags would coil and uncoil in front of Garl. Their blouses were ripped. They were carrying shreds on their shoulders. It wasn't fear that Garl could smell. It was dampness and piss. He would have punched and punched until September arrived and the season was over. He couldn't lay this kid on the tunnel floor.

Rags had wires in his torso, instead of tissue and bone. You hit him, and he would spring back at you just as hard.

Garl's left eye was closed. He had to stare at a target that jumped all the time. The skip was angry at himself. He couldn't tame the bad boy. The walls were sliding onto him. Garl didn't give up his punches, even as he fell. His own flurries had beaten him. And those tiny Amherst jabs. The skip sat on his rump, with five or six gaps in his mouth.

The kid had lost just as many teeth. Rags was mystified when Garl disappeared. His fists were clenched. They pushed at where Garl's face should have been. He didn't know what else to do. Someone directed his shoulder towards the clubhouse. "You decked him, Raggsy. It's over now . . ."

Scarborough had turned the kid around. He was as confused as any bat boy with a double ordeal. He had allegiances to his skipper and his roommate. But he couldn't help both of them. The kid was moving up the stairs, shoving Red Sox away. His shirt was like a series of rough bandannas that spilled down his back. His knees showed through his pants. One ear was so bloody, you would have sworn the lobe was gone. But he hadn't stumbled yet. So the brute took off his own jersey, rinsed it in the water fountain, and applied it to the bumps on Garland's head.

The skip blinked the blood and salt from his eyes. "I can see you, Chicken. You don't have to lean all over me."

"It aint the Chicken," Scarborough said. "It's your bat boy, skip. Now be quiet, or you'll hurt the blisters on your tongue."

"He's the worst cocksucker in the league," Garl said. "He's crazy mean, but he can box. I'm glad he didn't fight with Cobb. He'd have butchered the old man from Detroit."

"How do you know?"

A tooth dropped out while Garl laughed from his plot of land in the tunnel. "Scarb'ruh, you sure are hard to please. You have the goddamn evidence. Look at me ... am I on my ass, or not?"

And he coughed another tooth into the palm of his hand.

13

THE kid wouldn't go on the road with his team. Why should he warm the Sox's bench in Chicago, St. Louis, and Detroit? But those Dartmouth blows to the head must have softened his reasoning skills. He forgot that the bat boy had to travel with Hollis' men. The kid remained at the Brunswick without his roommate. It saddened him not to have the brute under his quilt. Scarborough was the last man in Massachusetts he could hold a conversation with. He grinned like a wounded jackal at everybody else.

Michaels, the house detective, knocked on his door. "You have a visitor, Babe."

"Is it a redhead?" Rags was thinking of his wife.

"Na, it's some Black. Says he's a friend of yours. Sorry, Babe, we couldn't let him sit in the lobby ... people might be upset. But I wouldn't chase out a friend. I don't care how black he is. He's waiting for you outside the porter's room." The elevator took Rags under the lobby. He found the porter's room and said hello to Carl Raines of the Cincinnati Black Giants.

"How's the Cincinnatis, Mr. Carl?"

"We're raking it in. There's no such thing as a bad year for my club."

"Should we find a soda shop? The Brunswick has funny ideas about its meeting places."

"This'll do," Carl said. He was the boss of the Giants, and no baseball hotel could get under his skin. "I hear you're on the outs with Hollis... and Garl is giving you a rest. Would you like to play for me?"

Old Carl's beautiful wife, Miz Emma, must have turned him crazy. Rags loved the Giants, but white men couldn't play on a Black team in the United States.

"I have a contract with the Sox, Mr. Carl."

"That don't concern us. You can jump the American League . . . how much is Hollis paying you?"

"Five thousand."

"I'll pay you six."

"It's not the money, Mr. Carl. I'd like to get out of Boston, but I can't. I'm signed to Hollis McKee. I wouldn't run out on the Red Sox."

"Love a duck," Carl said. "Do the white man's jig. That McKee will hump you blind. You got no future at Fenway Park. That's what my medicine man told me."

"You mean Samuel Sham, the witch? Hell, he couldn't even make the rain fly on us."

"Rain's a tricky business, little Rags. But Sam'l's good with futures. You aint got none."

The kid returned to his room and mulled over the witch doctor's words. Scarborough had stronger magic than Samuel Sham. So he went to the brute's speakeasy on Darling Street. "It's Ragland," he shouted through the peephole in the door. "Humpty Dumpty's pal."

The bouncer let him in.

"How's the Hump, Mr. Ragland?"

"He's on the road . . . with the Sox."

The bouncer's name was Herman, and he said, "It's a pity. We enjoy having the Hump around."

The bar area was packed with assorted shysters, floozies, and members of the Boston Braves, who were at home this week. These Braves, led by Cotton Charles, wouldn't acknowledge that Boston had another team. They were in fifth place this year. Cotton already had twenty-five doubles. A third baseman for the lowly Sox was less than invisible at the Darling Street saloon.

The kid sat at a table by himself. He drank soda water and white wine.

"That stuff's for grandmothers," Cotton Charles shouted to his mates. "Water and wine . . . hey, kid, is it true Garl caught the syph in Mexico last winter? Aint that why he's swinging a crippled bat?"

The saloon was cosier than Rags' hotel, and he didn't want to be banished from Darling Street for slapping Cotton Charles.

"Kid, what happened to your mouth? You have enough holes in there to park a bus."

One of the shysters told Cotton to shut up. He was wearing an orange suit. He had pink buttons on his vest and bold stripes. He came over to Rags and introduced himself as Billy Rogovin.

"I'm Rags. I play for the Sox."

"I know. You're the kid with the magic glove."

"The magic's dead. I can't even walk onto the field." Rogovin had gentle eyes. He seemed misplaced in an orange suit. Rags couldn't tell. Maybe Rogovin needed a shyster's uniform on Darling Street.

"The Sox are crazy to give up on you," Rogovin said. "They'll be stuck in the cellar for the next twenty years."

"Ah, it wasn't Garland's fault. He had to sit me down. I was scavenging . . ."

"How do you scavenge on a ball club?"

"It's easy. You beat up your own men."

"They probably deserved it. That owner of yours has a habit of collecting bums."

Rags and Rogovin had an afternoon of soda and wine. Their faces turned red. The shyster wobbled in his orange suit. "Come on. I'm taking you on a buying trip."

They clumped across the city, from Darling Street to Scollay Square. They passed tattoo artists, ten-cents-a-dance ballrooms for Army and Navy men, photo shops, a shooting gallery, boys who stood outside the burlesque houses, waiting for a peek, toothless old bums who did favors for prostitutes, wives who searched for missing husbands, and husbands with wives who'd gone to Scollay and never came back. Rogovin seemed to know all of them.

The distraught husbands would surround Rogovin and touch him on his orange suit. He had to push their hands away. But he didn't scream at them. They were customers of his.

"I'll find her, Sol. I'm working on it. I'll need another few dollars."

"I already paid you ten."

"Ten? Ten can't even get me into the alleys. You think I can shop around for every bitch who runs from Somerville and Braintree? It'll cost you, Sol, and it takes time." Rogovin led Rags into a clothing shop on Brattle Street. He bought silk pajamas for himself and cajoled Rags into an orange suit. He shouted for the tailor, who had to crawl under Rags and put chalk marks on crotch, shoulders, and cuffs. The tailor asked for six days.

Rogovin turned his gentle eyes on him. "Do it now." The tailor shrugged and went to his sewing machine, while Rags stood around in his underwear.

"Rogovin, I'm not on salary this month. I can't pay for this."

"Who says pay? It's a gift. If we're gonna become brothers, you gotta dress like me."

They walked away from Brattle Street in twin suits. "Fucking Hymie, he's a dog's tailor," Rogovin said, plucking loose hairs off Rags' orange sleeve.

The kid didn't get back to his hotel until three in the morning. The telephone rang soon as he opened the door. St. Louis was on the line. The long-distance operator prattled in his ear. Then he heard Scarborough's voice.

Rags shouted into the phone. "Hiya, Hump."

"Since when am I Hump to you?"

"Ah, I was at your saloon ... on Darling Street. That's your nickname over there ..."

"Raggsy, are you all right?"

"Sure," the kid said. "I made a friend while you're traveling with Garl and the Sox. I went to Scollay with him and he dressed me up in an orange suit."

There was a pause in the wires. "Who is this friend?"

"Don't get jealous, Hump . . . you're my roomie for life. They call him Rogovin, and he hangs out at Darling Street."

"I never heard of no Rogovins," the brute said. "Be careful, will you. Rags?"

"Guess what? The Black Giants offered me a job... old Mr. Carl came to the hotel and said I should quit the Sox and go with him."

"What did you tell the man?"

"Shit, Garl benched me and all... but I wouldn't desert my team."

The operator started prattling how three minutes were up, and Scarborough had to get off the line from St. Louis. Rags fell asleep with the telephone in his hand. He dreamt of his roommate. They were fishing from their windowsill at the Brunswick, and all they could lure into the room with their rope and their hooks were pairs of dirty pajamas. The pajamas might have been old players' uniforms. Rags flung them out the window.

He had coffee and eggs after he woke. He trotted to Darling Street in his orange suit. The bouncer winked at him. "You're spiffy today, Mr. Ragland."

He put a silver dollar into the bouncer's paw. "Thank you, Herman."

The bar was empty. Drinkers wouldn't arrive until noon. But Rogovin was there, eating an egg out of a cup. He looked unhappy, with thick, frozen circles under his eyes. The kid would have sworn that Rogovin had never gone to sleep.

Who knows where his bedroom was? The egg revived him. The yoke dripping onto his chin shook off some of Rogovin's gloom.

"Rags, when are they gonna lift that suspension and let you play?"

"After the Sox get back from St. Louis . . ."

"We're brothers now, you and me."

"I guess so," the kid said, with his morning smile. "Humpty and Dumpty with the same orange suit."

"Rags, your brother's in a rotten hole... I've been betting on the Sox to lose."

"That's a sure bet. The Sox are two and eighteen without me.

"I know, but I need a little more leverage."

"What kind of leverage, Billy boy?"

"Your glove."

The kid's eyes began to narrow.

"If you could fake a step, slow down a bit going for the ball. I'd have that leverage I need."

"I play to win," the kid said. "But don't worry. We're shitbirds this year. My glove can't change that."

Rogovin still had egg yolk on his chin. "You're right. Rags, forget about what I said ... I was only asking for a friend."

They marched to Scollay again, took off their orange suits, and slept with a team of Portuguese whores at a house on Franklin Avenue; Rags was grateful to his new brother. It was the first woman he'd had since those dishonored wives who lived with him on Quintana Roo. Later, they had pig's knuckles and Bavarian cream pie in the sunken part of the dining room at Jacob Worth & Co. Then they walked home to Darling Street.

Rags couldn't avoid the Boston Braves.

It was nighttime; Cotton Charles and his flunkies had half the saloon for themselves. They didn't bother the kid once they saw Rogovin with him, although Cotton smirked at the twin suits. The brothers had whiskey and orange juice at an end table. The bar ran out of juice, so they drank the whiskey with a little water on the side.

"Rags, who's the worst bum on the Red Sox?"

"Chicken Stallings. He can't throw the ball, and he likes to make lip farts in the shower."

"Let's get him on the phone ... and I'll warn him not to fart with his lips."

"The Chicken's in St. Louis. At the Buckingham."

Rogovin escorted Rags to the bar's private phone. He got the operator to ring St. Louis and the Buckingham Hotel.

"Chicken? It's me. Babe Ragland... I'm in Boston, where do you think? ... A pal of mine wants to say hello."

The kid handed the phone to Rogovin and waltzed back to his table. He had to go around Cotton Charles. Then Rogovin appeared.

"Billy, did you tell him no more lip farts?"

"I certainly did."

"Isn't he the biggest cluck you ever talked to in your life?"

"The biggest," Rogovin said, and he dug a swollen envelope into the kid's pocket.

"Billy, what's that?"

"A thousand fish. Do me a favor. Hold it for me. I don't trust the bastards in this place. They might lift it out of my pants. But they wouldn't touch you. You're the Babe . .."

"I'll hold it, Billy. It's just like Wells Fargo inside my pocket."

He walked around with Rogovin's money for two days. Rogovin never called for it. Rags couldn't find him on Darling Street.

"Where's Billy?" he asked Herman the bouncer.

Herman shrugged. "Billy boy does the sly every now and then. But he always comes back."

Rags had company at his hotel. It was the brute himself. Scarborough had returned to Boston ahead of the club. His face was more shriveled than it had ever been. Rags felt sorry for the brute. Scarborough had turned into an ancient, sobbing five-year-old dwarf.

"I shouldn't have left you here ... I should have said, 'Skipper, suspend me too, because Raggsy don't know beans outside of baseball' "

"Who says? I know boxing, I know bulls, I know Scollay Square. Can I help it if Hollis started humping me?"

"Mister, you humped yourself. When you walk with gamblers, you gotta pay the price."

"Who's a gambler?"

"That gink you put on the phone with Chicken Stallings. The gink offered Chicken ten thousand if he could get the Sox to blow any two games with the Tribe. Chicken squealed. Now Hollis knows, and Garl knows, and everybody is burning mad. Chicken swears the gink gave you a goddamn envelope for the Sox. A 'sweetener' he called it. Is that true?" Rags took the envelope out of his pocket.

"Sweetener? Rogovin asked me to hold this for him. He said it would be safer in my pants."

Scarborough was reluctant to feel the envelope. He shuddered at its thickness and shook his head at Rags. "Did anybody see the moolah change hands?"

"Yeah, half the Boston Braves."

Scarborough groaned. He wrapped the envelope in a towel, and hid the towel under the mattress, where the maids wouldn't have bothered to dust. Then he dragged the kid to Darling Street.

Humpty Dumpty didn't have his old sway at the saloon. The bouncer wouldn't let him in.

"Sorry, Hump, the vice squad's been here. Your boy's a no-no in this town ... tell the Babe to pack his valise and run to Colorado."

"Herm," Scarborough said, "who's this Rogovin?"

The bouncer closed the door on Humpty Dumpty. Humpty sat on the stoop.

"Somebody set you up. Rags, was it your father?... would he give you the royal screw?"

"Pa wouldn't connive with shysters like Billy Rogovin. He'd steal the Red Sox away from Hollis and send me down to the minors Billy said he was my brother. He shouldn't have fingered me with a gambler's envelope."

Scarborough climbed off the stoop. "He's probably a small-time Yid from Henchman Street. He sits with the gamblers at Fenway and he stooges for the cops. We'll never find him."

Rags rubbed the material of his orange suit. "I know a guy who can lead us to Billy."

"Who? The captain of the North End horse patrol?"

"No. The tailor that widened the crotch on these pants I'm wearing."

They sneaked into the clothing store on Brattle Street. Rags went up to the tailor. "Hymie, it's Ragland .. . how do you like me in your masterpiece?"

The tailor shrank from him.

"Don't you remember? Billy Rogovin brought me in . . . and you let out the crotch and fixed the cuffs on your sewing machine."

"This aint my merchandise," the tailor said, with contempt for Rags and his orange suit. "I don't put cheesecloth on my customers' backs."

He grabbed one of the kid's sleeves and tore it with his fists.

"Cheesecloth. I told you."

Rags would have pitched Hymie over his sewing machine, but Scarborough touched the kid's undamaged sleeve and led him out of the store.

"The rat's gone into the sewers. It's too late to flush him out. We gotta take care of you. The Judge's coming in tomorrow with the team."

"Which judge is that?"

Scarborough rolled his eyes to indicate what a rube the kid was.

"Mountain Landis himself, the emperor of baseball. You'll get the full inquisition in Hollis' office. Play the jester. Be his Uncle Tom. Yes him to death, you hear? Promise you'll report any gambler who winks his eye at you. And maybe, just maybe, you'll get off the ineligible list in a couple of years. Figure 1926 or '27. But for God's sakes, burn that orange suit."

Rags wore his player pajamas to Hollis' suite. He had to go upstairs all by himself. Bat boys weren't allowed in the front office. Furniture had been shoved around to satisfy the Judge. Hollis prepared a courtroom for Kenesaw Mountain Landis. An oak table served as the Judge's trial bench. You couldn't approach that table without a nod from him.

The Judge could have used Rogovin's Brattle Street tailor. Landis had teethmarks on his cuffs; they were bitten and frayed. His high collar had gone yellow against his scrawny neck. He was a small, frail man in a musty suit. The emperor of baseball clutched an old cane with rubber bands around the nob. If he flicked the rubber bands, it was a sign that he was getting impatient with you. He had a sharp beak, lots of silver hair, and a bulge in his jaw. The son of a bitch was chewing tobacco at Rags' inquisition.

He had Chicken Stallings, Cotton Charles, Hollis McKee, and the skipper on his left side. They sat in simple chairs. Hollis was like any other witness before the Judge. He'd lost the rights to his room. No president of the Red Sox could upstage Kenesaw Mountain Landis.

The Chicken leered at Rags. Cotton played with his fingers. Garl was the only one who seemed sad and uncomfortable in the emperor's court. He understood the ridiculous wrath of the Judge. Landis had come to Boston on the same train with the Sox. But he was too pure to mingle with them. The Judge rode in the engineer's caboose.

He let Hollis talk first. "Commissioner, the Babe kept busting people in the mouth. You couldn't go anywhere without Ragland having a fight. He got to be a real hyena. He attacked my Red Sox... beat up his own manager, didn't he, Garl?"

Garl wouldn't go along with his boss and savage the kid. "Rags had a bad marriage, Judge. It turned him wild ..."

The emperor began to flick his rubber bands. "A bad marriage is no excuse for hitting a man . . . continue, Mr. McKee."

"Well, we couldn't have a hyena on the field. We had to sit him down ... and he made more trouble for himself and the team. We have gamblers at Fenway, Commissioner. Every ball park does. But my Red Sox wouldn't throw a game. Ask the Chicken here. He blew the whistle on Ragland and his friends."

The Chicken was in his glory. He'd been a journeyman pitcher since 1917, with enough stuff on the ball to strike out Harry Heilmann every other year. Garl would use him in the late innings, when the Sox were ten runs behind or ten runs ahead. But now the Chicken would get his reward. He could declare his righteousness to the Judge. He rambled on and on, how he thwarted the gamblers in their attempt to bribe the Sox. .. Commissioner, he says there's money in it for you, ten thousand to spread across the board, and I say to Raggsy's pal, you go to hell. I hung up on him and I went straight to Hollis."

Then Cotton Charles sang to the Judge about the telephone call from Darling Street and the envelope Rogovin gave to the kid after the call was over. But he couldn't snitch on Rags without revealing his own trips to the speakeasy. The Judge's silver eyebrows curled up at him. "What were you doin' around bootleggers and gamblers, Mr. Charles?"

Cotton had to recant while his nostrils twitched and his ears were going gray. "It was just a hangout. I didn't talk to bootleggers, sir."

Mountain Landis mashed the tobacco inside his jaw. "Promise you'll never go near a speakeasy again."

"Hope to die if I ever do," Cotton said, with a look of misery settling between his gray ears.

"I fine you a hundred dollars for sittin' with bootleggers, Mr. Charles. But I'm not an ungrateful man. I'll rescind that fine and thank you for helping us shuck those gamblers out of baseball."

The emperor turned his eyebrows on Rags. The kid stepped forward. His knees were prickly from having to stand so long in one spot.

"I know your father, young man. I wouldn't want to shame his only son . . . Cedric Tannehill, did you put Chicken Stallings on the phone with a gambler?"

"I'm the Babe," Rags muttered. But the emperor couldn't have heard.

"Speak up," Landis shouted at the kid.

"Judge," Garl said. "He's twenty years old . . . the best third baseman the Sox have ever had. Whatever he did, he was acting out of ignorance."

The Judge went to his rubber bands. He didn't like busybodies in his court. "The boy has a tongue, sir. I'll beg you to be silent. We don't need interpretations of the law." Garl stared back at the silver eyebrows. He wasn't frightened of the Judge. The owners had elected him emperor after the White Sox lay down to the Cincinnati Reds and threw the World Series of 1919. Landis ruled from a tiny office in Chicago, with the single word COMMISSIONER on his door. He could descend upon any clubhouse and lecture players for an hour on the evils that might befall them. Whiskey and gambling were the two great sins. He had his private box at every ball park. He went from city to city in the engineer's caboose, high priest, emperor, and tyrannical god.

Garl didn't own a baseball team and he didn't have to bow to the Judge. Landis was a prick. But Garl couldn't help Rags through the emperor's court.

"Young Cedric, did you put Stallings on the phone?"

Rags was growing muddled on his feet. *Who's young Cedric? I'm the seventh Babe.*

"Billy was my friend ... why couldn't he say a few words to the Chicken?"

"So you admit it. You gave the phone to a gambler. And in return, he paid you off. Cedric, where's the money?" Rags took the envelope out of his baseball knickers. Landis seized the envelope, stuck his fingers in, and counted ten hundred-dollar bills.

"Billy said hold it for him ... there were some creeps in the saloon."

The emperor frowned. "Young Cedric, you consorted with gamblers, you aided and abetted them in a bribery scheme, and took filthy lucre from their hands ... are you sorry for what you did?"

Garl should have thrown Rags onto the floor and got him to cry in front of the Judge. You had to soothe the white-haired god, stroke him to sleep. But the kid wouldn't bend.

"Are you sorry?"

"No."

"Then I'll have to punish you ... Cedric Tannehill, as of this moment, the sixteenth of June, 1925, I declare you ineligible to play. You will not be allowed to enter any ball park in the major or the minor leagues. Do you understand? Baseball is finished with you."

Rags left the emperor's court, trudged down the stairs, thinking. *No more Red Sox, no more Babe,* and walked out of Fenway Park.

Rags and the Cincinnati Giants:

BOOK FIVE

14

He could have been a bullrider, or a copper engineer, like his pa, with Amherst, Tucson, and Abilene behind him. He'd have chatted with lawyers, had his own Mr. Griffey to watch over his affairs. Then he'd have taken a wife. Not a girl who'd sleep with the Red Sox. But a bride from Old Tucson, in a marriage that Griffey would have arranged. His pa would have come to the wedding, given Cedric a copper mine or two. The kid would have been safe among the Tannehills.

I don't want that.

He was leather, air, and horsehide on a ball. He was knickers and dirty brown grass, the first twist of a double play. He couldn't live apart from a baseball diamond. He was married to a fifty-cent glove.

Copper wasn't his birthright. *No.* He hadn't slept in any cradle in his father's house. He was born in a pile of mud near the pitcher's box. A baseball baby. Orphan Rags. And somebody had stolen his birthright from him. Now he'd have to go and hide in the Black leagues.

Scarborough blubbered when he saw Rags' face. He didn't have to hear the news: hollow eyes told him everything. The emperor had chased Rags, put him on the permanent ineligible list.

"He scratched you out of the game, didn't he?"

The kid's shoulders slumped under his Red Sox shirt.

"Raggsy, couldn't you play up to that old man? He didn't have a nickel's worth of evidence against you. Did he produce Billy Rogovin? Where's the famous gambler?"

"Who cares," Rags said. "I'm joining the Cincinnati Giants."

"What about Scarborough?"

"Hell, the Judge isn't after you. You can stay. You're still the Sox's bat boy."

"Aint we roomies?" Scarborough said.

"I have to play with sockamayocks. You don't. Whoever heard of anybody banning himself from the big leagues? I won't let you do it."

"It's a free country," Scarborough said. "We'll have to give notice to the hotel and buy ourselves a car." Scarborough didn't have to worry about the hotel; the Brunswick wanted Rags out. Any night was soon enough. The press had announced Landis' decision: FENWAY AND OTHER PARKS TO CLOSE THEIR DOORS ON THE BABE; RAGLAND BARRED FOR LIFE; CONNECTION WITH GAMBLERS HINTED AT; BOSTON POLICE WON'T ENTER COMMISSIONER'S BAILIWICK.

Rags didn't blink until he looked at Noel Finnbar's column. Finnbar called Rags a wifebeater and a rogue. BAD BOY STRIKES OUT. Rags reached for the baseball bat he always kept in the room. "I'm gonna knock some wood on Finnbar's head."

The brute struggled with him and grabbed the bat away. "Go on. It'll be wonderful with them photographing you in your jailhouse pajamas."

Scarborough resigned from the Sox, and they bought a three-year-old Hudson sedan. Rags was shunned by his teammates. Sheriff Smith wouldn't shake the kid's hand. Alvin Critz turned from him in the lobby. But Garland came up to the room. The skip seemed much more devastated than Rags or the brute. His team was dying on him. But it wasn't only that. The Judge had ruined a twenty-year-old boy. The kid would have to play with outlaws, or use another name on the field.

"Ah, don't you worry, skip. Me and the Hump are joining up with the Giants."

Garl stared at Rags as if he'd just been unwired. "John McGraw is tough, but he won't take on the commissioner of baseball. Don't have fantasies of playing in New York."

"Not New York," the kid said. "The Cincinnati Giants."

The skipper went pale in the mouth.

"You won't live out the year ... if the Cincinnatis don't kill you, the fans will."

"Hell, Garl, me and the Hump'll fight them all, back to back."

You couldn't dissuade the boy. Garl took him and the brute by their shoulders and squeezed, then he helped them carry down their bags. They got into the Hudson, with Scarborough behind the wheel.

"So long, skip."

And they drove out of Boston to marry up with the Giants.

They crossed seven states. They stopped at fairgrounds, circuses, cow pastures, and village greens. The brute tried the friends he had in baseball. No one could tell him where the Cincinnatis were.

The Hudson was eating up gasoline, and the kid grew disgusted with the search. "They're gone, those Cincinnatis . . . disappeared."

"How do you know? Maybe Carl Raines took them on a Cuban tour."

"You're crazy. Carl wouldn't run to Havana in June. He'd save it for February. I'll bet the Giants got into a fight with some town hke Springfield or Decatur, and the town chewed them alive."

"Bushwah. Decatur couldn't beat up the Cincinnati Giants."

"They're gone, wiped out. Scarborough, suppose we wiggled ourselves into one of the outlaw leagues along the Rio Grande? It's a natural. There's Texas baseball in my blood."

"You think the old man would let you do that? He'll hunt you down. The emperor's got agents everywhere. You can hide with a Black club, and that's it."

"I'm going to the Rio Grande."

But they got stalled outside of Louisville. Scarborough began to shudder in the driver's chair. He had to use every bit of force coming down from his crooked shoulder, or the Hudson would have gone off the road.

"I can smell him," Scarborough said.

"Who?"

"That magician. Samuel Sham. The Cincinnatis have got to be close. . . ."

Scarborough sniffed the air and arrived at a country barn. All Rags could see was a battered yellow bus. Where were those Buicks with mahogany on the outside?

Bossman Carl walked out of the barn.

"If it aint the bad boy himself... and Mr. Scarborough. Didn't I tell you Sam'l doesn't lie? Ditch the Red Sox, he said. And the Red Sox ditched you. I'm not sure I fancy having a renegade on my club. I'll give ya two thousand for the rest of the year."

"You promised me six."

"That was before the Judge demoted you. You aint worth much to me now. I can pick up an outlaw any time I want. Two thousand . . . and the hunchback has to blow. Sam'l won't tolerate him. He can't work his root with Mr. Scarborough around."

"Well, good luck to the Cincinnatis," Rags said. "Scarborough, are we on the road to Texas?"

Scarborough didn't move. "You ought to think about his proposition, Rags. I can always lumberjack."

"The heck with him and his Giants. Let's go."

Carl sprang in front of the sedan. "Three thousand... and we'll settle on a price for Scarborough."

They got out of the Hudson and peeked into the barn. "Where's Pharaoh?" The barn was filled with sockamayocks.

"Where's Yam Murray?"

Carl began to curse and spit. "Pharaoh jumped the Cincinnatis. He's with the Black Barons. Yam's with the Memphis ABCs. Muley Jones went over to the Buckeyes. There's a players' war going on."

"No wonder you came begging to my hotel. You lost your fucking team. And your seven Buicks, where are they?"

Carl stared at the ground. "Had to hock them for a while. They were getting too conspicuous. A town would spot my cars and say, 'It's them troublemakers, the Giants.' They'd send the sheriffs down on our scalps. So we switched to a bus."

"You don't need Samuel Sham," Rags said. "You have your own liar's root. You're in the poorhouse. You sold your cars, or you couldn't eat."

The witch doctor came stumbling out of the barn. He must have been whiskey mad, because the sight of Scarborough nearly riled him to death. He stamped his feet, brought up a dark blue bile, and began to whirl around the Hudson. Then he stopped to crook his finger at the brute. "Send him away, Mr. Carl. My liver is churning. My bladder is gone. I'm a ghost. My piss'll be black by tonight. I'll join the players' war, Mr. Carl, if you don't get that hump out of here."

"Go back into the barn," the bossman said. "Nobody's gonna steal a witch doctor off a losing team. Sam'l, this is the only home you got."

It must have made sense to the medicine man; he scampered into the barn with all the sockamayocks.

The boss' carpenters and groundsmen had also deserted him in the players' war. So the sockamayocks had to build a diamond and a grandstand for Carl. And they didn't have that magical way with a hammer, a trowel, and a scythe. The stands were lumpy down the middle, and the diamond had potholes near third base. The kid began to wonder if the holes were meant for him.

He was advertised as Mr. Babe Ragland, Refugee of the White American League, The Boy Who Was Driven out of Baseball by Kenesaw Mountain Landis, And Is Now a Fixture at Third Base for the Cincinnati Giants. Fans came to watch the Black players and their "fixture," Babe Ragland.

Rags got curious when the bossman didn't move from his barn. The Cincinnatis had run out of local villages to play. Scarborough told the kid not to ask. "It's probably got something to do with his wife."

Then, after the diamond lay empty for a week, Carl declared that Emma was supposed to meet him at the barn, and he wouldn't budge until his woman arrived.

The sockamayocks grew irritable living inside a barn like dairy cows. They couldn't attack their own boss, so they turned against Rags and the brute. "Randolph, you see them hug last night? My, my, they is a lovin' couple. There's more touchin' between those two than with Emma and Mr. Carl."

"Suck a tit," Rags said to the twenty sockamayocks, and they came at him with big nails, shovels, and scythes. Rags didn't jump out of the barn. He stood with Scarborough. They had their fists, Scarborough's hump, and a pair of Louisville Sluggers.

Carl was sleeping in the bus with Samuel, and he didn't hear that disturbance from the barn. The sockamayocks began to swish the scythes. Rags and the brute knocked at those blades with their Sluggers. The kid had a gash in his arm from a falling scythe. But three sockamayocks were on the floor, groaning, with bumps on their heads.

"Seventeen more to go."

The scythes kept swishing at them. A boom exploded through the barn. The ceiling buckled over the sockamayocks, who swore that heaven and hell had descended upon the Cincinnati Giants.

It was Emma Raines with a Colt revolver in her hands. She could steady that Colt as fine as any cowboy Rags could remember from his father's ranch.

"Go on," she said. "Carl's brave skunks, trying to cut up two little men."

The sockamayocks backed into a corner of the barn. They dropped their scythes and the other weapons they were carrying. They wouldn't take on Miz Emma, with or without her Colt.

"Thank you, ma'am," Rags said, shy around that beautiful woman who had Marylou's hair and creamy yellow skin. But she'd already gone out to wake her husband Carl.

A brittle truce was declared between the sockamayocks and the whites. Actually, it was Emma who forced a pact on the Giants. She had her husband vacate the barn and shove off for Tennessee. The sockamayocks would go with Samuel on the bus; Emma and Carl would ride in the white man's Hudson. Carl served as navigator. He sat up front, digging his fingers into different maps, while Scarborough steered. Emma and Rags had the back of the Hudson to themselves.

The kid forgot his wife and his lost pa and his dead career in the majors. The heated perfume that rose off Emma cured Rags of his ills. She would smile at him, kick off one shoe, and curl her toes under the Hudson's floor rug and Rags' foot, so her husband couldn't see. That woman had more fondling power in the twigs of her feet than any whore Rags had run into at Scollay Square. They couldn't pet or clutch hands in front of Carl, but the kid's blood was beginning to cook from all the caressing his ankles got before they reached the Great Smoky Mountains, where Carl decided to pitch camp.

The sockamayocks slapped at the grass, rolled a few dozen rocks, and built their crooked diamond on a hill outside Newport, Tennessee. Then they turned to hawking with placards on their chests, and sold the Giants in mountain villages. Carl had a crowd again. People were coming to hiss at the outlaw.

Rags solved the difficulty of playing on a hill. He ran along with the slant in the ground and took any ball off the weirdest hops. But the kid paid a price; he lost the feel of Emma's toes. How could she crawl into the Hudson with Rags, when Carl and the sockamayocks and hundreds of villagers were around on the hill?

"Take me to New Orleans," she sang in his ear.

The kid was forlorn. "I can't, Miz Emma ... I have to play."

She stuck to the Giants for a week, lived in the Smoky Mountains with her husband Carl, and then she disappeared. Carl's face wrinkled up, the kid bobbled a few, but the Giants were winning on their Tennessee hill.

A man with a satchel came up to Rags on a Saturday, wearing a black mourner's suit. He'd noticed Rags in the Cincinnatis' pants and shirt. "I'm awfully sorry, but can you direct me to Cedric Tannehill? ... he calls himself the Babe. Isn't he on your team?"

"What are you sorry for, Mr. Griffey?"

"My God, is that you?" Griffey said. Rags had dirt around his eyes and a sneer, and Griffey thought he was looking at a sockamayock.

"Hey Griffey, is my pa gonna buy off the Judge and put me back on the eligible list? Tell him to forget it. I'd rather play for the Giants."

"Cedric, your father is dead."

A shiver went from his throat and continued down to his knees, and the kid nearly fell. Griffey caught him by an elbow. Rags shook himself free. The shiver had gone out of him.

"My pa wasn't even sixty. Why should he die?"

"It was sudden. He collapsed ... no one could revive him."

The kid's shoulders began to heave, and he turned from Griffey, so his father's lawyer wouldn't catch him in the act of crying.

The kid stood with his knuckles in his eyes. He'd wet the collar of his gold and white baseball shirt. He realized the lawyer had business to discuss. Griffey wouldn't have brought his satchel to Tennessee for a simple death call. The lawyer may have been a toad for the Tannehill copper pits, but he wasn't a brute. He felt awkward with a satchel full of papers around a grieving boy.

"Cedric, I could come another time . . ."

"Na," the kid said. "We can go to my office." And he led Griffey into the back seat of the Hudson. The lawyer removed an enormous folder with sleeves that opened out like an accordion; there were envelopes stuffed into every sleeve.

"When did pa die?"

"A month ago," Griffey said, fiddling with the sleeves.

Rags grabbed the folder away; envelopes spilled onto the floor and made a pyramid around Griffey's feet. Griffey darted for the envelopes.

"Leave 'em there ... pa dies and it takes you a month to bring the news? I ought to hang you up by your funeral coat and let the bullfrogs jump into your mouth."

"Cedric, we couldn't find you, I swear . . ."

"Griffey, you could find anybody. I never heard of a soul escaping you."

"We had searchers out," Griffey said in his own defense. "We offered a big reward . . . Cedric, you're on a phantom team."

"You don't have to tell me that. Phantoms and sockamayocks and outlaws like me."

"I only discovered yesterday where the Cincinnatis were."

Griffey scooped up the envelopes, and Rags signed papers until his shoulder hurt. He wouldn't read any of the jabber written on them. That was for Griffey, not the kid. "I suppose pa cut me out for skipping Amherst and playing ball."

"On the contrary. You're president of Tannehill Copper ... I grant you, it doesn't mean all that much. Your father's industries are run by an independent board. But he wouldn't disown you. You can draw a monthly stipend if you come to Tucson. And the ranch, the ranch is yours ... you can't sell it, or trade livestock, but you can live on it whenever you like."

"Thanks, Griffey," the kid said, "but I don't think I'll get to Abilene."

"There's one more problem," Griffey said, turning shy. "You've inherited me. I'm your lawyer now."

"Well, if I can use a lawyer, Griffey, I'll give a yell. Until then you can push your rump to Tucson and sit on all that copper dust."

A regret began to eat at Rags after the lawyer was gone. *Should have asked him about pa.* He approached the witch doctor. "Samuel, how strong is that root of yours?"

"Stronger than angels and devils," Samuel said, showing off.

"What exactly can it do?"

"Curse the living and raise the dead."

"I want you to raise up my pa for me . . . I'll give you twenty bucks."

The witch doctor was contemptuous of the kid's offer. "Keep them twenty bucks. I don't work my root for cash. Any rootman does that, he's worth shit. Mr. Rags, you aint said a kind word to me before today. And you brung that Scarborough into camp. Why should I raise white folks for you?"

Even a lesser magician could have smelled the kid's disease: that lumpy, pathetic twist to Rags' body made Sam'l aware how heartsore he was. Samuel agreed to work his root. "I can't promise you nothin'. But I'll try. Come on with me." Rags followed the magician into the bus. Samuel found his root, which was in an old, cloudy jar, and he disappeared into the Tennessee woods with Rags.

He crouched near a rock and worked his root, fondling the outside of the jar. He chanted something that came out muddled to the kid. Who could understand a witch's tongue? The sky turned dark over the kid's head. A wind blew in the trees. The woods must have been full of owls. He saw their green eyes. They hopped along the branches, hooting at him. Rags wasn't going to be mocked by a company of owls. He swung at the branches with his throwing arm.

"Concentrate on your pa," the rootworker said.

It's a lie. Samuel can't raise a bean.

Sam worked and worked that root. It looked like he was bleeding his own jar.

The hooting stopped and a figure tumbled out of the forest haze.

"Pa?"

It was a woman, dressed in swamp weeds and a torn blouse. Marylou. The magician had conjured up a Cottonmouth. She swayed next to Rags in her damp clothes. Samuel hid behind the rock.

Her hair fell like rat tails around her shoulders. She smiled at Rags' uniform, the gold braiding of the Giants on his chest. "Harvard Jack," she said.

The kid had asked for his father, but he wouldn't refuse what he got. Rags didn't know how to talk to a ghost, so he winked and pushed with his tongue.

"Why did you go and drown yourself, Miz Marylou?"

"Garl wouldn't marry me."

"There's other men."

"Of course," she said, wiggling her rat tails. "Rotten lovers and a mean son-in-law. God gave them all to me."

She turned from him and ran deeper into the woods. Rags begged her to wait. He didn't feel as lonely with her rat tails around. But she wouldn't heed the kid.

"I'll have the swamps if I can't have Garland James," she said. "I'm going home."

Rags took the magician out from behind his rock. Samuel had a disappointed grin. "It aint my fault. No sir. That root sure is stubborn, Mr. Rags. It just wouldn't raise your pa."

"That's all right," the kid said, putting his arm around the magician. "I was glad to see Miz Marylou."

15

THE Giants prospered in Tennessee. Pharaoh Yarbull jumped back to the team. He could have earned more if he'd stayed with the Black Barons. But he wasn't happy with their kind of ball. They didn't fuss and fight and build their own diamonds. Pharaoh preferred the hurly-burly of the Cincinnati Giants. A few days after Yarbull, Yam Murray returned. Then Moses Cutshaw, Muley Jones, and Swimmy Welles.

The players' war was over. Pharaoh had cut out its heart. Carl began sending the sockamayocks away. His seven Buicks arrived from Atlanta on their own mysterious run. His carpenters were showing up, and his former groundsmen. Carl scolded them, called them traitors and skunks, but he took them in. Now he could afford to laugh at the kid.

"Where'm I gonna put you?" he said, stroking his chin.

"Pharaoh's the best third baseman in town."

"Put me on the bench," Rags said. "I've been there before."

But the Pharaoh wouldn't allow it. "Give him third, Mr. Carl. I like playing short this time of year."

With Yarbull around, the kid didn't dwell so much on his father and Marylou's ghost. Rags had that perfect team he'd always wanted. With Pharaoh, Yam, and Swimmy Welles, there wasn't a weak spot on the Giants. They had bats, they had brains and gloves. None of them smirked at the kid's white hands. They sucked Rags into their scheme of liquid motion. Legs and arms would melt around a ball. Nothing got through.

The diamond became a prison camp for enemy runners. Swimmy Welles would leap into the air over second, tag the runner, and throw before you realized he'd ever had the ball in his glove. He'd hide the catch by twisting his body away from the runner and the fools in the stands. But he was only a trickster compared to the man at short.

Yarbull wasn't double-jointed like Swimmy Welles. He didn't have to bend his shoulder back to lure a runner off the bag. He would leave you stranded wherever you were. The Pharaoh was an antelope on mud and grass. The Giants would shout to one another: "Is Yarbull puttin' on his hooves today?" He wouldn't have been human without the letters on his shirt. The batter would swing, and a bar of gold would pass in front of your eyes. That was Pharaoh on the move.

The witch doctor kept him alive. Yarbull's knees would buckle after a game. He would fall onto the diamond, and lie there, spasms going up and down his legs like malicious snakes under the skin, as if Yarbull had contracted epilepsy of the calves and thighs. Samuel would run out to him with a blanket and his root. He would place the root jar near Yarbull's left cheek, wrap him in the blanket, and draw those evil snakes out of his legs.

There wasn't another rootworker in the business that could touch Samuel Sham. He was the medicine man of the Cincinnati Giants and he could scorn his brother magicians, with their pathetic, shriveled roots. "Nobody can piss on Sam. I brung a white lady to life for three minutes."

The boss of the Giants had everything: Yarbull, Rags, and a magician. He announced to his club, "We aint goin' to Puerto this winter. The Buckeyes and the ABCs can have their Havanas. The Giants are stickin' to the United States."

It was after World Series time, and the barnstorming teams shunned the little man. Harry Heilmann had come back to play with his All-Stars, and he wouldn't consider arranging a postseason match with the Giants. The Judge had warned Harry never to go near a team that had Babe Ragland on its roster. Landis sent his agents down to reason with Mr. Carl. "Get rid of the Babe, and we'll find some competition for you." The boss didn't throw them out of camp. He had his financial stakes to consider.

Pharaoh had to knock on the bossman's shoulder. "Mr. Carl, that's a honey of a third baseman we got. I'd lose a step at short if you gave me a sockamayock."

Carl shut the doors of his Buick to the emperor's agents. "What you mean, fuckin' with my roster. The emperor aint got no business here. Mr. Rags stays with me."

The Cincinnatis were the only team in baseball that had defied the emperor and won. College towns, villages, and industrial teams outside organized baseball were eager to scrap with the Black Giants. They wanted an eyeful of Pharaoh and the Boston outlaw.

Rain, sheriffs, and the emperor of baseball couldn't halt the Cincinnati Giants. Samuel appeased the rain gods with his root. He could calm the worst storm, or push it over to another hill. If the rain did fall on the Giants, Sam would point to Scarborough. "It's him. The gods won't listen to my root, when we got a crippleback in camp."

Carl told his magician to shut up. The boss was satisfied. He could live with an occasional storm. If he fooled with Scarborough, Rags would walk off the field. Then the Pharaoh would bitch at him and start a second players' war. And Carl would have to give up his Buicks again. His ankles swelled on him every time he rode in a bus.

Let the rain gods get even with Carl a little for carrying a brute. They could blow as much as they liked, as long as they didn't steal his Giants away. Carl had the "winningest" team in baseball. He called the World Series a mockery in the placards he hung on his criers and his scouts. He challenged the Cardinals of 1926 to play Yarbull and the kid. "Hornsby aint nothin' but a big fat hen. I'll offer him two free games in a World Series with my Giants."

He knew the Judge would never allow the World Champions to play another series with a Black team, even if the Blacks didn't have a kid named Rags, so he could bark and bark. "I'll let my outfield snore in the grass. They won't touch wood with Yam Murray on the hill."

Carl had plenty of placards and plenty of blab. He didn't give a hoot about Rogers Hornsby. He was worried about Yarbull's knees. The spasms were getting worse. His carpenters had to build a stretcher to carry the Pharaoh off the field. Yarbull wouldn't budge until the fans had gone home.

Carl snapped at his magician. "Go to your root, Sam'l. You're not shakin' it as much as you could."

The magician was hurt. "You see how skinny I am, Mr. Carl. I'm working that root day and night for the Pharaoh. He runs during the game, don't he? When's the last time Yarbull missed a ball? My root can't fix him after innings is over. His knees are shot. The Buckeyes got a rootworker. Try him."

Carl wouldn't forsake Samuel Sham. You didn't swap magicians in the Black leagues. You might steal one off the ABCs if your witch doctor happened to die. But whoever worked a trade would bring boils, mosquitoes, and the flux to his men.

"Do your best, is all. If we lose the Pharaoh, we'll have to ride down the Mississippi, slappin' baseballs on a barge."

Three men stole Rags from the Giants. They waited until Scarborough was asleep. Then they opened the back door of the Hudson, taped Rags' mouth, wrapped him in a blanket, and carried him to another automobile.

Rags couldn't tell how many hours he was on the road with his kidnappers. They didn't feed him once. They kept the blanket over him when they pushed Rags out of the car. He had a short elevator trip. He was shoved into a chair. The blanket fell off.

The emperor of baseball had kidnapped him. Rags was in Chicago. He sat across from that cruel old man.

The Judge offered him steak and fried potatoes. The kid was hungry. He chewed on some steak with the Judge. It must have still been dark outside, or else those agents couldn't have smuggled him into Landis' Chicago office. "Would you like a cigar?" Landis said.

"No thanks, Judge . . . why'd you bring me here?"

"You're a stupid young man. You think you can run from me in the Negro Leagues? I heard your father died, and I wanted to give you a second chance."

"What kind of second chance?"

"To go back to your wife and the Red Sox."

"What's my wife to you?"

"Oh, we've been watching her ... I have agents in all the cities. She spends her summers on an island with somebody named Rhys."

Rags would have strangled that old emperor if the three kidnappers hadn't been with Landis in the same little room.

"My wife wasn't in the majors. Judge... you tell your men to quit following her."

"Then come to your senses, Cedric Tannehill."

The emperor grabbed his cane and thumped it against the floor. The room shook, and those silver eyebrows on the Judge almost leapt out at Rags.

"If you're feuding with Hollis, that's all right," the Judge said. "You don't have to play for him. I'll get you a spot on the Browns. Just sign a paper declaring you won't mess with gamblers again. Is that so hard to do?"

"Keep your Browns," the kid said. "I already have my spot."

The Judge looked at him. "Stubborn mule. I can reach into Black baseball... I'll throw a boycott around your precious team."

"Bushwah. You can't hurt the Black Giants."

The kidnappers took Rags out of the office and pummeled him a bit. He had to wear tape on his mouth and a blanket over his head. But they didn't abandon the kid. They brought him home to the Giants and disappeared in their car.

Rags wandered over to the Hudson. The brute wasn't inside. Scarborough came up to him after a while. "Raggsy, where you been?"

"I had my morning walk," the kid said.

"That's nice ... a morning walk in the middle of the afternoon. You missed the first game. I was worried about you. Carl's been screaming. You'd better get into your suit. . ."

He shouldn't have lied to the Hump. But he didn't want to re-tell the whole kidnapping story. It made him sick to think about the Judge.

There was an army of troublemakers in the stands for the after-noon game. They threw bottles down at the Giants and yelled evil things to Rags. The kid wondered if the emperor had hired them to stalk the team.

The troublemakers didn't fare too well. Yarbull got out of his stretcher to lead the Cincinnatis up into the stands. He had car-penters, coaches, and players with him. They knocked seventy-five men out of the grandstands. The Giants had to depart before the sheriffs arrived. But no one stalked them after that.

Only Rags had crazy lions in his sleep. The lions were on a beach. Someone had shaved their heads. Ribs showed through the deep hollows in their backs. They had an infielder's crooked paws. Give them jerseys and golden hats, and they could have played for the Giants.

Who could have dreamed of such lions? Comical beasts, their awkward bodies sinking into wet sand. They moaned like walruses. Then Rags recognized the beach. It was Tisbury town, where he'd never been. The lions were on one sandy wall. A redhead came over from her house to feed the stupid things. She wasn't wearing any clothes. She gave them gruel out of a smelly pot, sticking her fin-gers into their mouths. It was the kid's wife. The lions belonged to her. They were Iva's beasts, and they loved to eat from her fingers, lapping the gruel off her knuckle joints. And it horrified the kid.

His wife going naked in front of lions. They could see the beard between her legs. Who knows what kind of lustful thoughts a lion could have?

The kid felt a hand on him. Scarborough peered over the front seat. "Raggsy, you having a nightmare? You cried in your sleep."

"It was nothing," the kid said. "A dumb dream." And he pulled up his knees into his ordinary sleeping position. He didn't give a damn about horns with infielders' claws.

They circled the country for a year and a half, those Cincinnatis, drawing crowds wherever they could sculpt a diamond. A yellow woman with a bruised eye showed up at the camp they had near the Snake River, in Idaho. Carl grew agitated. It was Miz Emma. He didn't have the nerve to ask her about those missing eighteen months. It was the longest Emma had been gone from him.

Carl turned witless. He couldn't run the team. Yarbull had to care for the Cincinnatis, lying on his back. He sent hawkers out with placards and told each man who would sit and who would play. Then the boss recovered his wits.

Rags was in a deeper funk. He could smell Emma Raines upriver and downriver too. He couldn't stop thinking of her skin and her reddish brown hair. He lay in his bed on the back seat of the Hudson, with spasms that were almost as bad as the Pharaoh's. The brute would call to him from the front of the car. "Should I give you my blanket, Raggsy?"

"How's a blanket gonna cure me? I'll have to borrow Sam's root."

But the kid survived without a witch doctor. Emma crawled into the Hudson with him one night, and the spasms went away. She didn't have to fondle Rags with her toes anymore. Carl wasn't in the front seat. She hugged and kissed the third baseman. He watched her body in the moonlight. He loved how her ass jutted out, and the soft pull of her kneecaps that were like tiny animals trained to rub against the kid.

"What happened to your eye?"

"I got hit," she said.

"By what? A squirrel, or a circus bear?"

"By a man," she said.

The kid started to put on his socks. "I'll kill him ... right now."

She laughed. "It was a thousand miles from here."

"I don't give a turd about that."

He was into his clothes before she could protest. Rags wouldn't take off his socks again until she told him the man's name.

"Marshall Glove."

"I'll remember that."

And he found that snuggling spot in her shoulder where he could fall asleep. Emma was there in the morning, hugging him still.

"Don't you have to sneak back to Carl?"

"Why? He knows about us. I'd run to New Orleans if I couldn't stay with you. He'd rather have me in Idaho."

So Emma lived in the Hudson with Rags. It was her bedroom and her couch. The kid didn't hear the boss complain. Rags had his usual berth with the Giants.

It was Scarborough who began to grumble. *How can you have a roomie when there's a woman in the back seat?* The brute was like an extra wife. He listened to the sounds of their caressing, and then he took the kid aside.

"Raggsy, you think Carl would give me a few weeks off?"

"Where you going. Hump?"

"To visit Claudine in Havana."

"Who's Claudine?"

"My winter wife."

"This is July, you dope. Cuba's like an oven."

He couldn't hold on to Scarborough. The brute got Carl's permission to leave, and Rags had the Hudson for Emma and himself. He loved that high yellow woman, slept with her, ate with her, but he developed a slight twitch in his shoulder when Scarborough forgot to come back. It was the last days of September, and he was lonely for the brute.

The Giants had traveled down to Louisiana, and Emma began her whispering act. "Take me to New Orleans."

"I'll take you," Rags said, "when their police chief lets us in."

The police chief of New Orleans promised to string up Giants in Jackson Park if he saw one gold uniform near his parish.

"I didn't ask the team to take me . . . I'm asking you." Rags withstood her whispering into the month of October. He looked for signs of Scarborough, and when Scarborough didn't come, he said for the sake of argument, "Carl will fire me if I hop to Orleans with you."

"He won't," she said. "The Giants are half mine . . ."

Emma drove the kid and his Hudson from Baton Rouge to the Parish of Orleans. She parked on Iberville Street, a few blocks above the French Quarter. The Creoles wouldn't live so far up on Iberville. It was a black street at this end. It had mansions with peeling walls, empty lunch houses, and retired whore "cribs." The whores were driven out by the Navy in 1917. The whores didn't starve. They moved down to the Mississippi, in the Vieux Carré.

Emma took him through a gate in a high wall on Iberville Street. They walked round and round a patio and landed in a little house that was shut off from the street. They could have entered

another parish, walking round that patio. There were shutters on
every window in the house.

"Emma, did you borrow this cottage for us?"

"I didn't have to. It belongs to me."

She went marketing and returned with pots of food, while the
kid dusted off tables and chairs with his elbow. They had yellow
rice, shrimp, peppers, and red beans that Emma cooked on her
stove, and then they made love in a real live bed. It wasn't like
scratching around in the back seat of the Hudson, with nowhere to
put your arms and legs. They had sixty hours to themselves, behind
the shutters. Rags snored without the rhythms of third base in his
head. Baseball couldn't spook him on Iberville Street.

"Emma, what's the best restaurant in town? . . . not the biggest,
just the best."

She laughed at him. "Are you tired of my cooking so quick?"

"I want to go out with you . . . what's the best place?"

"Victoire's on Burgundy Street ... but they don't let brownskins
in there. You'll have to pick out fish bones by yourself."

"We'll see," the kid said.

"Honey, it aint smart for us to stroll into the Quarter together.
Trust me."

But the kid had decided on Victoire's. So Emma fixed her hair
and put on a green dress, and the kid found a reasonable suit of
clothes in his traveling bag. Emma pressed the trousers for him.
They walked hand in hand to Burgundy Street and stood in line
outside Victoire's. The Creoles next to him did nothing but stare.

"Honey," she whispered, "we'd better scat. They'll bring the
cops down on us."

"They're only staring because you're beautiful in your green
dress."

Emma realized how crazy the kid was. But she wouldn't shame
him in front of the Creoles and drag him from Burgundy Street.
The line brought them closer and closer to Victoire's door. Emma

anticipated the moment when Victoire himself would point at the sidewalk and say no to her. He liked to greet his customers at the door.

Victoire smiled when Rags and Miz Emma approached. Lord of Egypt and Jerusalem, Victoire hugged the kid and shook Emma's hand. "M'sieu le Babe," he said.

The kid was known in New Orleans.

Emma wasn't a prophet. How could she tell Rags was a hero to the Creoles, who loved baseball but despised its American commissioner and his despotic ways? The Creoles considered Rags one of them, a boy who had been shoved into a stateless society by the whims of a heartless judge.

They had the center table at Victoire's. M'sieu le Babe and Emma drank wine at Victoire's expense. Everything was on the house. Rags noticed a slight red tinge in the wine glasses of the Creoles.

"What's that?"

"Cassis," Emma said.

"White wine and cassis," he told the waiter.

Rags wanted pompano. The waiter shook his head. "Sorry, M'sieu, no pomp. The fishermen are lazy. They won't go out and catch pomp in the fall."

Rags had broiled trout, and Emma had redfish. Victoire drank a glass of wine with them, and asked the Babe to please come in January when they would have pompano for him, and the fishermen weren't so lazy. The Creoles were too proud to beg autographs from Rags. The waiters had to do it for them. Victoire gave up some of his finest linen to satisfy the Creoles. Rags scribbled on a dozen napkins. "To all my pals in New Orleans, Babe Ragland, October 17, 1927."

Another man came up to him. He was short and stumpy, but he didn't have a waiter's black sleeves. It was Roland Shakespeare, the police chief of New Orleans. "Shucks, Babe, when I put that edict out on the Giants, I didn't mean you. It's a delight, Babe, a pure delight, having you in town."

Rags had to sign a napkin for him. "To Chief Shakespeare, from the Boston outlaw."

The Chief chuckled over that. "People here is wishing the Judge drops dead . . . enjoy your meal, son."

Rags began to whistle after they got back to Iberville Street. "Didn't we chew on good fish? That's no lie." Somebody knocked on Emma's window. Rags heard her talk through the wooden slats. Her back humped while she talked. The cassis had mellowed the kid. "That a friend? Honey, invite him in . . ."

A dandy in a pink collar and yellow shoes marched into the little house with a pair of henchmen behind him. The henchmen wore ugly pieces of metal on their fists.

"Hi," the dandy said. "I'm Marshall Glove, and you must be Ragland, the baseball bandit what took my old lady into Victoire's and had a little trout... Emma, you should have told me you was back in New Orleans. That aint nice to ol' Marsh."

It was Marshall Glove who'd socked Emma and put that mouse under her eye. The kid hadn't forgotten that. He began to sneer. "You sure look pretty in your yellow shoes. Does it give you courage when you have to beat on a woman?"

Marshall didn't throw his henchmen at Rags. He stuck a dash of white powder into his nostrils and wouldn't say a word until he snorted three times, and the powder went up the tubes of his nose. It was the loudest snorts the kid had ever heard. The snorts weren't new to him. Carl's sockamayocks would snort cocaine through rolled-up paper dollars, but none of them had such quantities of powder to toss around and spill.

Marshall smiled. "Just because Chief Shakespeare kissed your skinny ass, it doesn't mean you own the bayou. Be a good boy and lemme borrow Emma for an hour. I'll bring her home, I promise . . ."

"You're not borrowing shit."

Emma moved in front of Rags, so the henchmen's iron knuckles would fall on her instead of him. "Honey, let me go with Marsh. I won't stay long . . ."

But Emma could see that dopey male pride burn through Rags. His head was like a cabbage shot with blood. He'd get himself killed in New Orleans. Emma took her Colt out of the kitchen drawer.

Marshall had a waxiness in his eyes. It had nothing to do with cocaine. "Baby, that's my gun. I gave it to you . . ."

"That won't hurt my trigger finger, Marsh. I can still shoot your ears off."

He made a slow move towards Emma. She cocked the revolver and lined the barrel up with Marshall's left ear. Marsh didn't waste a threat on Emma and Rags. He went out onto the patio with his henchmen and disappeared from Iberville Street.

Rags hunched into a corner of the little house. "Who's this Marshall Glove?"

"A sportin' man. A gambler, a thief, and a pimp."

The kid had a dread of asking her things. He didn't want to know about Emma's times with Marsh. She locked all the shutters and took the kid into her arms and stroked his eyes. "I'm a crib baby," she said. "I was born in a whorehouse attic on Robertson Street. My mama had the same yellow skin. I worked in a bagnio since I was old enough to crawl. It was a sportin' house for Black people. No whites was allowed. But it was high class. We had Black planters and all. I would run pitchers of wine into the bedrooms and watch the girls milk a man's prick to see if he had the clap."

"How old were you?" the kid asked.

"Five or six."

"Well, I don't want to hear any more."

Rags shut his eyes. "How'd you meet Carl?"

"He was visiting Stalebread's, the bagnio where my mama raised me... the Giants had more clout in them days. They didn't bust up cities so much, and the cops would let them in. They were a little unrefined for Stalebread's, but the landlady liked baseball men. She thought they were minstrels, or something. Carl kidnapped me out of the bagnio after his first look. I was thirteen. He married me the next day, in front of a Black priest and all."

"What about your mama?"

Emma giggled as she remembered Robertson Street. "Mama was glad to get rid of me. She didn't want no competition. I had hair in the right places, and the sweetest tits …"

"Didn't it make you cuckoo being with so many men?"

"One prick's as good as another," Emma rasped, and then she started to retreat from her own rough talk. "I was happy with Carl… but he got so jealous… how can you be a wife, a child, and a woman to one man?"

They kept to the upper ranges of Iberville Street. Every hovel they passed had a shuttered door. Emma wouldn't have him wander down to the Vieux Carré. Franklin was the dividing line. The streets below Franklin belonged to Marsh. They were safe up around these hovels.

"Can't we go to Victoire's again?"

"He invited you in January for pompano. If you eat there now, he won't let you pay, and he'll get resentful. That's how the Creoles are. They have codes that even they can't understand."

New Orleans was too complicated for the kid. Creoles and gamblers and Shakespeare the Chief. He holed up in Emma's alley. He had her warm body at night, and curling against her, with the skin of her shoulder in his mouth, he didn't look for anything else. Palm trees grew in the courtyard. They were lusher than the Boston Fens. He had a jungle in his woman's yard, and no swamp water to drown in.

They toured the black streets and visited a row of cemeteries. The cemeteries were strange to Rags. People were buried above the ground in vaults that reminded him of brick ovens. The ovens had begun to corrode. Most of the writing on their faces was in French. The kid found a pirate's grave with a poem on it:

Intrepide guerrier sur la terre et sur l'onde
Il fut dans cent combats signaler sa valeur
Et ce nouveau Bayard, sans reproche et sans peur,
Aurait pu sans trembler voir s'ecrouler le monde

Emma told him what it said. "The pirate Dominique fought in a million battles and could have watched the end of the world without shivering once."

"How'd you learn all that French growing up in a whorehouse?"

"This aint Cincinnati, you chump. It's Creole country."

The kid hiked on brown cemetery grass that could have been the Boston infield.

"My mama's buried in here," she said, and she led him to another aisle of oven graves in the cemetery across the street. The oven had no marker on it.

"It's the brownskins' vault. The whores had their own funeral society. Girls from Stalebread's go into the upper shelf."

Now Rags had a sense of the living and the dead in New Orleans. His muscles began to knot after a few more days, and his eyelids drooped.

"Look at you," she said. "A person would swear I gave you the gleet."

"What's the gleet?"

"The syph and the clap rolled into one... you're a baseball junkie is what you are. Rags, I can cure you of it. The midwife at Stalebread's taught me some gris-gris. She was our voodoo woman."

"It won't work," he said, but he had to do something about his shivers and his sweats. She cut the heart out of a turtle she bought on Villere Street and boiled it in a pot. She applied the gray,

bloodless heart like a compress over Rags' belly. It drew the baseball poison out of him. He didn't shiver for a whole night. But the
shivers came back in the morning.

Emma had to go to a voodoo shop in the Vieux Carré. She sprin-
kled a red dust inside his armpits and sang a little prayer about cat
whiskers and the intestines of a pig. The shivering left him and
returned, left him and returned, like before. He grabbed her hand
when she wanted to try another voodoo shop.

"I can't stay here... Emma, please. We'll go to Carl. I'll be his
goddamn slave if he'll let us live in the Hudson like married folks.
Come with me to the Giants."

"Not now," she said. "Honey, I'll join you in a while." The kid
drove up Iberville Street and got out of New Orleans.

16

Iᴛ wasn't the sockamayocks of 1925, a team that had gone invisible during the players' war, and shrank into the earth with their battered yellow bus. The kid had no trouble finding a caravan of seven Buicks. The '27 Giants were the idols of backwater villages all along the Gulf. No one talked of Ruth, Lazzeri, and Gehrig in Biloxi, Mississipi. It was "that wild Black gang" the Biloxians wanted to catch, boys that could hack out a diamond in the swamps and put on a baseball show.

The kid wondered at it: a baseball diamond in the midst of alligators and mud. The Giants were absolute engineers; they could solve any problem that had to do with foul lines and the pitcher's hill. They could have floated a diamond under the shabbiest bridge, or let a river run past second base.

Carl wasn't greedy. He gave third back to the outlaw and didn't mention his wife. The Buicks would have sunk forever without the pontoons the Giants built. The team was snug in its swamp home.

The Giants had to wear galoshes on the field; the magician frightened alligators with his root, or they would have eaten every base, but so what? The fans were coming in. And the blue swamp gas that made everybody cough seemed good for Yarbull's knees. The Pharaoh didn't take to his stretcher after a game. He could run off the diamond like any other Giant.

Biloxians enjoyed the notion that a team of Blacks would carry a white brute. Scarborough returned from Havana. The kid had a roommate again.

"How's Claudine?"

The hunchback was playing deaf.

"I asked you about your winter wife."

Scarborough shrugged unhappily. "She has a new man..."

"I thought you married her in church."

"Claudine aint no whore. She takes all her men to church. She's got wedding papers for nine husbands. I gave her a hundred dollars ... for her kids."

"Is that a special fund for bastards, orphans, and love babies?"

"It's my money," Scarborough said. "I can do what I want."

And they settled into their usual life of peace and irascible talk inside the Hudson.

Black baseball took Rags out of any specific order of time. Seasons didn't count. Winter and summer meant the same thing: baseball diamonds in the hinterland, Carl and his hawkers scrambling for games. February looked no different from July. The Cincinnatis searched out warm, leafy spots, away from sheriffs' offices, and near a village or two. The kid was waiting for Emma to show. It was 1929. Or did he have the wrong year? Scarborough was better with calendars. Scarborough kept up. The brute would feed Rags baseball stories.

"Hollis McKee lost the Sox. He had to sell out. They were gonna throw him into receivership."

The kid shrugged at the news. Emma was what he cared about. He was miserable in the back seat, without her hands to stroke his eyes. He considered a journey to Iberville Street whenever the Giants played near the Gulf. But he was terrified somehow. He couldn't tell what he would meet behind her shutters. Marshall Glove, or another man? He wasn't scared of Marsh and those boys with the iron knucks. He was scared of Emma Raines and the look she might give him. If she turned cool to Rags, the kid would die.

"Raggsy, you know it's bullshit about Babe Ruth. He went to St. Mary's, but he wasn't an orphan ... he had a mom and a dad. It's in all the papers. His dad owned a bar, and that monkey would steal from the till. So they tossed him into the bad boys' school. And he'd say, 'I'm too ugly for my pa to visit.' It must have rattled the monk. When he got to the big leagues, he told everybody he was a bastard."

"You can't put him in jail for that. It's not a crime."

"I know, but the rest of the league's been jumping on his tail, shouting, 'Bastard, bastard, bastard . . .'"

Rags had a vision of Iberville Street, and he lost most of what the brute was telling him. But he did hear the name "Garl."

"What's that about Garland climbing the flagpole in center field?"

"It was a trick he had before you came to the Sox. He would hide behind that pole and shimmy right up to the middle if the ball was coming his way. He'd stiff-arm that ball and do his 'flag' catch. But he twisted his foot last year and fell down the pole. Garl aint with Boston anymore."

"Did the Brownies pick him up?"

"I don't think so."

"Then he must have gone back to Dartmouth to study Greek."

"No. Garl's disappeared."

"Who told you that?"

"Hooks Poland. He opened a hobby shop in Shreveport. I bumped into him yesterday on the road."

"You sure Garl isn't at Dartmouth under another name?"

"Raggsy, Hooks wouldn't lie to me. The skipper's disappeared."

"I know where he went," Rags muttered. "Hey, are we in 1930?"

The brute figured he had Rip van Winkle for a roommate. Rags must have gone into a great snore since he returned from New Orleans.

"We're in 1931," Scarborough said, not wanting to plague the kid.

"And what month is it?"

"Rags, people have been out of work for two fuckin' years . . . half the country is living on apples and water, and you juggle baseballs and run around with cardboard over your eyes . . . it's June. Wake up, and don't be such a jackass. You're twenty-six, and you already have a gray hair on your head."

Rags wandered through the bushes and found a country store. The store had a telephone. It took him twenty minutes to get an operator on the line and another ten to place his call to Tucson. He heard her squabble with the receptionist at his father's company. "I have a collect call for Mr. Martin Grilfey from Cedric Tannehill. Will you accept the charges, hon?"

The receptionist had never heard of Cedric, and the kid had to break into the conversation. "I'm the president of Tannehill Copper," he growled. "Get me Griffey right away . . ."

After five more squabbling minutes. Rags screaming he was president, president, Griffey took the call.

"I was with a client," Griffey said. "You should have given me a little warning."

"Didn't you say you were my lawyer now?"

"Be reasonable, Cedric. You haven't been in touch for so long."

"Well, I need you. Griff. Find me a small college in Massachusetts or New Hampshire that could use a Greek teacher and a baseball coach."

"You do have a charming way about you, Cedric ... I suppose I could find this miracle college in a year or two."

"Have it by tomorrow. Griff." And the kid hung up.

He got a booking out of Galveston to Quintana Roo. He must have been on a smuggler's run. The ship stank of whiskey, and the sailors carried machine guns. But they all remembered the American League.

"Rags, I saw you play the Indians in 1925. What a glove!"

Being sailors, they were curious about the fist a third baseman had. They examined the rough claws on his throwing hand. He drank rum with them out of their private stock and took target practice aboard the *Sweet Marie*. The machine gun turned hot and shivered in his arms. But he did destroy two straw hats and the captain's old pajamas. He borrowed a dinghy from the pirates, and they dropped him into the water about a mile from Quintana Roo. They were wary of other pirates, who jumped out like flying snakes at any ship that touched near the coast.

So the kid thanked the good pirates and rowed his dinghy onto the beach at Quintana Roo. The beach wasn't as deserted as it had been during his last vacation. It had the same dumb sand that couldn't support a lizard or a cockroach. But it was congested with human beings. They weren't the zombies of 1925, kind old men with bald spots and vacant looks, exiled governors and poets and conquistadors. These were a rough band of men. The rats had come to Quintana Roo. The beachcombers were vicious this year.

They carried sticks and cumbersome knives that they shook at Rags. He wasn't to join their party. They babbled in some devil's tongue and fought among themselves for what little food was around: inland berries, roots, nuts, chewable leather. You couldn't see too many faces under the thick beards they wore. How was the kid supposed to uncover Garl?

He shouted at these ratty men.

"It's the Babe, Garl. I'm on Quintana Roo."

No one bothered to answer him. They continued their babble of tongues, and menaced him with their sticks and knives.

Rags developed a kind of intuition on that dumb gray sand. Garl was hiding with these rats, he was somewhere in that body of beachcombers. He didn't want to expose himself to Rags.

The kid stomped up and down, yelling "Pharaoh, Harry Heilmann, Hollis McKee." He was getting hungry. But he couldn't borrow a nut or a root off these terrible men.

Garl, I understand. I remind you of baseball too much. I'm your own fucking history that you came here to outrun.

Didn't the brute say Rags was twenty-six? That single gray hair in his scalp had to mean something. Rags was no orphan in the sand. He'd wrestled baby bulls on his father's ranch. He'd hit seven home runs in the major leagues. He could survive on Quintana Roo.

He went searching for berries and nuts. The hinterland was even more godforsaken than the beach. What happened to the village where Garl had found an adulterous wife for Rags? The kid returned to the beach with one sickly root. It seemed like a prize to the starving beachcombers, who were making ready to dismember Rags with their knives. The knives never touched Rags. Garl picked this moment to reveal himself. He was as ratty as the rest, with a long brown beard, but he began hurling beachcombers into the sand. The entire gang fled from this loco who turned on his own people for a boy with a root.

"Shit, Garl, you didn't have to lose your friends on account of me. I would have socked a few of 'em before they whittled me down with their pieces of tin."

Garland chuckled under that beard, and the kid recognized his old skipper.

"I hear you fell off the flagpole," Rags said.

"Who told you that?"

"Scarborough did. He got it from Hooks Poland."

"Hooks was always a blabbermouth," Garl said. "What the hell are you doing in this miserable place?"

"I've come to bring you out of Quintana Roo."

"Why? Are you offering me a spot with the Giants? I'm finished with baseball. Rags, I've paid my dues. I can live on a beach. My mother is dead, my grandpa is gone, and my three brothers are out of school."

"What happened to Dartmouth and Greek?"

Garl began to sputter words from a play called *Philoctetes*. The kid answered him in Greek. "They do that finger talk at Amherst too ... I had a whole month of Sophocles."

"Well, Sophocles can sleep without Garland James," Garl said. "I'll pick roots in the territories and swallow sand..."

"No you won't. I'm not leaving by myself. We don't have the Boston tunnel, Garl, but we can fight up and down the beach . . . until I drag you off Quintana."

"I have fifty friends over there with knives. I think they'd side with me."

"Maybe. You buried a dozen heads in the sand. Those beach rats might not forget so fast... Garl, there's a college in New Hampshire named Calliope that's looking for a Greek and Latin scholar and baseball coach. Guess what? They've decided on you . . ."

Garl scratched his cheek.

"I inherited my father's company," the kid said. "I have some pull. But that's not it, Garl. You beat out all the contenders by a country mile. There's not another scholar in the world who went to Dartmouth, studied Greek, played center field, and skippered the Red Sox."

They broke the kid's root and sucked on the bitter ends for nourishment.

"Garl, where's that village with the bad wives?"

"They moved into the interior. They couldn't stand the smell of so many gypsies on the beach... how's the Black Giants?"

"Going at six hundred games a year ... I'm in love with Carl's wife. She lives in New Orleans now. She won't stay with the Giants."

"If you can take me off Quintana, why can't you steal her from New Orleans?"

"She's got a pistol, Garl. She'll shoot me in the nose."

"Who says you need a nose to play third?"

Rags couldn't answer the scholar. They got into the dinghy and started to row. The kid had made arrangements with the pirate ship. He wagged his shirt for half an hour until the good pirates appeared and picked them out of the sea.

17

THE Giants had snaked over to Mississippi while the kid was down in the Yucatan rescuing Garl. He discovered his own Hudson outside Hattiesburg, but where was the baseball diamond? The Giants were in mourning. They didn't go around in gold and white. They had dusty black suits and black chapeaus, hats that were snug on their foreheads and hid one eye. They weren't in a talking mood.

The kid had to slide into the Hudson and catch Scarborough in the front seat. The brute also wore black.

"Hump, what's going on? I left a team and come back to a funeral station."

"Mrs. Carl is dead. '

That name didn't draw blood at first. *Mrs. Carl? Who's that?* Then the kid remembered who Mrs. Carl was. "Emma Raines?" he said, and his lip turned swollen. He went to Carl.

The bossman lay in the head Buick, with his body in the frozen attitude of a corpse. It took him a while to unbend himself and respond to the kid. They smoked a reefer together. The cigarette didn't take Carl from his sorrows, but it did get him to talk.

"The police come looking for me . . . they found Emma in her yard with a necktie on her that was a little too tight. They don't keep a body long in Louisiana . . . they put her in the whores' vault, where her mama is ... on the Black side of the cemetery."

"Who strangled her, Carl?"

"The cops wouldn't tell, but it must have been her fancy man ... the gambler she was living with."

"Marshall Glove?"

"I never heard his name," Carl said, and he grew corpselike again.

The kid ran to the Hudson and tried to push Scarborough off the front seat. "Get out. Hump. I'm goin' to Orleans to kill a man."

"Who?"

"The gambler, Marshall Glove ... I'm sure he strangled Emma Raines."

"Nobody arrested him, Raggsy. If he's a gambler, he's got an in with the police. Kill him, and you'll die in New Orleans."

"It's none of your business."

"Who says? Roomies don't have secrets. Your business is my business . . . where does he live, this Marshall Glove?"

"I don't know."

"Some murderer you are .. . come on. I'll help you find Marshall Glove. But don't you kill him. Just break his bones a little ... that way you won't have a murder charge sittin' on your head."

"Who taught you so much about criminal justice, huh Hump?"

Scarborough took the wheel. "It aint criminal justice. It's common sense."

They left the Hudson behind a watermelon shed in the French Market. Rags crossed the railroad tracks and stood on the levee, watching the slow brown run of the river. There were rafts and houseboats for sale near the Toulouse Street wharf.

"Wish we could buy a houseboat," Rags said. "I'd park it down-river, and then we'd have a home somewhere."

The brute dragged him from the levee. "Houseboat, my eye. After we finish with Glove, you won't be able to rent a frog off the river."

"How are you gonna get to Marsh?" Rags said. "With your hump?"

"You'll see," the brute muttered. They walked from bottle shop to bottle shop on St. Philip Street. Girls hung out from the balcony windows with nothing on, and showed their pudendas to Rags and the brute. Scarborough wouldn't stop for a look. At the fifth or sixth bottle shop he found a dwarf. He signaled to Rags, telling him to stay on the street. Rags could smell peaches and horseshit in the Vieux Carré. The brute came out smiling from the bottle shop.

"Glove lives on Barracks Street... but it's no use trying to catch him there. He hangs out at a gambler's den on Dumaine. Two in the morning is the best time to parlay with him. He goes out for a piss in the street and a friendly poke with the ladies."

"Hump, do you have a detective's license? How did you learn all this?"

"From the dwarf. Little guys like to help each other out."

"Let's go to Victoire's. It's not the right time for pompano, but we can have the best trout in New Orleans."

They waited on line outside Victoire's window. Rags couldn't understand why the Creoles on line with him inched their bodies away from the brute. Victoire wasn't at the door to greet his customers. Had the restaurant changed hands? A different Creole stood watch. He seemed reluctant to let Rags and Scarborough into the restaurant. He pointed to a card in the window that claimed gentlemen had to be properly attired after dusk. The kid was in his baseball shirt. "Where's Victoire?" Rags growled.

The Creole shrugged. "The old man has been dead for a year. His son hardly comes to the restaurant."

"Don't you recognize me? I'm Babe Ragland. I defied the Judge . . ."

It meant nothing to this man. The Creoles had forgotten the kid. Then a waiter peeked through the door. "Ah, M'sieu le Babe." He brought them into the restaurant but they had to sit at an end table, next to the cashier. The waiter produced a scarf and a coat for Rags. He bent over and whispered to the kid. "It's your friend. The Creoles are superstitious, M'sieu. Hunchbacks frighten them out of their wits."

"Should we leave the table?"

"No, no. Victoire would return from the dead and cut off our tongues if we offended you."

Rags ordered white wine and cassis. The brute liked that pink taste in his mouth. He had two halves of a blood-red Texas grapefruit, chicken gumbo, and a crabmeat casserole. The name *Victoire* was printed on his water glass. A fan with wooden blades spun over his head, stopped, and spun. He could see his own ears in the mirror on the wall. The mirror had hooks for a gentleman's umbrella. The grandfather clock behind the cashier's booth wouldn't toll the hour. The chimes stood still.

A Creole lady stared at her pocket watch. "Darlin', it's ten minutes till nine."

The kid had his trout. He sucked on the lemon that came with the fish. "Good for the teeth," he said. "It stops yellow scurvy."

Scarborough was annoyed at the kid's arrogance. "Any dumbbell knows that."

They paid the bill and sneaked out of their hidden corner. Rags left the coat and scarf on his chair. Conversation stopped when the two of them passed among the Creoles.

They still had hours to kill.

"Hump, we'll go to Marsh's sportin' club and feel the place out."

"What if he recognizes you?"

"He'll be too busy making dollars and sniffing nose powder."

They didn't hop on a trolley to Dumaine. They decided to walk. They couldn't avoid the "crib" girls of Conti Street. Haggard women would leap out at them from windows and low balconies. They were more interested in the brute than in Rags. "Hello, Hot Papa, want a good ride?"

Scarborough wouldn't flirt with them or examine their tits.

They followed him down the street. "Half a dollah, half a dollah, and you can go round the world."

The brute had to give them the change in his pocket, or they would have torn pieces of his flesh. He cursed the whores of the Vieux Carré.

"It's not their fault," Rags said. "The Navy chased them out of their own District. So they relocated, and got new cribs. Emma told me that. . ."

"Well, I don't like it much when painted women touch me in the street."

They arrived at Marshall's hangout, the Royal Fox. It was part speakeasy, sporting house, and gambling den. The Fox had a cherrywood bar, competing nests of whores and pimps, cocaine dealers, river rats, smugglers, gamblers, and the impoverished sons of Creole sugar men. It also had a pit near the bar for wrestling and boxing matches, and dog fights. The champion boxer of New Orleans, a Cajun named Mario, stood in the pit without his clothes. His ears had been chewed off. A nostril was gone. He had dents in his skull that were as deep as a human hand. His back was ribbed with scars that read like some crazy scripture. Who would want to challenge such a man?

Marshall Glove stood near Mario, with wads of paper money and gamblers' notes stuck in his fist. He was the main betting man at the Fox.

"We're out of luck," the kid said. "What if this Mario is his bodyguard?"

"Uh, uh," Scarborough said. "The gambler is bettin' against the Cajun."

"Well, show me the man Marsh is bettin' for?"

A roly-poly woman started to undress. Rags had assumed she was a barmaid. People called her Alice. She didn't have a line on her gentle face. All her pubic hair had been cropped. Alice's cunt inflamed the brute. He couldn't take his eyes from that baldness between her legs.

The river rats told Scarborough that Alice was ruined for life. She'd gotten on the bad side of certain voodoo mistresses in the French Quarter, and the mistresses laid a curse on her: they "sealed her up" so that no man could enter Alice.

The brute said he didn't care. He'd find a way of loving her if she would marry him. He'd ask her after the fight.

"There aint gonna be nothin' left to ask," the rats said. "She won't have arms, she won't have legs , . . she'll be a puddle of water and shit. No one can beat the Cajun."

"What odds are you giving?" Scarborough said to the river rats.

"Eighteen to one."

He bet a dollar on Alice.

She went into the pit with Mario the Cajun. There wasn't a referee to watch over them. It was a curious fighting they did. They could only box and wrestle with one hand, because they had to attack and cover their genitals at the same time. The Cajun was a head taller than Alice, and his reach was almost double. He could slap and kick at her before she got close. But it wasn't Amherst vs. Dartmouth at the Royal Fox. Alice didn't have to depend on any science and rules of fisticuffs. She took the slaps and the kicks. Her mouth turned bloody. The Cajun laughed at his fat target. He could have danced in the pit and waited for Mardi Gras to come. Alice couldn't absorb every one of his blows.

Mario drank a glass of beer in the middle of the fight. The rats applauded when he belched out an aria for them. They begged him to finish Alice. They wanted their money. So the Cajun resumed his kicking act. Alice's skin went black around the knees. Mario got careless. He slapped at her with both hands. Alice burrowed in like a bulldog and caught him where he was hung. The Cajun screamed. He jumped into the air, his neck muscles quivering, and fell out of the pit. His handlers might have revived him. But it was too late. The laws of the house wouldn't let Mario reenter the pit.

The brute collected his eighteen dollars and went over to Alice, who sat on the cherrywood bar with her legs open. The rats had lied to him. Alice wasn't sealed.

"Ma'am, would you consider marrying me?"

Alice figured the brute wanted to rent her for half an hour. "Sure, honey," she said. "I'm tired right now. I'll marry ya tomorrow."

The brute returned to the river rats. You could see his discouragement in the twitching of his shoulder. His hump had dropped a whole mile. How could he marry her tomorrow when he'd have to run like the devil from New Orleans?

It was only midnight. They'd have to hover near the bar until Marsh strolled out for his two A.M. piss.

That dwarf on St. Philip Street knew his man. Marshall didn't stir. Then, at the stroke of two, he walked out of the Royal Fox with fat Alice, who had gotten dressed in the meantime.

"Damn," the brute said, "*she's* his bodyguard." But he wouldn't disappoint the kid. He'd have to jump on his espoused wife and wrestle with her, or the kid would never reach Marshall Glove.

They slinked behind Marsh and Alice. The gambler turned around. He thought the two men were out to steal his money. He gave these two men to Alice. She stood with her hands on her hips. "Go on home, little boys."

She didn't recall Scarborough. He could have been any hunchback on the street. The brute tried to rush her. He leapt at Alice. She plucked him out of the air and threw him into the gutter, with the dead cats, the garbage, and the shit. He rolled over, slid off a dead cat, and rushed her again.

The kid had his chance. While Alice was busy flinging Scarborough everywhere. Rags got to Marshall Glove. He climbed on

Marshall's back, clung to him, and socked him in the kidneys. He could hear Scarborough shout.

"Don't go for the head ... you'll kill him, you'll kill him . . . don't go for the head."

Even in his fury to hit Marsh, the kid followed Scarborough's instructions. He socked the gambler into the sidewalk, going for the kidneys, the back, the shoulders, and the heart. Alice couldn't help her boss. The brute was like a small octopus. As far as she hurled that slippery man, the faster he would rush her. She'd try a different strategy. Break off his miserable hump. She hadn't reckoned on that tough bark under his shirt and coat. She held him in her arms, but she couldn't snap off any piece of him. He wiggled out of her grip, and using his hump as a battering ram, he knocked her into the street. Alice was stunned. She'd destroyed the Cajun tonight. She couldn't believe a common hunchback would humiliate her.

"Raggsy, are ya through with the gink?"

The kid sat over Glove, and pulled on the gambler's scarf. "Did you enjoy strangling Miz Emma, you son of a bitch?" Glove's eyes dropped back into his head. It was like pulling on a blind man. The gambler mumbled something. What if the kid had been wrong, and some mad Creole murdered Emma in her patio? "Marshall, it's me . . . Ragland, the baseball player."

He couldn't get Marshall to admit a thing. The gambler began to shudder on the sidewalk. Was it cocaine fever, or guilt over Emma Raines? Rags climbed off of him. "Hump, let's go."

The kid was running somewhere. The brute had to follow. He waved to Alice sitting in the garbage. Where was east and where was west? The kid was going the wrong way. The Hudson was parked near the Mississippi River.

"Raggsy, this Alice aint gonna lie down in garbage too long. She'll send an army after us ... where the hell are ya running to?"

The kid wouldn't answer him. He called to a flower girl outside a bagnio on Dauphine Street. The flower girl couldn't have been more than six or seven. What was she doing here so early in the morning? The kid demanded all her goods. He didn't settle on a price. Rags wouldn't bargain down a six-year-old girl. He put twenty dollars into her hand and grabbed a hill of half-dead flowers. The brute had to walk with a rotten sweetness in his nose.

Rags took him into a graveyard with knobby walls. The graveyard had brick houses in it. The kid stumbled from row to row, searching for a particular house. There wasn't much of a moon in New Orleans, and Rags had to squint into the shadows under and over the bricks. He paused, stooped, and put the fucking daisies at the bottom of a house with a crumbling roof. "Emma's inside."

Scarborough pulled Rags away from Emma's brick house. They took a wide, circular route down to the levee. The Hudson was still there.

"Raggsy, stop dreaming on your toes. We got gamblers and fat ladies after us." Scarborough shook his head. He stowed Rags in the Hudson and got behind the wheel. "Jesus, don't you want to play for the Giants?"

Bossman
and Magician:

BOOK SIX

18

THE scythes lay dead in the Buicks. The grass was unshorn. The groundkeepers hadn't cleared a line for first base, and they didn't grow a hill for Yam Murray. Carl wandered in and out of his Buick in bedroom slippers. The boss was incoherent most of the time. His speech jumped from whorehouses to curve balls and Mississippi mud. He would rant and cry and threaten his players, and then talk of "lending" the team to Pharaoh.

Worst of all, the magician had run off and left his root behind. It was unheard of to function in the Black leagues without a witch doctor to chase the storms into another district, cast a spell on your enemies, and heal the lame.

Samuel hadn't committed a senseless act. It was shrewd of him to go. The Giants had deteriorated in front of his eyes, fallen to a nothing club, and who would be blamed for it?

Samuel Sham. They couldn't hire another magician. No dependable witch doctor would come to the Giants.

Pharaoh met with Swimmy and Yam. They offered the root to Scarborough. The hunchback wouldn't hear of it.

"I'm a bat boy, trainer, and first baseman," he said. "I won't fuck with clouds."

"Can't you do a little magic with your hump?" Swimmy asked.

"I aint got voodoo in my blood. I wouldn't know how to talk to a root."

"I'll be your magician," Rags said, and he took the root jar into the Hudson's back seat. Then he pointed to his chest. "This magician swears Texas is for us. We have to hold down until Carl recovers his head."

"Where in Texas is that, magician Rags?"

"Gents, we're goin' to Abilene."

It was seven dirty Buicks and a Hudson that arrived at his father's ranch. The foreman didn't know what to make of it. He never saw so many Blacks leaning out of automobiles. Was it a minstrel show coming through central Texas? He had enough scatterguns and Colts behind him to let these Blacks fly like gooney birds up into the Panhandle.

The foreman had to hesitate. There were two white boys in the Hudson sedan. A skinny fella and a brokeback. The skinny one got out of the car.

"Where's the owner of this cattle farm?"

"Aint your business," the foreman told him.

"I'm making it my business," Rags said. The scatterguns were raised to the level of his neck. But Rags wouldn't back off.

"Look at me, you ... I'm Cedric Tannehill. And this is my fuckin' place."

The foreman and his ranch hands slapped their knees. They chuckled so hard, their scatterguns wavered and dipped. A gun went off. Rags thought he was standing on top of an earthquake. The boom split the ground under him, and turned the kid deaf for a minute.

"Liar," the foreman said. "Cedric wouldn't bring Blacks to his daddy's house... he's in Boston playing for those Red Sox."

An old Black cowboy in leather pants came up to Rags, sniffled at him, and hugged him around the shoulders.

The foreman scolded the Black cowboy. "Benjamin, what the hell are you doin' now?"

Rags smiled. "How are you, Benjy?"

"Still walkin', Mr. Cedric," the cowboy said.

Rags turned to the foreman. "Jack Tarr, you were always a scumsucker and a prick."

And the foreman had to eat crow. He'd failed to recognize young Tannehill around Blacks and a brokeback. It was still confusing to him. Had the shines taken over Boston? Did the Red Sox go Black? He muttered to his own Black cowboy. "Benjy, what team is this?"

"Don't you know, captain? The Cincinnati Black Giants, champeens of the world."

Jack Tarr would have broken into guffaws, but he couldn't insult this millionaire kid, who had come out of the dust with seven jalopies and a run-down sedan. *The Cincinnati Black Giants*. What could you do about these eccentric millionaire sons? Old Mr. Marcus died with the grit of copper on his tongue. There was a man. Drink his whiskey and sit on a bull's back. And the son plays catch with Blacks.

"Cedric, we got your father's room all prepared for you ... the team can bed down in the number-two barn."

"Thanks, Jack, but I'll sleep in the barn with the Giants." Jack couldn't have a Tannehill breathing cowshit. He had to relent. "Aint no bother. There's room for everybody in the big house."

So the Cincinnatis stopped being nomads for a while and moved onto the ranch. The Spanish maids and cooks prepared a hundred flapjacks for the Cincinnatis alone. Jack Tarr took his food at the opposite end of the table. The ranch was suddenly a lonesome place.

Rags wouldn't sleep in his father's bed. He occupied his old room in the northwest corner of the house. Scarborough shared the room with him.

The kid wouldn't have his breakfast without the old Black cowboy. "Mr. Yarbull, this is the man who taught me how to hold a bat ... Benjy, where are those other guys? .., Clarence, Dummy, and Spot ... with their neckerchiefs ... bullriders who could hit and field."

"They're gone, Mr. Cedric. Clarence is in El Paso. Dummy joined another outfit. Spot's dead . . ."

Yarbull looked across the table at Rags. "Why'd you come to the Giants when you have all this? . . . flapjacks, clean sheets, and enough bulls to keep every shorthorn in the state of Texas happy."

"I'm a ballplayer," the kid said. "I don't breed bulls." And he finished his breakfast without mentioning baseball again.

Carl didn't regain his wits at the ranch. He cried in his room and clutched the few articles of Emma's that he had: a kerchief, a ripped dress, a bottle of toilet water that was going scummy, a pair of whore's stockings he kept around ever since he lifted Emma from that bagnio in New Orleans. But his mind wouldn't crawl back to the Cincinnati Giants.

Rags went to Yarbull. "He's not getting any better... and we can't rebuild the team if we stay off the road and live in this house. How can you barnstorm from a Texas ranch?"

"We need lights," the Pharaoh said.

Rags blinked at him.

"The best Black teams are carrying their own lights these days. The Monarchs started that. Now the ABCs have them, the Memphis Sox, the Nashville Elites ... we won't survive if we can't fit night games into our schedule."

"How much would it cost?"

"I aint no accountant, but the ABCs might sell us their lights."

It took Yarbull thirteen phone calls to find out.

"We can have their lights, their poles, and their generator for a thousand dollars cash."

The kid didn't have a thousand on him. He had to telephone his Santa Claus, Martin Griffey of Tucson and Tannehill Copper.

"The Giants are in trouble. Griff. We can't operate without a portable lighting system. It'll take a thousand in cash. Am I entitled to a loan? Or do I have to beg for it?"

"You'll get your money, Cedric ... off the books. I wouldn't want your phantoms to play in the dark."

"I have one more problem. Griff. The boss of the Giants is out of his mind. Would Tannehill Copper like to buy a baseball club?"

"I'll discuss it with the board, but to tell you the truth, I don't think we'll go into baseball this year."

"Then I'll have to buy the Giants. What would you say we're worth?"

"That depends. What have you got?"

"We got plenty... Pharaoh Yarbull, for instance. He's the Black George Sisler . . ."

"Can he break into the major leagues?"

"Don't fool with me. Griff... you know he can't play in the majors . . . and I've been barred for life."

"Cedric, give the crazy man who owns the Giants two hundred dollars. That's a fair price."

"Listen, Griff. The phantoms have rolling stock ... seven Buicks and a Hudson sedan."

"What vintage? How old are the cars?"

"Ten years old, I suspect. . ."

"That'll add another two hundred to your baseball company. I'd say the Giants are worth four hundred dollars on the open market. .

"Then you'll have to lie a bit. . . stretch the inventory, Griff. You know how. And give Carl Raines twelve hundred for his Giants."

"That's robbery," the lawyer said.

"Who cares? I'm president of Tannehill Copper. I have to have a little leeway."

There were no documents to sign. Nothing could be transferred over to the kid. Carl had ruled by fiat. His ownership didn't come from a piece of paper. Rags stuck Griffey's twelve hundred dollars into an empty tobacco tin and gave it to the Black cowboy to hold for Mr. Carl. "You take care of that man, Benjy. I'm leaving him on the ranch. He was like a pa to m e... I stole his wife for a few weeks. I'm sorry for that. . . ."

And the Giants got out of central Texas to pick up their lights from the ABCs. Rags saw a converted fire truck with ladders on the sides and a gasoline generator sitting on top, and some shaky poles and strings of light bulbs.

The kid was dubious about the lights. Pharaoh reassured him. "The deal was made Black to Black, boss. They wouldn't burn us. We got a first-class system, you'll see."

"Shouldn't we test the stuff?"

"Boss, we can't insult the ABCs."

The Cincinnatis rode off with their lights; the poles rattled and the fire truck leaked. Every Giant, from the carpenters and ground-keepers to the players, the hunchback, and the magician-boss, had to cradle light bulbs in his lap. Glass shivered and popped on the bumpy roads. Rags cursed Yarbull, the ABCs, and his new lights. He should have been a farmer, not the entrepreneur of a wandering baseball club.

They camped in a small desert patch outside Colorado Springs. The groundsmen left their scythes in the Buicks. There wasn't enough grass to monkey with. They threw up a diamond in the middle of the desert floor. The carpenters stuck the poles into the ground, screwed in the lights, stretched out the cable lines that snaked from pole to pole, and hid the fire truck in deep center field.

Their placards had lured a team of deaf mutes into camp. Rags could let his generator sleep during the afternoon. The mutes played ferocious ball. They lied, cheated, and wanted to fight Swimmy Welles. They had six thousand of their brothers in the stands.

Scarborough was amazed. "There must be a whole army of mutes in Colorado Springs."

The Giants had to beat them twice, or the mutes wouldn't go home. The kid had strawberries on his legs from the way those rough little bastards slid at him. He ate a can of sardines and prepared for the night game that was scheduled with a bunch of semipros.

The semipros arrived at six o'clock. They were bandits and outcasts from a dozen leagues. Not one of them had a decent baseball jersey. Rags didn't care. He was more interested in his lights.

A carpenter went into the bowels of the fire truck and switched the generator on. The fire truck shook; ladders fell off. A noise came out of the truck that was like the scream of a hundred women. Rags had to hold his ears, but Yarbull hadn't tricked him. The truck was alive. It fed the cables and the poles, and produced a terrific blaze of light. The Cincinnatis had a second afternoon on the diamond.

They were destroying the semipros, who showed themselves to be sickly bandits. But the generator had a coughing fit after the third inning. The fire truck stopped shivering, and the lights went dead. Rags swore he'd sue the ABCs. Carpenters hopped about. The Giants' golden uniforms looked like strips of lead in the dark. The generator began to cough again. There was a hiss around the poles. The lights blazed up. The Giants finished murdering the semipros.

Yarbull's legs.

Rags couldn't cure them with a generator and a string of lights. He didn't have Samuel Sham to pack the Pharaoh's brittle knees with a variety of ointments, spices, and medicinal gums. The kid had to be his own magician. Scarborough would give the Pharaoh rubdowns between innings, and wait with him until he was carried off the field. But these were temporary measures. Rags was the only one who could go to the root.

He concealed himself in the back seat of the Hudson, sang to the root jar, and stroked it with his claws. The Pharaoh hit three home runs. The Cincinnatis gaped at Rags. The new bossman was a regular witch. Swimmy found the solution. Rags was crazy enough to work black magic with a white man's claws.

Yarbull didn't have to lie down in the stretcher more than two hours a day. He could twist around faster than he ever could. But Rags didn't trust himself as a magician. Yarbull's eyes were old. The skin near his lips was tough as shoe leather. His hairline seemed to push right into his skull.

He was leaping for a ball in another game with the mutes, and you could hear his body rip. It was like the grinding of ferocious teeth, as if an invisible shark had cut through his legs and into his groin. He dropped to the ground in a swoon.

The kid ran to the Hudson. The root jar revived the Pharaoh. His tongue was homier than a toad's head. Rags scooped water into the Pharaoh's mouth with his own magician's hand.

"We'll get a doctor," the kid said.

The Pharaoh said no. All he needed was a carpenter and the kid's root. He'd wear stilts under his baseball pajamas. "Boss, you'll have to put me on third ... I can hold the base line, and that's about it."

"Who'll play short for us?" the kid blubbered, thinking of Yarbull's ripped knees.

Pharaoh got his smile back. The horniness had gone out of his tongue. "Don't bellyache," he said. "You'll have to be the shortstop, Mr. Rags."

So they worked a switch. Yarbull stood on his carpentered legs. He was like a snowman in gold and white. He didn't melt. But he couldn't do more than stretch an arm or hop on those stilts under his pajamas. Rags had to cover the Pharaoh's ground. He scrambled after bunts and jumped out at balls that flew over third. But no one could say the Giants didn't have Yarbull in the field.

He couldn't go for singles anymore. How can you beat out a hit with boards taped to your legs? It was a home run or nothing for Pharaoh Yarbull. He would sock the ball into the next prairie and hobble around the bases. That was Yarbull's only chance.

It didn't hurt the Giants. They won with that snowman on third, and crept into 1934, while other Black teams dropped out of sight. The big leagues were also having a troublesome year. Babe Ruth was thirty-nine, and the Yanks had become the old men of organized baseball. The Cardinals took the World Series from Detroit. Their ace, Jerome "Dizzy" Dean, had put together a barnstorming act with his brother Paul. The Dean brothers weren't afraid of Mountain Landis. They met with Rags on the sly and agreed to appear once with the Cincinnatis for a purse of two thousand dollars. The game site was a pasture outside Enid, Oklahoma, where Landis' agents were unlikely to come.

"What happens if we lose?" Scarborough asked.

"I'll have to hock the team ... or cry to Santa Claus, Martin Griffey."

"Suppose you cry to Santa a little too often?"

"We'll have to risk that," the kid muttered. "Now go and tape up Yarbull's legs."

The Dizzy Dean All-Stars arrived in a huge traveling van. The van had a washroom and couches for Dizzy and Paul. The Dean boys liked to rest their arms on the road. The All-Stars that hopped out of the van didn't impress the kid. They were the usual sockamayocks. He couldn't have told you their names. Rags had already been out of the majors nine and a half years.

The sockamayocks were a decoration Dizzy could afford. He won thirty games this year, and he also had his brother Paul. He was six feet two, and when he came over the hill with his long right arm, batters had to sing a prayer. His smoke was the best in the league, but he didn't have to depend on it. He had a slider and a screwball that broke into your cuffs, or disappeared altogether. He could turn that horsehide into a "ghost."

If Dizzy liked you, he'd let you call him Jerome. He was twenty-three years old, and he'd been following the Cincinnati Giants since he was a boy in Arkansas. He worshiped Pharaoh Yarbull and Yam Murray, and he was fond of Swimmy Welles and the kid. He swore he'd learned half his stuff from Yam.

But Yam was nearing fifty. He couldn't compete with Jerome and Paul. He had to go to his emery board because even a sockamayock can buy a lucky hit.

The game started at four in the afternoon. Paul shouted to his brother. "You be tender with the Giants, Jerome. We aint got insurance for broken skulls."

Dizzy went through the Giant batting order and struck out all nine men. Rags noticed a piece of wind. He could smell the ball. It seemed to drop around his toes. He couldn't accuse Jerome's umpire. Rags had his three cuts. The ball looped and looped and was gone.

Yarbull might have hit the great Jerome. But he was handicapped. He couldn't push his elbows very far with those stilts he was carrying. He had to taper his swing, or fly on his ass.

Fucking Jerome, the kid sang to himself. The Dean brothers wouldn't have bet two thousand dollars on a team of sockamayocks if they weren't sure Pharaoh was wearing stilts. The money was in their pocket. They could have Yam scrape the ball, and tickle it with his emery paper. The sockamayocks would get to him after a while. All they needed was a run.

But old Yam Murray surprised the Deans. He made those sockamayocks slap the ball on the ground. Swimmy and Rags gobbled everything out of the grass.

Rags had his generator switched on at seven o'clock. It was the nineteenth inning. Not a single son of a bitch had reached first base. The sirens, those crazy women inside the fire truck, began to wail. They couldn't disturb Jerome. He put down Giant after Giant with his screwball, his sinker, and his smoke. He ate a candy bar between innings. He would have gone back to the hill and pitched until morning if he had to.

Yam was dying on his feet. His arm had stiffened up, his knees had withered to a kind of paste. Rags fed him sardines and water. The brute seized Yam's shoulders and rubbed and rubbed.

They got him to pitch again.

The sirens wailed.

The lights in the outfield began to dim.

The diamond was turning gray. Yam couldn't see his catcher's fist.

The wailing from the truck inspired Rags. He had Scarborough pinch-hit for Muley Jones. Dizzy peered down at Scarborough from the hill. He winked to his brother Paul. It was the bottom of the twenty-fifth. Jerome hadn't pitched to a hunchback in his years with the Cards. He was searching for a reliable target. Should he throw to that bubble the brute had on his back? Or aim for the gold letters on Scarborough's chest? His smoke couldn't harm the brute, and his sinker bounced in front of the plate. He walked Scarborough in five pitches. The hunchback ruined his perfect game.

The sirens had blessed the Giants. After twenty-four innings they had a man on first. But Rags couldn't take Scarborough's hand and lead him around the bases. How could they bring him home?

Rags swallowed wind for the tenth time. Jerome struck him out. It was the Pharaoh's turn. Yarbull took off one of the stilts. He had to have the opportunity to bend a knee. The stilt he wore was like a peg leg now. It anchored him to the plate, but it didn't poison the cut of his bat. Jerome went over the hill and gave Yarbull a screwball to eat.

The clap of wood on horsehide was the sweetest sound Rags could hear. Scarborough scampered to second. He stopped, coughed, touched his heart. Rags waved him to third. "Go on, Hump, g o..." The sockamayocks looked and looked for that ball in the outfield. The dim lights baffled them. They tripped and stumbled and climbed in and out of gopher holes as the brute jumped on home plate. His head was blue from all the running he did.

"Shucks," Dizzy said to Paul. "Yarbull tricked us. Aint a damn thing wrong with his legs."

The Pharaoh was lying on the ground. The tremble of the bat had traveled like a shock wave through his body. The remaining stilt dropped off. He was in a cold, cold shiver. Muley Jones carried Yarbull into his Buick. Rags poked his face in the window. He'd won two thousand from Jerome and Paul, but he seemed miserable.

"I'm fine, Mr. Rags," Yarbull said. "I think I'll sleep a little." And he managed to pull down the Buick's window shade.

The caravan drove to a spot near the 'Bama state line. They were outside a village of sheds and cardboard houses. You could sniff the burning of pork. It was Yarbull's hometown. He wouldn't go into the village with the Giants. He got out of the Buick and stood on the road with his bossman-magician.

"Stop worrying, Mr. Rags. I won't get lost."

He couldn't hit and field any longer on those ravaged knees. And he wasn't going to watch the Giants play while living in a stretcher. Yarbull rubbed his cheek.

"I started playing for money when I was twelve. I had three road wives, and my main woman is in this here town. We got five kids ... it wasn't those stilts that put an end to me. I could have played with my whole body in wood. But I'm sick of it. A man likes to hold his children more than once a year. Please don't wait with me, boss. Some kid will pass by and bring ol' Pharaoh into town. You'll frighten him ... a white man and a pack of Buicks."

So the kid left Yarbull on the road and took off with his caravan of Cincinnati Giants.

Rags went back to third base, and the Giants got themselves a new shortstop, a seventeen-year-old boy named Ira Sharp. He was surly and began to fight other Giants until Scarborough cured him of the habit by flinging Ira over the roof of the Hudson one day. The boy respected his elders after that. He developed good hands and feet. He could charge the ball and throw his face in the dust. Other Black teams began to court Ira Sharp. The Homestead Grays wanted him for their spot in the Negro National League. They offered to triple his salary. Ira wouldn't jump to the Grays. "I'm with the white magician," he said. "I play for Mr. Ragland and his Black Giants."

But no amount of magic could thrust a calendar into the kid's head. "Hump, what year is this?"

"1937."

Scarborough had become the bookkeeper-first baseman of the Giants. "You're thirty-two," he said.

"Thirty-two? We got years and years to play . . ."

The root jar kept the Giants strong. The kid was a powerful magician. He could pull sheriffs and the Judge's lackeys off a baseball diamond. He could turn a swarm of locusts away. He could heal cuts and wounds. But why had Scarborough begun to limp?

"What's the matter?"

"A Charley horse," the brute said.

But he was coughing and breathing hard at first base.

"I'm sittin' you down, Hump. Tend to the books. That's enough."

"I'm a first baseman," Scarborough said. Rags was in a pickle. How could he bench his own roommate?

Scarborough coughed up blood after a game and wobbled towards the Hudson. The brute was giddy. He shoved his narrow hips like a wild boy, gassed on some strange wine. He labored, knee over knee, frightened that Rags would find the spots of blood on his baseball shirt. *Nobody's benching the Hump.*

He had a fist inside his back. The fist had a mouth, and the mouth was full of teeth. It clawed under his shoulder, and ripped his chest. *Raggsy, aint I cute at first base? I helped you beat Dizzy Dean. You can't throw strikes to a hunchback. That's the truth.*

He couldn't make it to the Hudson. His knees twisted out. The kid ran to where the brute had fallen. Scarborough was dead.

The magician got his root. He leaned over Scarborough, kissed him, and fondled the jar. Not one nerve in Scarborough twitched. "Hump," Rags said, "get up, get up, get up . . ."

He threw the jar into the dirt. It wouldn't break. Swimmy picked up the jar and put it back in the Hudson. Then he grabbed the kid's arms and led him away from the corpse.

19

DISASTER struck the Giants. Locusts ate the wood off a Buick. Diamonds would freeze up and split along the base lines. Storm clouds followed the team. Bullfrogs would leap out of the mud to plague the magician and his men. Swimmy stubbed his toe, trying to avoid the frogs.

All these visitations only served to harden Rags. He would slip on a frog's head, roll in the mud, and denounce the root. The Giants had to plead with the magician. "For God's sake, boss, don't mock that thing. It's got legs and arms like any Black man. You can't beat the devil without Sam'l's jar."

So Rags took out the jar to save his team. He wouldn't fondle it. But he did rub the sides a little. The storm clouds disappeared. The frogs burrowed into the mud and left the Giants alone. Without his knowing it, Rags grew kinder to the root. Hairs sprouted on one of its three forks. These were the only blossoms a root could have.

Rags would have been satisfied with a simple ghost. It didn't have to carry the brute's smell. Just give it a voice and the beginnings of a hump. Rags sang to the jar.

They were outside Des Moines. The groundsmen had combed the earth. There wasn't a split in the diamond. The local all-stars had challenged the Giants. Swimmy, Ira, and Rags performed seven double plays.

A brute came loping out of the stands. He wore a homburg, but no felt hat with green feather and a beautiful crown could hide his twisted back. It was Scarborough, Scarborough in fancy clothes. Rags got his wish. He had Scarborough's ghost on a hill outside Des Moines.

He hugged the little man and kissed him on the forehead. "Hump, how does it feel to be dead?"

The brute had a sour face. "Lay off, will ya?"

It wasn't Scarborough's voice. But Rags had to consider the alterations of heaven and hell. He hugged the little man again.

"Jesus, will you give a guy some air? Are you crazy, or what?"

The joy began to drop from Rags. The brute had a crow's-foot at the end of each eye. Scarborough's wrinkles were terrific, but they weren't so severe. He hadn't looked seventy when he was with the Giants.

The kid was talking to Henry Watteau, Babe Ruth's old bicarbonate of soda boy. He'd flourished in the last fifteen years. His handkerchief was pure silk.

"Ragland, where's your brute?"

"Gone," the kid said. "He had a hemorrhage and a heart attack on the same day."

Watteau lifted his hat. "I told him to get out of baseball. It's a killer for us . . . you can't live long with a toadstool sitting on you that squeezes your heart every minute."

Brother, how did you survive?

"I got nineteen garages," Watteau said. "And two diners. Ragland, I'm worth a million ... I owe it all to the Babe. The sweetest man what ever lived, Mr. George Herman Ruth. I come out of the hospital and he gives me a grubstake ... heart of gold. Say a bad word about him and you get a kick in the balls . . ."

He presented Rags with his signature on a little card. "That's worth a free meal at one of my diners. But do me a favor. Don't bring the Blacks."

Rags tore up the card after Watteau left the diamond. The kid wouldn't eat without his Giants.

He didn't die at third base. A lefty couldn't hurl that ball around the horn the way a righty could. But Ragland hugged the line like no other human being in the majors, the minors, or the Black leagues. He was the white Pharaoh Yarbull, without Yarbull's stilts. It didn't matter that he had a glaze in his eye, that he would think and think of his roomie while he covered the bag. "Come on, Hump... where the hell are you?" The glaze didn't interfere with his glove.

A world of Scarboroughs could have tumbled in the kid's head, and he still would have completed the throw to first. He lived in the Hudson on cans of sardines. He heard mumblings about some kind of war. His Amherst days hadn't deserted him. He'd studied maps of China and Japan.

Ira was kidnapped from the Giants. It had nothing to do with a scalping party in the Black leagues. The shortstop was going overseas. Swimmy Welles was safe. He had a wife and three kids. But he had to scribble out an itinerary for his draft board in St. Louis. The War Department was asking him to stay in touch.

The Cincinnatis began to lose their evil reputation. Towns and villages had gotten gentler to the Giants. Baseball was good for the home front. Rags was allowed to parade his men on village greens. Schools lent their diamonds to him, as long as the Giants showered somewhere else. Rags thought the schools were crazy. The Giants hadn't showered in three years. It was their habit to bathe in the nearest stream.

But this new glory did nothing for Rags. Town life was no comfort to him. He missed the Hump. He didn't want another roommate. Swimmy would have moved into the front seat, but the kid preferred to live alone inside the Hudson.

Once, in a fit of isolation, when he would have been happy to give the team over to Yam, he showed up at an Army induction center in Hannibal, Missouri. He had the gold and white of the Giants on his chest. His face was wild, as if an animal had come in off the street. You couldn't have guessed his age. He was like some mad, ancient boy walking in his own fever.

The Army nurses humored him as he stood on line.

"Can we get you a cup of tea?"

"Get me into the war first."

The medical examiners didn't have to listen to his heart. They peeked at those claws of his. They hadn't encountered a normal person with such gnarled hands. It was a mystery. The nails were black. The knuckles had horns on them. The fingers themselves bent in curious ways. Every joint must have been broken once or twice.

"I can catch a baseball," Rags said. "Why couldn't I throw a hand grenade?"

The examiners thanked him for coming around. They couldn't accept cripples in this man's Army.

Rags went into a soda shop and had five chocolate sundaes. The soda clerk studied his gloom. "Mister, I can get you as much tail as you want."

There was a one-room whorehouse right above the soda shop. The kid marched upstairs. Why couldn't he rest with a woman for an hour or two? He wasn't unkind to whores. Hadn't he been in love with a crib baby, Miz Emma Raines?

He knocked on the door.

"Honey, come on in . . ."

Two women were sitting on a bed in flesh-colored peignoirs. The kid turned sly. He looked again. It was a woman and a girl. Their faces were suspiciously alike. God, a mother and daughter team in Hannibal. All he could think of was red hair. *Iva and Marylou*. He ran out of the whorehouse shrieking to himself.

He heard a familiar tune outside the soda shop.

Eveline, Eveline, won't you wait for me?

Rags stepped across the street.

He was on the sidewalk of the Hannibal Playhouse. He saw posters for *Eveline*. Hallelujah! Hollis' play about baseball wives had come to Hannibal. A hit on Broadway, the posters declared. *The miracle of '42*. But he couldn't find Hollis' name.

The kid paid half a dollar to walk in on the matinee. This wasn't the same *Eveline* Hollis had brought to the Morosco in 1923. The actors who played the Red Sox were much leaner in Missouri. Their blouses were ragged. Their shoes were unlaced. The kid could have died. These weren't fat boys out of any acting school. They were the original ragamuffins, Hollis' team of orphans and fools. Ferdie Willis, Eveline's husband and the hero of the play, could have been Chicken Stallings, or the kid himself. He had the rough, garbled voice of a ballplayer:

Evy, Evy, stay with me.
It's hell in Chicago
Grief in Detroit
Without my darlin' wife.

The kid couldn't control himself. He was sobbing by the middle of the second act.

Fortune stuck with the Giants. It wasn't on account of the hairs in a root jar. The magic was in the receipts Rags collected at the end of every Giant game. The war had made them popular. Those phantoms, the Cincinnati Black Giants, were pushed into American history.

They appeared at schools, colleges, big city stadiums, and prison farms. Convicts were their greatest fans. These embezzlers, murderers, and thieves remembered Pharaoh and old Carl.

"Where's the hunchback . . . where's Carl's wife?"

The phantoms were playing a team of convicts inside the penitentiary at Springfield, Massachusetts, when the kid recognized his lost brother, Billy Rogovin, among the population. Rogovin wasn't wearing his orange suit. He had gray pajamas in the prison yard. He tried to sink back into the crowd of convicts.

It was the sixth inning, and Rags had interrupted the game to grab hold of Billy. The gambler from Darling Street had aged. His lips were pudgy. He was like a fat, rotting toad without his orange suit. Where were the prison tailors? Couldn't they have found other pajamas for Billy to wear?

No one considered it strange that Rags should talk to a convict. The trusties and prison guards didn't interfere with the owner of the Black Giants. The kid held Billy by his pajama tops.

Rags didn't have to query him, or repeat old, old stories. Billy volunteered to mumble the truth. "Your boss Hollis .. . he paid me to fuck you out of the American League."

"Thanks, brother Bill."

The Giants didn't have Ira Sharp to plug their hole at short. They had to jump around like Chinese bandits to beat the jailbirds, 2-1.

The caravan stopped in Weymouth. It couldn't have been five hours since the Giants collected their bats and said goodbye to the warden at Springfield. A man in a twill suit rapped on the window of the Hudson with his ring.

"Babe Ragland, I'd like a word with you."

Rags welcomed him into the car.

"I'm Howard Pile . . . from the commissioner's office."

Howard Pile had the most beautiful hands in Weymouth. His nails were pink as an Alabama sky, and he didn't have the slightest bump or horn on any of his knuckles.

"You work for the Judge?"

"Yes sir, and he's mighty sorry what happened to you, son."

Son? Who's calling me son?

"What the hell does that rascal want from me, Mr. Pile?"

"We're conducting an investigation against Hollis McKee . . . we'd like you to help. You'll have to file some papers against your old boss ... we can't put you on the active list until that man Hollis goes before the Judge."

"Active list?"

"The Judge means to reinstate you ... let you play again in the American League."

"What year are we in, Mr. Pile?"

"I don't understand . . . year? This is 1943."

Rags didn't have the Hump to calculate for him.

"Is it May or June?"

"Son, it's the middle of August."

"I must be thirty-eight... they'll laugh at me. Grandpas can't bust into a training camp."

"There's a war on. Teams are dying for third basemen." The kid threw that agent out of the Hudson. Then he sat on top of him and started to bite Howard's ear. It was a bullrider's trick, something he'd learned from wrestling baby bulls on his father's ranch.

It was lucky for Howard that the carpenters were close. They kept the caravan in tiptop condition, banging dents out of twenty-five-year-old Buicks, and sealing up cracks in the mahogany with some kind of paste.

"Mr. Rags, that's a man lying under you . . . you'll bite his ear off and we'll have to run to Missouri."

Rags let Howard go. "You tell the Judge I don't need redemption from him."

The carpenters applied Mercurochrome to the agent's ear.

"How'd you learn so fast that I talked to Billy Rogovin? Does the emperor have spies in the Springfield pen? I'll handle Hollis McKee on my own. . .

The Giants had a free day in Boston. The kid wouldn't visit the Fens. He wasn't afraid of alligators rising out of the swamp. It was something else. He didn't want to meet Marylou's ghost. He went to the Ritz-Carlton in his gold baseball suit and asked for Hollis McKee. The clerks shrugged their shoulders. They didn't remember Hollis at the Ritz.

A bellboy who must have been fifty winked at Rags. "You'll find him in Scollay Square ... try the Mackerel bar on Franklin Avenue. That's his new address."

Rags handed the bellboy a paper dollar. "Hollis lives at a bar?"

"Why not? He's a whiskey bum."

The kid walked down to Scollay. He had to go through the Mackerel twice before he could spot Mr. McKee. Hollis didn't have a tooth in his mouth. He sat with an empty glass and sucked on his cheeks. The kid had a bottle of whiskey brought to Hollis' table. The bum drank and drank.

"Hollis, look at me . . ."

Those raw whiskey eyes took Rags in.

"The gracious son-in-law," he said. "The lefty comes home to Boston . . ."

"Dumbhead, I was your property, your kid at third . . . you sabotaged your own team when you hired Billy Rogovin to set me up. Why did you do such a crazy thing?"

The whiskey eyes began to clear. "I wanted you out, out for good . . . you destroyed my poor dead brother's girls."

"Go on, drag in Judah Cottonmouth's ghost... poor dead brother." Rags wished he had his root on him. That jar couldn't find the Hump, but maybe it would bring Hollis' bloodbrother into the Mackerel, so Rags could look at those Dartmouth twins, Hollis and Judah Cottonmouth, and decide which one was the bigger prick. "I

ought to hang you from the ceiling . . . you created Iva and Marylou . . . you slept with the mother and turned the daughter into a
nagging child."

Hollis clutched the bottle and cursed Rags with whiskey on his
tongue. He was in a panic. He'd guzzled and slobbered so much,
most of the bottle was gone. The kid ordered a second bottle for
the whiskey bum.

"Hollis, you should be rich . . . *Eveline* is everywhere."

"I sold my rights to it for a hundred dollars ... I'm glad. It was a
stupid show." *Evy, Evy, stay with me.*

"Hollis, where's my wife?"

The bum started to grin. "She's down the block."

"What's Iva doing on Franklin Avenue? .. . it's August. Iva
should be in Tisbury town."

"She gave up the Vineyard years ago . . . she was living with her
mama's servant. You remember Rhys ... he squeezed the last penny
out of her and ran off to Rio with a banker's wife . . ."

"What happened to the house on Beacon Hill?"

"She lost that too ... Iva's come to Scollay, like the rest of us . .
. can you blame her when she has a husband who wears knickers
all the time? ... I should have sold *Eveline* to you . . . changed the
third act, put in material about the orphan who abandons his wife
. . . gives her to Rhys."

Rags lifted the bum out of his chair. He could have hurled him
across the Mackerel. It wouldn't have cost Hollis. The bum had no
more teeth.

Customers watched a man rise over a table. It was no whiskey
dream. The magician's forearms kept Hollis up in the air.

"What's Iva's address?"

"Who knows? She works at the hash house two doors to the
left. . ."

The kid put Hollis back in his chair. How could you take your
revenge on a twisted root of a man? He went to Iva's hash house,

the Harbinger Inn. The shock of her red hair made Rags shiver in his gold and whites. She was behind the counter, feeding sailors and bums. The pout lines had disappeared from her face. Delivering ten-cent hamburgers to the bums, she had all the concentration of a dutiful child.

Iva looked up and saw a grown man in pajamas. She thought he was a Black from the way he had shuffled in; it was only the standard crouch of the Cincinnati Black Giants, a gesture of suspicion and a pattern of flight that were necessary for a team that lived on the run. The kid walked and moved like any other Giant. His eyes were hidden from her. His jaw slanted away from the counter.

Iva recognized the meaning of his pajamas: a baseball player. She stared hard at the slant of his jaw. It wasn't a Black who had come in for the twenty-cent special: coffee and baked beans. No. It was the seventh Babe. Cedric Tannehill Rags. She rushed out at him with a meat chopper in her hand, muttering, "Baseball, baseball, baseball..." The kid ran for his life.

Iva blamed her goduncle. Ragland would never have found her on his own. He couldn't see past third base. Hollis must have led Rags to the Harbinger Inn. Iva took her apron off and went to Hollis' perch at the Mackerel.

She was convinced that both of them had been born under the same tree. They were wastrels, Iva and the old man. They'd pissed their fortunes away. Hollis lost his team and backed one abominable show after the other. And Iva had her gigolo, Rhys. Funny, she didn't even like to kiss that man. But she gave him everything. It was only Cottonmouth cash. It didn't keep her mother from drowning in the swamp. What could it do for Iva?

"Hollis McKee, why did you tell that baseball player where I was?"

The goduncle grinned at her. "I thought it was about time Scollay had a marriage broker."

"Well, do your brokering for someone else. I've had enough husbands in my life."

"Iva girl, you were only married once . . ."

"Don't talk. You didn't have a third baseman in your house."

"But I had him on my team. That was worse. I could never stand a fanatic. He would have played for free if I'd let him . . . will you buy some whiskey for an old gent?"

"No, but I'll feed you a hamburger if you'll get the hell out of the Mackerel and go down the block with me."

Hollis wouldn't leave his perch. So Iva had to bring the hamburger to him. But a toothless man couldn't swallow a whole patty of meat. Iva mashed it for him with a spoon. Then she had to go back to her job. The sailors and bums at the Harbinger Inn wanted their hamburgers and bowls of soup.

20

RAGLAND learned how to follow the railroad tracks. The Giants would go from one whistle-stop to another. It was good business. You could always find a team of grandfathers, school boys, and military rejects in a railroad town. The kid began to wonder why so many of these towns put diamonds up near a churchyard. Was it recreation for the dead? It bothered Swimmy Welles to blink at tombstones all the time. Rags got used to it. Why should he care if the dead yearned to watch phantoms in gold and white?

The Giants caused a miracle in Maryland, Kansas: the Chicago Limited hadn't stopped at Maryland for over twenty-five years. People collected around the engineer's caboose. It was painted red and Denver gray. The engineer himself stepped down from the caboose. He asked for Cedric Tannehill.

The town of Maryland didn't have any Cedric Tannehills to give away. "He's with the Black team," the engineer said.

Townsmen brought the engineer into the Giants' camp. The engineer looked at Rags. "Cedric Tannehill?"

"Who wants him?" the kid said with a scowl.

"Judge Landis."

"Tell him to go suck on an egg."

"He's been riding for a week now, young man ... he had to call the president of the railroad. You think it's so easy to make a special stop? It was a favor to the Judge. The president of a railroad's got small power these days. The goddamn government runs this line ..."

"Maybe I ought to snitch on you and the Judge."

"You are an ungrateful young man," the engineer told Rags. "The Judge is sick ... and he's been waiting to see you."

"Let him wait ... that son of a bitch threw me out of baseball."

But the kid was foxy when it came to the Giants. He realized a red caboose was handsomer than a ballclub. The Cincinnatis would have to crawl into the churchyard and sleep while the Chicago Limited was around. So Rags went along with the engineer.

He climbed up into the caboose.

The caboose looked like a rich man's den. It had rugs and drapes and a small cherrywood bar that could have come from the Royal Fox, that sporting house where Rags saw the Cajun lose to fat Alice, when the Hump was still alive. Rags had to peek into the corners to find Judge Landis. The emperor lay on a reclining chair, with blankets over his legs. You couldn't have recognized the Judge without his silver scalp. The rest of him was puny and dry.

Rags came up close; he would have sworn some dead Indian was underneath the blankets. But dead Indians don't cry. Rags couldn't mistake the sobbing of that old emperor man.

"Something hurt, Judge?"

Landis wiped his eyes with the ragged edge of his sleeve. The emperor didn't have a decent handkerchief "It's seeing you in that Black boy's suit, and knowing I'm the cause."

"Well, don't let that bother you. Judge. I like the Cincinnati Giants."

"... I was hasty. I didn't stop to think it could be Hollis trying to ruin a player of his. Cedric, can you forgive this old crackpot. . . I'm a pompous, self-righteous ass."

"Nothing to forgive. Judge. I would have been miserable if I had to stay with the Sox."

The emperor began to sob again. "I have twenty years of reports on you ... my men shouldn't have hounded you so much. But they did reach that gambler ... what the hell is his name?"

"Billy, Billy Rogovin."

"They discovered him in jail . . . why didn't you let us prosecute dirty Hollis?"

"I couldn't, Judge. It's got to do with family. That's personal business between Hollis and me."

But the sobbing didn't stop.

"Shit, Judge, don't cry ... I forgive you."

A blanket had fallen off. Rags stooped, got the blanket in his gnarled hand, and covered up the emperor's knees. Then he walked out of the caboose.

"Mustard and buttermilk, that's my diet. I can't swallow anything hard."

The Judge couldn't have told you if he was having a dream on a railroad car. He'd done a lot of crying lately. It was like a rheumatism attack. They called him baseball czar. Do czars have chilly feet? Sons of bitches, who else had preserved the national sport? He'd made an outlaw of this Ragland. But what else could he do? He had to bite at every gambler who approached a ball park, or the game would sink into the muck again. It was gambling, or baseball. You couldn't have both.

He remembered Ragland's hands. *Loved to watch that kid.* The first and last lefty in the corner. The seventh Babe. Imbecile. Why hadn't he suspected Hollis McKee? Anybody who mixes baseball and musical comedies can't be good.

The train left in a quarter of an hour. But that miracle happened twice. The Chicago Limited stopped at Maryland station on its return run. It was heading for Albuquerque. The Giants hadn't gone out of Kansas yet. They were at the diamond near the churchyard when the train stopped. The engineer signaled from the caboose. Half the town rushed over. The emperor of baseball was dead.

"Went in his sleep... like a baby. Give that news to young Cedric. He'll want to know."

The townsmen ran to the diamond and interrupted a game between the Giants and the military rejects.

"Ah," Rags said, after hearing about the Judge. "He wasn't such a bad egg."

The game started up, and Rags socked the ball into the churchyard for a home run. He felt jittery as he hopped around the bases.
Something roared in his ears: it was the sound of the emperor crying, under the whistle of a train.

Rags sat out the last two innings. The Giants could take on military rejects without the Babe.

No one had to tell Rags the war was over.

A boy in military shoes met the caravan near St. Cloud. Ira
Sharp had been returned to the Giants. The shortstop got out of his
military shoes. He went deep into the hole to deny a base hit to the
Black Pygmies of St. Cloud, Eau Claire, and Duluth (the Pygmies
had to represent three towns in order to survive).

It was almost like having the Pharaoh again, only this Pharaoh
threw with his right hand. He could sock triples, steal second base,
hold cannonballs in his glove. The Giants didn't keep any stats; the
number of strikeouts and double plays meant nothing to a phantom team. Yet Ira had to be batting .600 on the road. Rags couldn't
remember when his shortstop had less than two hits in a game.

A man was following them around. He watched the Giants in
Omaha, Beatrice, Hastings, and North Platte. He saw them in little stadiums and under the Giants' own lights. When there was an
overflow crowd, he would stand behind the fire truck in deep center
field that carried the old gasoline generator. He couldn't have ignored the sirens inside the truck, the crazy voices that generator
provoked, the sound of shrieking women.

Rags caught him near the truck. It was Howard Pile, the commissioner's man. What the hell did he want? Landis was dead.

Howard started to shake. The kid had to grab his shoulders
and give a pull, or Howard might have had a seizure in center field.

"Howard, I promise not to bite your ear off. Why are you following us?"

He handed Rags a card that had the nose and cheeks of an Indian on it, the emblem of the Boston Braves.

"I'm a scout," he said. "We're looking for Black boys . . ."

"Why?"

"The Dodgers are picking up Blacks like crazy and hiding them in their farm teams."

"What the hell for?"

"Son, this isn't 1922 . . . you're gonna have an explosion of Black boys in the major leagues. We'd like to take Ira Sharp off your hands, give you three thousand for his contract . . ."

"I don't have contracts with my men. You can deal with Ira yourself."

Ira wouldn't go.

"Mr. Rags, who needs the Boston Braves? Only an idiot would give up the Black Giants."

"Well, idiots are growing smart this year . . . take the man's money, Ira. The Black leagues are shrinking fast." He argued with Ira for three days, until Ira grew depressed.

"Don't you like me anymore, Mr. Rags?"

"Like you? Next to Pharaoh, you're the sweetest shortstop I ever had . . ."

"Then why are you working so hard to get rid of me?"

"Because. They're scumsuckers in the major leagues, but that's where you belong. Now will you go with the man?" Ira left with Howard Pile, and the phantoms had a broken team. Rags put a sockamayock on short. He had no one else. The big leagues were grabbing away all the good Black prospects.

The sockamayock owned a pair of wooden feet. Rags and Swimmy Welles had to dive into that hole at short. Rags' knees would whistle. A peculiar wind would blow through him as he hopped around the infield.

Soon I'll be like the Pharaoh, and I'll have to play on stilts.

The kid went to his root. He caressed the jar and sang to it. "Baby, if my knees give out, we'll land in a pile of shit."

The whistling stopped. The kid developed a healing glue in his knees. He had the stamina of a rookie boy. He rode bulls at third base. He ran after prairie dogs. He snorted and tumbled in the grass.

Swimmy had to caution him. "Boss, you aint no chicken. Slow down a little."

"Bushwah," Rags said. He ran onto the field and tossed a bullet to first base. The fire truck shrieked at him. The sirens started to yackety-yak. He could hear a constant word under the scattered breath of their song. They didn't throw the Hump's name at him. These women had a different shriek. *Iva, ha, Iva.*

He went back to the root. "Tell those bitches to leave me alone."

He began to dread night games and the grinding of the generator. The sirens were eating him up. They were the true magicians. They could beguile him with their music, trick him with a roar. Scarborough spoke to him out of the fire truck. The bitches had faked his voice.

"Raggsy, go to your wife."

The kid's body rattled at third. He would have poured lead in his ears to drown that music. Let the sirens mock him. He loved Scarborough's voice."

"Where are you, you little guy?"

"Raggsy, go to your wife."

"Have a heart, will you? . . . she chased me with a goddamn cleaver. The woman would have turned me into chopped meat."

Swimmy watched his boss hold a conversation with himself. Mr. Rags was overworked. The big leagues were kidnapping Blacks all over the place. The Giants would be reduced to an old folks' home for sockamayocks and aging outlaws. But how could Swimmy tell his boss to shut up and play?

The mumbo jumbo didn't hurt the Giants. Whatever passed between Raggsy and the fire truck, he still chased ground balls. He would sing to Scarborough and claw a high chopper out of the air.

The Giants should have been going into their winter act. It was November, but they didn't shoot for the bayou country. The caravan pushed east. The sirens were charting the Cincinnatis' course. The groundsmen had to sculpt their diamonds on hills of snow. The kid could frighten blizzards away with his root, but he couldn't take care of freezing weather. The sirens purred their undersong in the cold. *Iva, Iva, Iva.* The Giants had to wear extra shirts.

Rags got to Boston on the last day of a blizzard. He only had his baseball shoes, and Scollay was adrift in a white field that snaked along the streets just like the Mississippi going around the bend of New Orleans. The kid arrived at the Harbinger Inn with snow on his head.

Iva growled when she saw those silly pajamas on Rags, and his wet stockings. She didn't reach for that butcher knife behind the counter. His face was hollow, as if he'd lost his cheeks somewhere in the blizzard. She gave him a cup of soup. He drank the soup with frosty hands and said hello.

Some bums at the counter began to paw Miz Iva. She was used to it. She slapped them on their dirty gloves. The bums didn't like having the kid around. He was an intruder in their hash house. They pawed Miz Iva again. The kid seized them by their collars and shoved them into the wall.

"Don't get rough," Iva said. "They're old men."

The kid apologized. He picked up the bums, dusted off their pants, and returned them to the counter.

"Where's Scarborough?" she asked.

"Dead," the kid told her.

"Do you have another roommate?"

"No."

She couldn't say why he seemed handsome in his pajamas. He was skinny as ever. But that pile of bones appealed to her in some crazy fashion.

He began to stutter. His lips were cold. Miz Iva had to help him out.

"Are you proposing to me?"

Rags could hear the bitterness in her voice. "No, ma'am . . . I'm looking for a roommate, that's all."

She smiled and took her apron off.

"I'll be your roommate," she said.

She announced to no one in particular that she was quitting her job. The bums blinked at her. Scollay was turning upside down. You couldn't depend on a coffee girl anymore. It would be a miserable winter for them. Miz Iva grabbed her coat and said, "Henry, Tom, Victor, Paul, you be good . . . I'll come back and spank you if you don't behave." Then she walked into the blizzard with that pajama man and the bums started to cry.

Glory, Glory and the Browns:

BOOK SEVEN

21

RAGGSY had a new partner inside the Hudson, a different kind of brute. An ex-waitress with red hair, a bride from some lost century, a wife who wasn't a wife. She gobbled sardines with the kid. She sewed patches on his uniform. But she wouldn't sleep with him.

He didn't quarrel. He didn't push. He didn't climb over to her portion of the car. She would have thrown a shoe in his face. All he could do was sniff her red hair. Miz Iva wouldn't peek into an old ballplayer's heart. She was a roommate with her own territories. She hadn't promised to kiss and fondle Rags. There was nothing about husbands and wives in her "contract" with the Giants.

Rags was like a rookie with a blue prick. The magician couldn't seduce Miz Iva; she'd have none of him. He didn't go to his root; the jar was next to worthless on women with red hair.

He had the back of the Hudson to himself at night, and more than Iva to disturb his head. The rolling stock was falling apart. A Buick had to be junked in Topeka. The fire truck had a terrible cough. But the kid couldn't replace his rolling stock. Santa Claus was gone. Griffey died the same year as the Judge. How could Rags ring up lawyers in Tucson he didn't even know?

The caravan was losing its tail. But Rags kept the Giants. He wouldn't let go. And he learned how to exist with that brute in the front seat. His desire shrank into his gold and whites. His prick turned a natural color. The blueness wasn't there.

A telegram caught up with him in Battle Creek. It had lots of numbers on it and crooked lines. He could read the words *St. Louis Browns*. But he couldn't deal with the crooked lines. "Iva, what's this?"

"The Brownies want you to join up . . ."

Rags giggled to himself. "Maybe they think I'm a Black short-stop . . . tell them Ira Sharp went to the Braves."

"They know who you are . . . they're offering you ten thousand dollars to finish the season with them."

"Lunatics," Rags said. He was ready to tear that yellow paper in his fists. "What name is on it?"

"Briggs Josephson."

"Is Briggsy still managing the Browns?"

Iva squinted at the telegram. "He's the owner now."

"They're paying me money to pick up with them in June?"

"Husband, it's July."

How come I'm her husband when she reads a telegram?

Rags got the long-distance operator to dial St. Louis. The Brownies were on the road. A clerk in the front office gave him their schedule.

Rags took off his gold and whites. He felt peculiar in civilian pants. "Iva, I can fix our rolling stock for ten thousand ... get a few light bulbs. Will you take care of the club while I'm away."

"Of course," she said. "What am I supposed to do?"

"Make sure we have enough sardines... Swimmy will do the rest."

He left the Hudson with Miz Iva, grabbed a Buick, and drove to New York City. He found Briggs in his private suite at the Concourse Plaza. The old skipper's back had gone crooked. He walked with a cane now. And this was the sweetest third baseman the Browns would ever know. He tortured the American League with his bat and his glove before he went over to Hollis' Red Sox and discovered Babe Ragland in the middle of Arkansas.

They gave each other a third baseman's hug.

"You bum, didn't I say you'd come to the Browns? . . . heck. Rags, where you been?"

"Everyplace and no place, boss."

"Goddammit, we need your glove."

"I'm an outlaw . . . they won't let me into Yankee Stadium."

Briggs looked at him. "Bushwah. The Judge cleared you right before he died."

"Who's gonna be my roommate?" the kid asked.

"Don't be silly. You'll room with me. And when we get to St. Louis we'll have a Babe Ragland Day. Free bats for the first two thousand kids. How does it feel to be a rookie all over again?"

"Is Ty Cobb still around? I don't think I'm strong enough to fight that son of a bitch."

"Did you know the truth about Cobb? His mother shot his father in the head when Ty was a boy. She mistook him for a burglar. Ty loved the old man, and it turned him mean."

It made the kid sorrowful to hear about Cobb's mom and dad. "I'm tired," he said. He took a nap in Briggs' suite.

He must have been Rip van Winkle, like Scarborough once said, because Rags didn't even know night games had come to the American League. He was issued a uniform by the Browns' equipment boy. It had a number on the back. He was No. 12 of St. Louis. You didn't wear knickers anymore. The Brownie pajamas dropped below the calf and narrowed at the knee. You couldn't fly in them.

Iva had circled the year 1949 in the kid's pocket calendar. Rags had to be coming on forty-five. Wasn't that old for a rookie? What was he doing on the Browns? One glance at his teammates and Rags knew why. Briggs had to be desperate. His Browns were the modern dogs of baseball.

Nine men on stilts could have clobbered them.

Rags didn't linger in the clubhouse. He walked through the tunnel at Yankee Stadium and borrowed a mitt off a left-handed brother on the Browns. He didn't like the gloves of 1949: the

282 THE SEVENTH BABE

fingers were banded together, and the pocket was webbed. You could have squeezed a grapefruit in a glove like that.

He sat out the first three innings, while the Yankees climbed on the Browns for six runs. They had DiMaggio, Henrich, Woodling, Rizzuto, and Jerry Coleman. The names meant little to Rags. What could Rip van Winkle declare about the wonders of white baseball?

He couldn't find a single Black man among the Yankees and the Browns. Were they hiding their crop of Blacks on some baseball farm? Would the Blacks revolt and start a new players' war? How could Rags tell?

He didn't complain when they put him in the field. He wished he had his generator with him. The kid preferred his own lights. The glare from the roof bit into his eyes. He took his familiar monkey crouch. He stabbed at ground balls. People didn't notice his crazy left hand. He was a journeyman infielder, recently arrived on the Browns. Who would have remembered that other Babe Ragland?

He scratched a single and struck out twice. He looked into the Yankee dugout. Where was Henry Watteau?

Rags didn't travel to Boston on any train with the Browns. He rode in his Buick and avoided the Brunswick Hotel. The Red Sox had moved out years and years ago. They were rich men who lived in the suburbs of Boston during the hot months. The Browns had inherited the Sox's old hotel.

The kid couldn't stay there. He had a grievance against this hotel. The Brunswick had turned on him in 1925, after the Judge threw Rags out of organized baseball. He slept in the Buick.

Night games were still unpopular in Boston. The kid was grateful for that. He wouldn't have a rotten glare in his eyes. But the gods of Fenway had done terrific damage to the park. "Duffy's Cliff" was gone: left field lay completely flat. It couldn't have supported a hill of toads. And what had happened to Garl's old spot? Center field seemed forlorn without a flagpole. It was a naked pie of dirt and grass.

Loudspeakers hurled the kid's name through Fenway Park. Did they fire Bull Weingarten? Bury his horn in left field? Such loudspeakers wouldn't mention the kid's past. Rags was forgotten history. Jesus, how many Babe Raglands could there have been?

He started for the Browns. What was forty-five to the kid? He had the legs. He dove towards the line and took a double from Birdie Tebbetts. He twisted left and right, charged suicide bunts, raced into shallow left field.

The Sox scratched their heads: who is that funny old man? Do the Brownies have any more amazing grandpas? Dom, will they lend us one? Isn't that loony throwing with his left hand?

Rags didn't get much pleasure out of it. A wind blabbered through his skull. He heard Bull Weingarten's voice. *Batting sixth for the Browns and playing third base, out of the Negro Leagues, our former bad boy who bloodied many noses in his three years with us, Ragland himself, the seventh Babe.*

He wouldn't jump the Browns without telling Briggs. He had to go into the Brunswick Hotel to find the bossman. The lobby had fallen to shit. No wonder the Sox fled from here. It was a haven for parasites, roaches, and bums. Whores barked from the lobby chairs. The kid wouldn't have been surprised to meet shysters in orange suits. A bellboy touched his shoulder. "Good to see you. Babe. It aint been much of a hotel without you and Mr. Scarborough."

Rags couldn't remember him. Didn't bellboys ever leave their jobs?

"Are you Stanley?" There must have been a Stanley at the Brunswick.

"No, I'm Ned."

He shook the bellboy's hand. "Good to see you, Ned."

And he went up to Mr. Briggs. The old skipper seemed disappointed that Rags couldn't stay with the Browns. "Aw, we could have had some fun ... a Babe Ragland Day. You deserve it, kid. The American League pissed on your head."

"It's only yellow water, skip. You can blow it off when it dries."

Fenway hadn't spooked the kid. He just didn't care about the major leagues.

He raced like the devil to Battle Creek. Rags had only been gone six days. He got into his team's pants and shook off the dourness of Boston and New York.

"Iva," he said, "I'm sorry ... I couldn't hold on to that ten thousand. I like Briggs. But the Browns aint for me."

Iva was an independent girl. She could have run the Giants without Mr. Ragland. Hadn't she grown up on baseball? Sat with her mother in Hollis' box at Fenway Park? She would have stolen Rags' pajamas and installed herself at third with his little glove if she had to. Lefty, righty, it didn't matter to her. She could throw either way. She invited herself into the back of the Hudson after they finished a can of sardines.

The kid was surprised when the wife's hand went under his shirt. He could have yodeled to her from the back seat for half a century and she wouldn't have listened to his songs. You had to wait until the girl made up her mind to crawl in with you.

It took twenty-six years.

She held his roughened body. He was all skin and bones.

A wire tuned to jump in the grass. She'd missed her roommate Rags. She didn't mind being married to a man with a glove. *Don't call me Eveline.* She wasn't a baseball widow out of Hollis' musical show. She lived with her husband in an automobile. Miz Iva was part of the team. She went on the road with the Cincinnati Giants.

They kissed and scratched, like the children they used to be. Rags had tender claws.

New Man in the National League:

BOOK EIGHT

22

THEY were a couple of barnstormers.

Rags would lie down with the wife, his gnarled fingers in her red hair. They had no interest in a permanent home, with pantry shelves and potatoes in the ground. Iva could make her pantry under the seat. They had the front and back of Raggsy's Hudson.

The kid was glad he got out of white baseball. He couldn't understand its habits and hidden rules. The majors were buying up Black ballplayers, and then these ballplayers turned invisible. How long could you hold them on a baseball farm? The kid didn't have to worry. Black ballplayers began to leave the farm. Rags heard Swimmy Welles talk of Luke Easter, Monte Irvin, Sam Jethroe, Don Newcombe, Larry Doby, Willie Mays, and Ira Sharp, who was now a shortstop with the Braves.

The kid was approached by the Negro National League. Teams were drying up, and they wanted Rags to be the new man in "organized" Black baseball. They never would have come to him if their league hadn't been in such rotten shape. The bossmen of the National League had scoffed at the Giants, called them desperadoes and trash. But those bossmen needed the desperadoes to stay alive.

"Hell," Rags said. "I'll play with them. It's no skin off my ass."

He liked the idea of having tournaments with the Black Yankees, the Pittsburgh Stars, and the Philadelphia Elites. "Maybe I'll get into a World Series before we die."

But it was a crazy, helter-skelter league. Rags couldn't be sure who would show up to play. Teams would move in and out, join other leagues, lose players, crumple, and start up again. The Pittsburgh Stars became the Jersey Bisons, and ran off to the Negro American League.

The kid managed to squeeze in seven games. He was back at Yankee Stadium to battle the Black Yanks. There couldn't have been more than a thousand faces in that cavern. The kid scowled at empty seats. He couldn't perform in a graveyard. Balls rocketed over his head. He didn't turn over a single double play. He had cotton wool inside his bat. He hit baby balls to the pitcher's box. But he wasn't as feckless as the Black Yanks. He forced his men to keep awake, and they drubbed the Yankees, 6-0.

He resigned from the National League.

The league would have grown thin with or without the Cincinnati Giants. The bossmen couldn't compete with Willie Mays. They'd had Ragland for a minute, and nobody else. Would Ted Williams jump to the Negro National League?

Black ball began to suffocate. It couldn't survive on its own bitter sweat. A few mavericks remained. But how could they support their magicians, their lights, and their players' sardines? Only the Giants wouldn't give it up. Rags had his root jar and his wife. The Hudson died on him somewhere in 1954. The kid moved into a Buick.

He had the fire truck soldered and stitched. Ladders would break. Fenders would disappear. He'd crawl under the truck and stroke its stomach with the root. The Giants would have perished without their lights.

They were baseball dinosaurs, the last of the barnstorming teams. You couldn't find another crew like them. Their money bag was low. Rags couldn't promise his men anything more than a share of sardines. His eyes would hurt him off the field. Miz Iva drove the Buick.

But the kid had his spot. He ate ground balls. He went into the hole, his glove snapping like the meanest turtle in America. He was Ragland of the Black Giants. If he had a dizzy spell, he would blink twice and then sock a triple over a barn or a chickencoop. Iva had to rub his legs in a vinegar solution to bum away the charley horses.

The Cincinnatis built a stretcher for their boss. Sometimes they had to carry him off the field. The wife would come with her vinegar and roll up the kid's pajamas. He'd shut his eyes and think of Yarbull, the Mississippi River, Texas, and the Hump. He had a ball club. No one could make him retire to his father's ranch. He'd have to buy lemons to go with the sardines. He didn't want his men to suffer from yellow scurvy.

The kid opened his eyes.

He wasn't a Brownie or a Red Sock. Rags hated schedules and choochoo trains. He had more fun in the heartland. With his desperadoes. His legs twitched from the wife's vinegar solution. When the twitching stopped he stood on one knee and broke the stretcher his men had made. It bothered Rags to be surrounded by sticks of wood. Those sticks reminded him of the Pharaoh's career. "I'm too young to start wearing stilts."

He rolled his knickers down and walked away.

Elbows and claws.

He was an old wizard in kneepants, defying nature with a root. By every conceivable law the Giants should have vanished, and their magician corralled somewhere with grandpas. Only madmen and children would have persisted with all that barnstorming in the mud. Who cared about the Cincinnati Giants? You couldn't get more than fifty people at a game. *Fuck the receipts.*

The dinosaurs went from town to town. The old hurly-burly was gone. They were lucky to finish a game. Baseball was a disease in the magician's head. Incurable by now. He'd have played fungo in the grass if no other team would walk onto the field with his Giants. High schools were better equipped than Ragland's men. They didn't have to survive on sardines. The Cincinnatis were stitched together like their own fire truck. They wore patches on every sleeve. They would come into town with soot on their faces from a long, long ride. Refugees from nowhere. You would have thought fifty sheriffs had been chasing them. But no one was on their tail except that bossman-magician. *Play your game,* he said. He didn't bother to send out hawkers and criers. What the hell is a crowd? He had Miz Iva and his lights.

He came to Arkansas with his men.

The wizard wanted to see Sackville Forest one last time. There wasn't a trace of that old Boston tryout camp. Sackville Forest was sinking into the ground. It had a few huts and a grocery store. Rags couldn't find the Sox's boardinghouse. It must have blown away.

Iva prepared a big pot of beans for the desperadoes. The smell of her cooking brought a gang of old men out of their huts. They weren't vagabonds, like the Giants. They were citizens of Sackville Forest. But they didn't refuse the beans Iva offered them.

The wizard got into a conversation with the old men, who were amused by the threadbare gold and whites the Giants wore.

"I guess the Sox ruined your town," the wizard said.

"How you mean?"

"When they pulled out and went to Florida."

None of these old men could recall the Red Sox.

"It's that demon what killed us," they said. "We got a monster in the forest."

"What does he look like?"

"He's small and rough... and he knocks you on your ass. He's good to little kids. But little kids can't run no town."

"Does he have an odd shape?" the wizard asked.

"Who can tell? He bumps you so fast."

Rags ventured into the woods. He had to fight through a thicket of low, twisted trees, with branches slapping against his neck. He shouted at the trees.

"You in there, Scarborough? Are you the guy who scared this town to death?"

But the demon wouldn't come to him.

The wizard tumbled into a bear den. He was up to his belly in dry leaves.

He saw ten sharp toenails dangling over his head.

The monster of Sackville Forest was hanging from a tree outside the bear den. It was Scarborough. He'd strung himself up by his baseball pants. His neck was all blue. But he wasn't gagging, or spitting blood. He smiled at the wizard.

"Remember me?"

Rags was afraid to look. "Doesn't it hurt?... hanging like that. . ."

He tried to pull Scarborough down, but he couldn't reach those ten sharp toes. The baseball gods were punishing Rags for being greedy and playing so long. They'd brought back Scarborough's ghost without any black root. The kid was powerless. He'd have to watch Scarborough hang. He couldn't save the Hump this time.

"Raggsy, don't you worry. It only hurts when I yawn."

"Why are you spooking this place?"

"I feel like it," the demon said.

"Don't you want to climb down and talk to me?"

"I can talk from up here."

Rags was confused. Did the demon count as Scarborough? Or was it a dumb masquerade? But the kid would rather have this Scarborough, than no Scarborough at all.

Scarborough's tree began to shake. Rags heard a bitter laugh. "Pretzelhead, you should retire your glove. You're blind, you know that? The Cincinnatis are a piece of shit."

The baseball pants ripped from the tree, and Scarborough jumped into the bear den with Rags. "You wanna wrestle, or box?"

The kid wouldn't fight with his roomie. He didn't care what kind of demon Scarborough had become.

"I can take your little Amherst jabs," Scarborough said, flicking his paws into the wizard's face.

"You think I'm Garl, huh? You can't punch me into no tunnel floor."

He barreled into Rags. The wizard was up to his belly in leaves again.

This aint Scarborough.

The monster turned gentle all of a sudden.

"I didn't mean to deck you, Raggsy. I had a fit. It's hard meeting your roomie after you been hving alone in the woods."

"Hump, I could camp around here if you like... keep the Giants in this state."

"Na," Scarborough said. "Don't come to Sackville no more . . . I'll have to bump you, Raggsy. That's my job."

How did Scarborough get to be such a demon? Was it the kid's fault? Some curse that baseball had put on him? Was it better to bump people and hang from trees as the monster of Sackville Forest, or lie dead in the ground? Even a wizard couldn't answer that.

Scarborough leapt out of the bear den with a crazy somersault.

"Goodbye, Raggsy."

The kid couldn't hope to follow him. He had to work with his claws to scale the bear den's high crooked wall. He didn't go chasing Scarborough. What's the use?

Rags left that tiny forest. He nodded to the old men around Iva's bean pot and ate the leftovers. The wizard chewed and chewed.

The gods of baseball could go to hell. The kid was glad he saw Scarborough in the woods. But he wouldn't haunt the brute. He took his dinosaurs out of Sackville Forest.

Call him devil. The Hump didn't care. He owned these woods. He was ferocious. He banged into ladies and old men who put their feet inside his forest. He was Scarborough, first baseman and lumberjack, formerly of the Red Sox and the Giants.

He couldn't tell you how he got here. He was playing first for Raggsy when he dropped to the ground. He woke with leaves on his forehead. His body ached. He didn't have any compulsion to look for the Giants. He was like a forest animal now. He'd have wrestled foxes and bears if these animals had been around. The woods were empty of them. He could only prey on people.

He recognized this forest the minute he awoke. It was the same woods where he tried to hang himself years and years ago, when he was still with the Sox. The devils must have stolen him from first base. They didn't have to instruct the brute in the art of being nasty. He bumped whoever came close. But he couldn't get baseball out of his head.

He *knew* Rags would come. He had to wait until the root jar turned cloudy enough and Rags felt the urge to bring his desperadoes. The Hump put on a show for his roommate, pretending to swing from a tree.

Who was the bigger magician, Raggsy or the Hump? He heard himself cry. It was a rough, snorting sound. Something a bear would make. He had a new wish. To get out of the forest and recapture first base. But he was bound up in these woods. Doomed to bump into people until the whole of Arkansas disappeared from the earth.

He should never have given up lumbeijacking to join the Sox. The devils couldn't steal a lumberjack. But the hell with it. He wouldn't have met Raggsy without Briggs and the Sox. He was Scarborough, Scarborough, bumping with his body and holding baseball inside his head.

He'd shove his brains out onto the road, taste the leather on his mitt. Who could stop him? Devils couldn't order him around. He'd have his first base in the woods. The hidden Giant, running, jumping, knocking into trees.

On a Field in Holyoke, Massachusetts:

BOOK NINE

23

"DRINK your honey and hot milk, Mr. James."

Fuck off.

Garl wasn't impolite to the fat nurse. He sipped the beverage she had prepared for him. He was seventy-nine years old. His three baby brothers had put him in Holyoke House last year. Garl paid the bills. He had a small pension and something of a bank account. His brothers would phone him from time to time, ask him about the pain in his legs, but they wouldn't come to Holyoke. It was too far away. Shem was a lawyer. Laurence was a brain surgeon. Theodore was a stock and bond man who was retiring to the Florida Keys.

How could Garl have been close with his brothers? He played ball summer and winter to see them through college. Shem, Laurence, and Theodore established themselves, made long careers, and Garl was happy for his brothers. He spilled the honey and hot milk into a flower bowl after the fat nurse had gone.

There was Red Sox fever in Holyoke and all of Massachusetts. Boston sat on top of the American League, thirteen games ahead of its rivals. The orderlies at the nursing home remembered that Garl had once played center field for the Sox. So they considered him an expert on anything to do with the club.

"What about Yaz? Jesus, he'll be thirty-nine this month . . . And Jim Rice? Can you believe that man's power? . . . and who's a better catcher than Carlton Fisk? ... the Boomer at first and Hobson in the corner . . . banging in a hundred and twelve runs . . ."

"His arm is weak," Garl said.

The orderlies looked at the old man. "You crazy? He's a goddamn hero . . . going with a hurt shoulder."

"Bushwah, he can't make the throw."

"Wise guy, who won the Man of the Year Award, Hobson or you?"

They had a conference among themselves. They didn't want to rile the old man. They heard how he fell off a flagpole fifty years ago. They were crafty with Garl, leading him away from the current Sox.

"Who's the best third baseman you ever saw?"

They figured he'd say Brooks Robinson, Billy Cox, or Graig Nettles, their enemy on the Yanks.

"Pharaoh Yarbull. No one could chew his glove."

The orderlies were mystified. "What team was he on?"

"The Cincinnati Black Giants."

He was spiteful and shrewd, this old man, reaching into the Black leagues to arrive at a third baseman that none of them could have known about.

"Was your Pharaoh a righty or a lefty at the plate?"

"He hit from the left side," Garl said.

"Then he had to change hands when he took the field."

"No, he was lefty all the way."

The orderlies knew their baseball. They weren't toys for any flagpole man. A lefty third baseman? Only Blacks would tolerate such a freak. "How did he go around the horn with that left hand? He'd have to be an acrobat."

"He could go around the horn, through the horn, anywhere you like."

Demented. They had to feed orange juice to an old fool. They began to doubt he'd ever been on the Sox.

"Who's your next choice, old man?"

"Babe Ragland."

"Was he a lefty too?" they tittered.

"All the way."

"With the Black Yankees, or what?"

"Ragland was with the Red Sox."

A fury began to grow inside the orderlies. In a different year they might have ripped off his clothes and allowed him to bake on the lawn. Why should they give a crap? Boston was destroying the American League. The old man could invent all the lefty third basemen he wanted. Would they forget a Babe Ragland if he'd held down third for the Sox? They scratched their heads and pulled fiercely on their chins. "Hey, there was a guy ... he came up from an orphanage, hit a lot of singles, and was thrown out of baseball by the commissioner himself."

"That's the Babe."

This obscure mouse was better than Cox and Nettles and their own Butch? Demented. They'd have to keep the old man from climbing another flagpole. They wrapped the blood-pressure cuff around his arm, squeezed the bulb, took four individual readings, put a check on the old man's chart, laughed to themselves, *Babe Ragland, Babe Ragland,* and told Garl to stick to a diet of lettuce and orange juice.

He was glad when they removed their trays and bottles and cuffs. They didn't torture him at Holyoke House. But he despised the charts, the hot milk, and the sound of their blood-pressure bulb. His legs had caved in, and that's the reason his brothers conspired to get him into a nursing home, so Garl would stop falling in the street. He refused to sit in a wheelchair. He had a cane, and he would hobble about. But mostly he stuck to his room.

He'd been forty years a baseball coach and master of Greek at a college in the Hampshire hills. Garl had never married. Women stayed with him. He would hug their bodies at night. But nothing seemed to last. He was ashamed to admit that he'd forgotten them. It wasn't the fault of his dotage. Garl remembered every busher he had played with. And one redhead. Marylou. Her lips would peck at him in his sleep. Old man as he was, he would eat off her body. Look for freckles on her shoulder.

He was a hunter in a nursing home, killing off old taboos. Garl had fucked himself. He'd denied the redhead and starved whatever passion there was in him. He should have married Marylou, taken her off the roster at Fenway Park, severed her from Hollis McKee. Garl always had the good excuse. He was a gypsy ballplayer with a family to support. How could he anger Hollis?

He lost Marylou to the swamps. He'd enter his eighties with the mark of her lips on him: a tired center fielder married to a redhead in his sleep when he could have had a waking-time wife. He was a constant boarder, living in hotels, rooming houses, and a nursing home. His wandering had brought him here, to Holyoke House. Hot milk and honey.

There was a tumult downstairs. A convict was loose in the nursing home. It sounded unreasonable to Garl. What would a convict be doing at Holyoke?

"Hiya, skip."

He did see a man in a convict's suit. Was it for Halloween? Impossible. It was August now. The man reminded Garl of his brother Shem. Shem wouldn't come to Massachusetts.

The convict began to keen at him. He was reciting garbled bits of Sophocles ... a freshman could have done a better job. The convict mixed up Ajax and the wound in Philoctetes' leg.

Garl wouldn't correct him. He liked how this convict sang in Greek.

"Babe, you son of a bitch. You scared the hell out of everybody."

Ragland was wearing the pajamas of the Cincinnati Black Giants. The orderlies had sneaked upstairs with huge frying pans. They were ready to pounce on the kid.

"Go away," Garl screamed at them. The orderlies disappeared.

"Shit, I was only trying to visit you, Garl."

"People aren't used to the old-fashioned uniforms, kid."

The kid had to be seventy, or seventy-two. His back wasn't curled over. He didn't have wattles on his neck. His fingers were hooked and powerful: the proper claws of any third baseman.

"Babe, what's up? You didn't come all the way from Alabama or Wyoming to visit an old brother you once knew on the Red Sox and the Harry Heilmanns . . ."

"Ah, we're having an exhibition with some boys from Amherst summer school... a night game, Garl. And it's in the field next door. I was hoping you might come down and watch."

Garl jumped out of bed. He put on shirt and pants and grabbed hold of his cane. He hobbled behind Rags.

"I could carry you, Garl. It wouldn't be difficult."

"I can walk."

Garl met the orderlies on the stairs. "Come on with us," he said. "We're going to a night game."

Three orderlies. Rags, and Garl passed the nurses' office and ducked away from Holyoke House. It was a party of five scratchy men. The Babe led his party to a field across the road. The Amherst summer-school pickup team was waiting for the boss of the Black Giants. These scrappling, bignecked boys were anxious to beat the ass off a band of country Blacks. But the Cincinnatis had gone half white. Garl stared at them and recognized the kid's dilemma: these Giants were the rejects of a hundred tryout camps. "Sockamay-ocks," Garl said.

The kid agreed. "You take what you can get, skip."

Where were those landscape artists, the men who could sculpt a baseball diamond on any field? The kid had four lumpy bases, crooked foul lines, a batting cage with holes and wounds in the metal fabric, and a pitcher's station that looked like dirt off a chickencoop.

Garl noticed an ancient fire truck in deep center field, a rat's nest of cables, and lighting poles that gave the impression of giant toothpicks in the ground. The fire truck had bronchitis. It coughed a lot. What about the Cincinnatis' mahogany Buicks? There were only three of them left, and the mahogany was bitten off. The Buicks seemed naked to Garl.

A redhead came out of the first Buick. Garl had to go to his cane, or he would have flopped into the grass. *Marylou.* He prayed some local god would toss a curtain over him, so he wouldn't have to see that red hair. He put an elbow in front of his face. The beautiful witch was no longer satisfied to peck him in his sleep. She followed Garl out of the nursing home. Who could say what unholy thing she'd do to him in the field?

"Since when are you so shy, Garland James? You used to look at my mother."

Ah, it was only the girl. Marylou was dead.

"Sorry, Miz Iva, I didn't realize you were traveling with the team."

"You know Raggsy. He can't survive without a roommate."

Both of them laughed.

Shouldn't the girl have had some gray specks in her hair? She had to be seventy, or sixty-nine? Did you kick old age in the pants when you traveled with the Giants?

And who was on the hill for them, warming up his right arm? Yam Murray's hundred-year-old shadow? Garl's legs were twisted and all, but pathetic kneecaps couldn't interfere with his eagle eye: he spotted the emery board in the pitcher's glove.

Garl hobbled over to Rags. "Don't confuse a sick old man. Who's working for you on the hill? If it's not Yam Murray, it has to be his son."

"Wrong," Rags said. "It's the grandson."

"What's his name?"

"Yam Murray."

"Jumping Jesus," Garl said. "Whole generations of Yams ... he kicks like his grandpa. And I like the way he goes into the stretch.

Rags, are you holding him a prisoner? ... why isn't he in the majors right now?"

"Shoulder trouble," the kid said. "He screwed around with knuckleballs and got himself hurt. The Dodgers had to let him go. That's all right. He can pitch for me."

The kid couldn't blab too long. He had to play his spot. He lumbered off to third. The Amherst boys chuckled as he went into his crouch. They hadn't figured the boss would be part of the Giant infield. They could blow him down with the wind from their bats. They shouted to him, "Pop, do you have disability insurance?"

The kid told them to play ball.

"Then bring up the lights . . . it's black around home plate."

"Sorry," the kid said, and he signaled to the sockamayock in center field. The center fielder ran behind the fire truck. Garl heard a hiss. The poles shook in the ground. A light with a soft blue haze burned all over the diamond. This blue didn't hide the base paths; it was as if a mellow fog had rolled onto the field at noon time.

The summer-school team was satisfied.

Yam kicked from the mound and threw his emery ball into the cuffs of the first batter. He chopped at the pitch and banged a hard grounder into the hole. It would have gone through the shortstop, but the old man at third angled his body and it became a fucking knife that could stab a ground ball, recover itself, and hit the first baseman with a strike.

"He learned that from the Pharaoh," Garl said with a scowl. The Amherst boys shrugged. It had to be the night for graybeards. How else could you explain the catch? The orderlies touched Garl on his shirt. "Who is that old geezer?"

"Babe Ragland."

Two more innings of play and Garl had converted them.

"He's the best," the orderlies whispered. "... tell Nettles to move over, or Ragland will make the All-Star team."

The kid hopped, twisted, tossed strikes from between his legs. Amherst barely had the courage to go on with the game.

Garl could swear his kneecaps were on the mend. He was dancing near the third-base line. He listened to a crazy knock from the fire truck. The knock turned into a song. Women were serenading him from inside the truck. *Go with the Giants, go with the Giants.* Garl assumed his blood pressure was running high.

The sockamayocks beat Amherst summer school, 11-1. The center fielder switched off the lights. The truck was calm again.

The sockamayocks moved about the field like busy ants. They unearthed the lighting poles and carried them to the truck, dismantled the batting cage, picked up the pillow- bases and stored them in a Buick.

While Garl rocked on his feet, the orderlies were growing tense. They'd have to include Babe Ragland in their "immortals" list, put him ahead of Billy Cox, but what about the fat nurse? She would scream at them if she discovered that Mr. James had fled Holyoke House to watch college boys, scamps, Blacks, and old men play on a warty field.

"Garland baby, we'd better shuffle back to the house."

Garl stared at the orderlies. "I have to say goodbye to the kid."

That medicine from the fire truck, the generator-song, had begun to wear off. Garl felt a burning in his leg. The flagpole injury was flaring up. Was it bravura or stupidity to fall off a pole in center field? Whenever the umps tossed him out of a game, Garl would sit near the piss trough at the neck of the tunnel and relay his signals to the bench. He was the captain of piss and manager of the Red Sox. Did he drop from that pole out of spite, after his brothers' education had been finished?

What could he declare about his own folly? That he loved Greek and the foolishness of cramming Sophocles into the skulls of boys? That he wanted his center field without the rigmarole and politics

of a major-league club? He hadn't fallen off any pole. He'd jumped.
To cripple himself and shout "fuck you" to Hollis.

"Skip, what's the matter?"

The Babe was standing in dusty pajamas.

"Rags, you should have left me on Quintana Roo ... I'd have had
a ripe old age among those bandits, eating shrubs and roots. I'm
not partial to nursing homes... honey is bad for your teeth."

"Why don't you come with us?"

"I wasn't trained to be a bat boy, Mr. Ragland . . ."

"I could give you center field."

"How?" Garl muttered. "With a dead knee... and a stick in my
glove hand?"

"I'd rather have Garland James on one leg than any sockamayock... if the knee acts up, you can always manage the Giants. I have
enough to do at third."

Crazy team. Crazy fire truck. Would they like him in Colorado when he turned eighty-six? He got into the Buick with Iva and
Rags. Four sockamayocks sat in the back. Iva drove.

The orderlies were dumbfounded as the caravan took off. The
Giants had kidnapped *their* old man. They chased the Buicks and
the fire truck down the road. It went on for half a mile, until the
wind was out of them. It was a fool's errand. They couldn't outrun
a caravan. They'd have to return emptyhanded to Holyoke House.

They argued, pushed each other on the road. A furor was upon
them to think up a story. How do you tell a nurse that you lost one
old man? *Vanished.* That's the word. The old man had vanished on
a walk in the fields. They could afford to whistle. Who cared about
a nurse? They had their story now.